The Virgin Mary in
the Perceptions of Women

The Virgin Mary in the Perceptions of Women

Mother, Protector and Queen Since the Middle Ages

JOELLE MELLON

McFarland & Company, Inc., Publishers
Jefferson, North Carolina, and London

LIBRARY OF CONGRESS CATALOGUING-IN-PUBLICATION DATA

Mellon, Joelle, 1971–
    The Virgin Mary in the perceptions of women : mother, protector and queen since the Middle Ages / Joelle Mellon.
        p.   cm.
    Includes bibliographical references and index.

    ISBN 978-0-7864-3502-9
    softcover : 50# alkaline paper

    1. Mary, Blessed Virgin, Saint — Devotion to — History.
2. Christian women — Religious life — History.   I. Title.
BT645.M45   2008
232.9109 — dc22   2008000840

British Library cataloguing data are available

©2008 Joelle Mellon. All rights reserved

No part of this book may be reproduced or transmitted in any form or by any means, electronic or mechanical, including photocopying or recording, or by any information storage and retrieval system, without permission in writing from the publisher.

Cover art ©2008 Pictures Now

Manufactured in the United States of America

McFarland & Company, Inc., Publishers
  Box 611, Jefferson, North Carolina 28640
    www.mcfarlandpub.com

To my sister, Katie.
You will always be the other half of my brain.

Acknowledgments

There are many people and institutions without whose generosity this book would not have been written. Linda Main, Deborah Hansen and Anne Simonson served as advisors for my master's thesis at San Jose State University, where this idea began. Danny Fahs gave me endless support and encouragement, as well as making what seemed like endless photocopies. He was called upon several times to translate passages of French for me, including one instance of medieval French that I thought he would never manage. I was wrong. The wonderful folks at the Dorset Writer's Colony in Vermont were a true inspiration, and I can never thank them enough. I am eternally grateful to Richard Wiffen and Faye Levine, who served as "beta readers" for the early drafts of my chapters. I would still be adrift on a sea of confusion if not for their insightful comments. I also wish to thank the staff of the Knott Library at St. Mary's Seminary and University in Baltimore, Maryland. Your assistance got me through more dark nights of the writer's soul than I can ever mention. Julie Brown of Chant Art provided me with essential help in obtaining visual images for this book. I appreciate all the efforts of the staff, administration and students of Grace Episcopal Day School, who provided me with support, encouragement and pastry. Finally, of course, there are my parents, Christine and Dennis Mellon — you believed in me before anybody else did. To anyone I may have forgotten to mention, I trust you will forgive me. May Mary's blessings rain down upon you all.

Table of Contents

Acknowledgments — vi
Preface — 1

1. Explorations: Why Mary Was Lost — 5
2. Beginnings: Mary in the Bible — 23
3. Devotional Objects: I Carry Her with Me Always — 36
4. Marian Places: The Virgin at Home and Abroad — 61
5. Marian Times: Days, Months and Life Passages — 81
6. Context: Relationships with St. Anne, St. Joseph, Eve, and the Devil — 97
7. The Virgin's Virgins: Nuns and Mary — 115
8. Mystics and Miracles: Touched by the Virgin's Hand — 132
9. Transformations: From Pagan to Christian to the Uncertain Future of Mary — 154
10. Two Marys: The Virgin and the (Repentant) Whore — 169

Chapter Notes — 185
Bibliography — 201
Index — 209

Preface

Everything you've ever heard about the Virgin Mary is probably wrong. I constantly wanted to stop people in the street and say this to them while I was working on my thesis. I had decided to do a book history project as a sort of culminating experience for my master's degree in library science at San Jose State University. Because I found late medieval and early Renaissance Books of Hours so appealing, I was focusing on them. Eventually, I narrowed my topic under the direction of Linda Main, my primary thesis advisor. What I was specifically studying turned out to be how images of the Virgin Mary changed over the course of three centuries in Books of Hours commissioned by female patrons. For over a year, at San Jose State University's libraries, I looked at medieval and Renaissance manuscripts, ranging from the 14th through the 16th centuries, that featured Mary.

Eventually, I continued my work at the Knott Library at St. Mary's Seminary and University in Baltimore, Maryland. As a result of my research there, I came to the realization that what women had been taught about Mary over the centuries had changed astonishingly. My book, *The Virgin Mary in the Perceptions of Women: Mother, Protector and Queen Since the Middle Ages*, is the end product of my theological and historical exploration. It investigates a time when God had a female face and good Christians were taught that they should pray to a Holy Mother. Only a few hundred years ago, the Virgin Mary could be found everywhere—from the most private of sacred books to gardens, pub signs, jewelry, and spiritual vacations known as pilgrimages.

Official Church encouragement of what has come to be known as "the cult of the Virgin" led to an explosion of Marian devotion. It crossed all economic and social boundaries—everyone from the Pope to the lowliest of peasants had Mary at the heart of their spiritual lives. Medieval women especially looked to her to answer their prayers, be their role model, and serve as their advocate in heaven. They prayed to her several times a day and slept with Marian devotional objects on their bodies at night. She was invoked at all major life passages—baptisms, weddings, childbirths, and funerals.

Mary became such a radical and powerful force in the world that centuries

The "Mantle Virgin" offers her blessings to people of all ages, cultural backgrounds and economic levels (courtesy Chant Art).

of religious authorities dedicated their lives to exterminating her influence. The rise of Protestant religions in the sixteenth century brought about the first radical change in ideology. Protestant leaders considered the veneration of Mary idolatry, so they declared war on her. Marian statues were smashed, paintings of her were defaced, and plays honoring her were banned. Anyone who clung to her previous beliefs was systematically executed. For centuries, staunch Marianists were forced to continue their devotional practices in secret. Bloody battles were sometimes fought for the right to openly venerate her.

Ultimately, however, it was not Protestant intolerance that cast Mary out of most contemporary people's spiritual lives. In an effort to "modernize" the Catholic Church of the early 1960s, its foremost authorities declared a drastically decreased role for the Virgin Mary. She was henceforth to be considered nothing more than a particularly pious member of the early Church. For some people, especially women, this officially sanctioned demotion was heartbreaking. For the first time in recorded history, women born into Catholic families were provided with no sense of a Divine Female Presence, unless it was secretly imparted to them by defiantly Marianist mothers or grandmothers.

Due to the popularity of works of fiction like *The DaVinci Code* and *The Secret Life of Bees*, the issue of female spirituality is once again on many people's minds. Many books on Mariology (the study of the Virgin Mary) have recently been published, such as the excellent works *Missing Mary* by Charlene Spretnak and *In Search of Mary* by Sally Cunneen. Beverly Donofrio's *Looking for Mary*, though far less academic in tone, contains a great deal of insight about contemporary women's perceptions of the Virgin. *Alone of All Her Sex* by Marina Warner should probably be considered the seminal text of postmodern feminist Mariology. There has even been some Marian fiction that is solidly based on academic research, such as *Our Lady of the Lost and Found* by Diane Schomperlen.

Although the primary readership of such books is made up of women with some Christian background, there is a growing sense of interest among men and women of other faith traditions. After all, the role of women in spiritual life is something that touches all religions. At the beginning of the third millennium, many are noticing a void in their spiritual lives. Women are often not able to relate to God simply because, unlike Mary, He is nothing like them. Providing them with the information necessary to envision a seemingly new paradigm (that is actually hundreds of years old) is the ultimate purpose of my book.

1

Explorations

Why Mary Was Lost

There are many reasons why contemporary women feel distanced from the woman who used to be commonly referred to as their "Divine Mother." One of the primary ones, however, has to do with the rise of Protestantism in the modern world. Since the Renaissance, one of the main ways in which Protestants have differentiated themselves from Catholics is that they do not venerate Mary. Some Protestant leaders have even referred to the practice of worshiping her as "Mariolatry," casting it in the same sinful light as the adoration of golden idols. As a result, women who have been brought up in Protestant homes usually know little about her. Recently, quite a few of these women seem to have become keenly aware of this and are eager to talk about it. Over the past five years, there has been a virtual flood of fiction and nonfiction work by women, in which they write about their separation from her. Based on what they are saying, it seems that their knowledge of her is generally confined to her small role in the New Testament. In Diane Shoemperlen's recent fiction book about Mary, *Our Lady of the Lost and Found*, her unnamed Protestant heroine states that she grew up with little awareness of the Virgin. She adds that Catholic friends had to inform her about things such as Holy Cards featuring Mary and the Rosary.[1]

But it is not only Protestant women who have been distanced from the idea of a Divine Presence that is female. The Marian scholar Sally Cunneen argues that the current rift between Catholics and the Virgin Mary was created in the 1960s by Vatican II, when Pope John XXIII deliberately downplayed her role in the Catholic Church. This was primarily an effort to modernize Catholicism and, perhaps more importantly, decrease the differences between Catholics and Protestants. However, his declarations brought about a sharp decrease in Marian sermons and devotions in Catholic churches throughout the world. Millions of women who had grown up with such comforting rituals as Rosary recitations and May processions were suddenly forced to live without them.[2] Cunneen writes that after Vatican II, she put her Rosary away with other mementos of her childhood and "more or less forgot about Mary except at Christmas and in times of panic."[3]

Perhaps the most extreme disconnect between contemporary women and the Virgin began during the late 1960s and early 1970s. Many, especially young women of that time, were discarding the previous generations' traditional values. As a part of this, they utterly rejected Mary as a part of the whole outdated package. Some feminists even began to claim that she was not an appropriate model for women. In her article *The Marian Tradition and the Reality of Women*, Elizabeth A. Johnson sums up the primary feminist critiques that have been put forth against Marianism since the late 1960s: 1. The Marian tradition has been intrinsically associated with the denigration of the nature of women as a group; 2. It has dichotomized the roles of men and women in the Christian community; and 3. It has "truncated" the ideal of feminine fulfillment and wholeness.[4]

Other female scholars wrote articles and even entire books denouncing her role in women's lives. Marina Warner was one of the most notable, eloquently expressing her frustration with the Virgin in her groundbreaking 1976 book, *Alone of All Her Sex*. This work was so influential that it transcended the academic audience. Widely read in the 1970s, it is still in print and readily available in most bookstores today. Warner states that women who view the Virgin Mary as their ideal are forced into a position of hopeless yearning and inferiority. This begins a vicious cycle, in which their feelings of inadequacy further increase their need for the consolations of religion.[5] Despite her disgust with the role in male-dominated society that Mary had come to represent for her, however, her rejection of the Virgin apparently caused her a great deal of personal anguish. She states:

> So potent was [Mary's] spell that for years I could not enter a church without pain at all the safety and beauty of the salvation I had forsaken. I remember visiting Notre Dame in Paris and standing in the nave, tears starting in my eyes, furious at that old love's enduring power to move me. But though my very heart rebelled, I held fast to my new intimation that in the very celebration of the perfect human woman, both humanity and women were subtly denigrated.[6]

For decades after this, women who had been influenced by feminists such as Warner continued to denounce the Virgin Mary's role in women's spiritual lives. In her 1984 article "Mary and Femininity: A Psychological Critique," Patricia Harrington asserts that "the kind of femininity Mary represents serves to perpetuate patriarchal social structures and to inhibit full psychological maturity."[7] She concludes her article with the scathing statement:

> Mary does heal, but she also destroys. She comforts, but she also weakens and enslaves. Her girlish trust of God and her maternal gaze of love, familiar throughout the Catholic world, can help perpetuate a patriarchal system in

which women's lives are restricted and distorted into passivity and dependence.[8]

In a more popularly accessible way, Beverly Donofrio, the former teen mother of *Riding in Cars with Boys* fame, has written about her rejection of the Virgin Mary during the 1960s and 1970s. She hung a bust of the Madonna and Child on the wall of her apartment as a kind of visual irony. She says, "Mary's image on my wall was a joke, a kind of kitschy reference to an impossibility, an iconic ideal mother I could never be, the type of mother I scoffed at: a passive, sexless, adoring — or weeping, wounded, and suffering — mama."[9] In a more vitriolic moment, Donofrio threw a clock which featured images from the lives of Jesus and Mary into the garbage and dumped potato peels on top of it. She asserts:

> I hated Mary. I despised her abdicating her will to God's. Not that I'd believed in her since puberty, but she was a figurehead for a mythology I wanted nothing to do with: woman as ever-loving wimp.[10]

In a more scholarly work, Elizabeth A. Johnson analyzes contemporary women's objections to having the Virgin Mary as an important spiritual figure in their lives. She argues that their rejection of her primarily stems from the current patriarchal Church's insistence on emphasizing her roles as "handmaid of the lord," virgin, and mother, which leads to "a wreck of oppressive expectations."[11] She goes on to lucidly elaborate why these roles have become unacceptable for most any woman of the twenty-first century. The idea of Mary as the handmaid is derived from her statement to the angel Gabriel when He announces to her that she has miraculously conceived Jesus while remaining a virgin. "I am the handmaid of the Lord," she humbly replies, meaning, essentially, "I will do whatever God says." With this one statement, she has (perhaps unintentionally) characterized herself for millennia to come as obedient, passive, submissive and deferential.

Contemporary women frequently earn their own money, insist on marriages of equal partnership, and fight a continuing battle against sex discrimination in all areas of life. Naturally, such strong people find this role of "handmaid" unrealistic or even absurd, given their daily realities. For centuries, however, this version of Mary has been considered by male spiritual leaders to be the ideal all women should emulate. African American women, with their racial history of slavery, often find the "handmaid" particularly intolerable. Many feel that this image has been used against black women for far too long. Traditionally, the "handmaid Mary" was held up to their grandmothers to encourage their acceptance of slavery-era roles such as cook, housekeeper, wet nurse, and concubine.

Women are also frequently angry about the Catholic Church's emphasis on Mary's role as a virgin. Instead of celebrating virginity, contemporary women are happily reclaiming "their own sexuality as part of their blessed human and spiritual wholeness."[12] In an era when contraception is available to practically everyone and children are largely a choice, virginity no longer seems as liberating as it did to women in past centuries. Only a few generations ago, women rejoiced in virginity, since it meant freedom from pregnancy and subservient dependence on a husband. By contrast, Elizabeth Johnson brings up several examples of women who are now infuriated and bitter about Christian emphasis on Mary's virginity. Johnson cites a wonderfully expressive South African nun, who says that she is angry about the fact that she is not even supposed to utter the word "vagina," as if God had created a body part so evil that it could not be mentioned. Another woman living in New York airily dismisses the whole idea of Mary's virginity, saying that Mary's sex life is nobody else's business.[13]

The third role for Mary which a lot of women find off-putting, somewhat surprisingly, is that of mother, probably her most strongly emphasized modern role. Mary as the Madonna is still everywhere, from Christmas cards to candleholders to jigsaw puzzles. For many women, however, this emphasis on motherliness is highly objectionable. It is not that they dislike the idea of motherhood in general — plenty of women in today's society are happy to be mothers. More specifically, what they object to is the idea that, like the Madonna, motherhood would become their defining characteristic, eclipsing or even blotting out their other accomplishments and identities. Such a wide range of women have become mothers that characterizing them entirely by their children is simply absurd. There are women who live in marriages that are true mutual partnerships, women who combine motherhood with careers, those who live with female partners and those who have the formidable task of running single-parent households. The very fact that such a range exists forces a redefinition of motherhood. Quite simply, motherhood cannot possibly mean the same things it did when Mary took it on, when having children meant devoting all your time, energy, and mental resources to them.[14]

If contemporary women ever manage to think of the Virgin Mary as anything other than a wholly negative influence, they often regard her as a distant and mysterious figure whom they have to seek out. Titles of many recent Marian books by female authors consistently refer to the idea of looking for her or even stumbling upon her unexpectedly. Sally Cunneen's popular scholarly work is called *The Search for Mary*, while Beverly Donofrio's spiritual memoir is entitled *Looking for Mary*. In fiction, Diane Schoemperlen refers to the elusiveness of Mary with *Our Lady of the Lost and Found*. Even the title of Sue Monk Kidd's bestseller *The Secret Life of Bees*, with its protagonist's black Madonna picture concealed in a tin box, suggests something that must be sought out. In her poem "Mary of the Mirrors," Nancy G. Westerfield poignantly describes looking for the Virgin Mary in herself.[15] There is definitely a strong sense among many women that somehow, somewhere, in our society's rejection of traditional values, Mary has been mislaid.

Even Beverly Donofrio, with her initial extreme animosity toward the Virgin, eventually felt compelled to go on a pilgrimage to Medjugorje, Yugoslavia, to look for her. What Donofrio experienced there moved her strongly enough that, upon her return, she found herself handing out Rosaries to all her friends.[16] She found that what had truly been keeping her at a distance from the Virgin Mary was that aspects of her had been missing in our culture since Vatican II.

A woman who lived in Europe during the late Middle Ages would have found the idea of having to seek Mary out laughable. The Virgin was positively everywhere. Books such as *The Hours of the Virgin Mary* and *The Mirrour of Our Lady* were produced at a minuscule size, so that they could be constantly carried on women's belts (and frequently were). Even poor, illiterate women were seldom without their wooden Rosaries, which they often wore to bed. Their more wealthy contemporaries had ones made of precious metals and jewels. Under their feet were plants and flowers that had names associated with her, such as rosemary, ladyslippers, and Our Lady's hair. One could even nip down to the pub and have a drink at establishments such as The Virgin, Our Lady's Inn, and the Salutation, which referred to the angel Gabriel's famous greeting, "Ave Maria."[17] Far from viewing Mary as an oppressive force, medieval women, in every sense of the word, adored her.

During the Middle Ages, no distance was perceived between women and their Divine Mother. For any problem, large or small, one of their first courses of action was a prayer to her. If the cow was sick, Our Lady of Perpetual Help could cure her. More serious problems, such as prolonged infertility, might require a pilgrimage to a popular Marian shrine, where sincere prayers and a small offering would sort things out. Women believed that Mary was directly and personally involved in their lives. As early as the eleventh century, she was credited with a diverse catalog of miracles that were beneficial to humankind. She returned lost fortunes, cured the sick, restored severed body parts, and saved women from being raped. She personally bestowed holy gifts upon mankind (most notably the Rosary). Female saints believed that she appeared to them often to provide inspiration and advice.

Most secular women, however, loved the Virgin especially because of their strong belief that she would successfully plead with Jesus to spare the souls of even the worst of sinners. No matter what sins they or their family members committed, they knew they would go to heaven if they trusted Mary to intercede for them. The Middle Ages abounded with wildly popular miracle tales in which Mary spared utterly unworthy sinners from hell. Marina Warner states:

> The more raffish the Virgin's suppliant, the better she likes him. The miracles' heroes are liars, thieves, adulterers, and fornicators, footloose students, pregnant nuns, unruly and lazy clerics, and eloping monks. On the single condition that they sing her praises ... and show due respect for the miracle of the Incarnation wrought in her, they can do no wrong.[18]

This point of view was not contested by Church authorities of the time. Indeed, respected Biblical scholars instructed all clergy to encourage their sinful parishioners, especially women, to appeal to Mary. Biblical authority, specifically in the story of the wedding at Cana and the Song of Songs, was frequently cited to prove that Mary would save a sinner that her Son would otherwise condemn to the fires of hell.

At the wedding at Cana, Mary encouraged Jesus to perform His first miracle. When the stores of wine ran out at the reception, Mary told her son, "They have no wine." Perhaps somewhat irritated by his mother's unspoken demand that he remedy the situation, Jesus replied, "Woman, what have I to do with thee? Mine hour is not yet come." Despite His initial reluctance, however, He turned water into wine to please His mother. Mary's power over her Son, to make Him do something even when He preferred not to comply with her wishes, was not lost on the clergy of the medieval era. They reasoned that if Mary could make Jesus perform his first miracle against His better judgment, she could also persuade Him to judge sinners more kindly than He might otherwise be inclined to do.

Although the reasoning is more symbolic and obscure, medieval theologians also believed that the Song of Songs in the Bible expressed Mary's mediator role between sinners and Jesus, especially on Judgment Day. Indeed, many scholars of the time believed that the entire Song of Songs referred to this role. In his essay, "The Marian Interpretation of the Song of Songs in the Middle Ages," P. Fidelis Buck states that, according to medieval logic, Jesus was generally considered to be the "head" of the Church. The neck of the bride is particularly mentioned in Canticles 4:4 and 7:4. Mary was therefore thought to be the "neck" which joined Christians ("the body") to the head.

Highly influential Church authorities of the day urged priests to teach women to appeal to the Virgin Mary. Thomas of Perseigne argued that, as air is breathed in and out through the neck, through Mary's mediation, mankind's interior devotion is presented to God, and God's mercy is transmitted to man.[19] Twelfth-century Biblical scholar Eadmer believed that Christ the Judge became partial when the name of Mary was invoked by a sinner. Eadmer felt that calling on the Virgin could bring salvation more quickly than appealing to Christ directly. His contemporary, the great theologian Anselm of Canterbury, urged, "let him who is guilty before the just God flee to the tender Mother of the merciful God."[20] A century later, scholar Conrad of Saxony proclaimed, "She prevents her Son from striking sinners; for before Mary there was no one who dared thus hold back the Lord."[21]

The entry for the Virgin Mary in Miriam Van Scott's *Encyclopedia of Hell* is quite extensive, since it has traditionally been believed that she has a large role in saving the condemned from its fires. The "Hail Mary," best known of all Marian prayers, ends with a supplication to "pray for us sinners, now and at the hour of our death." Many popular legends throughout history have

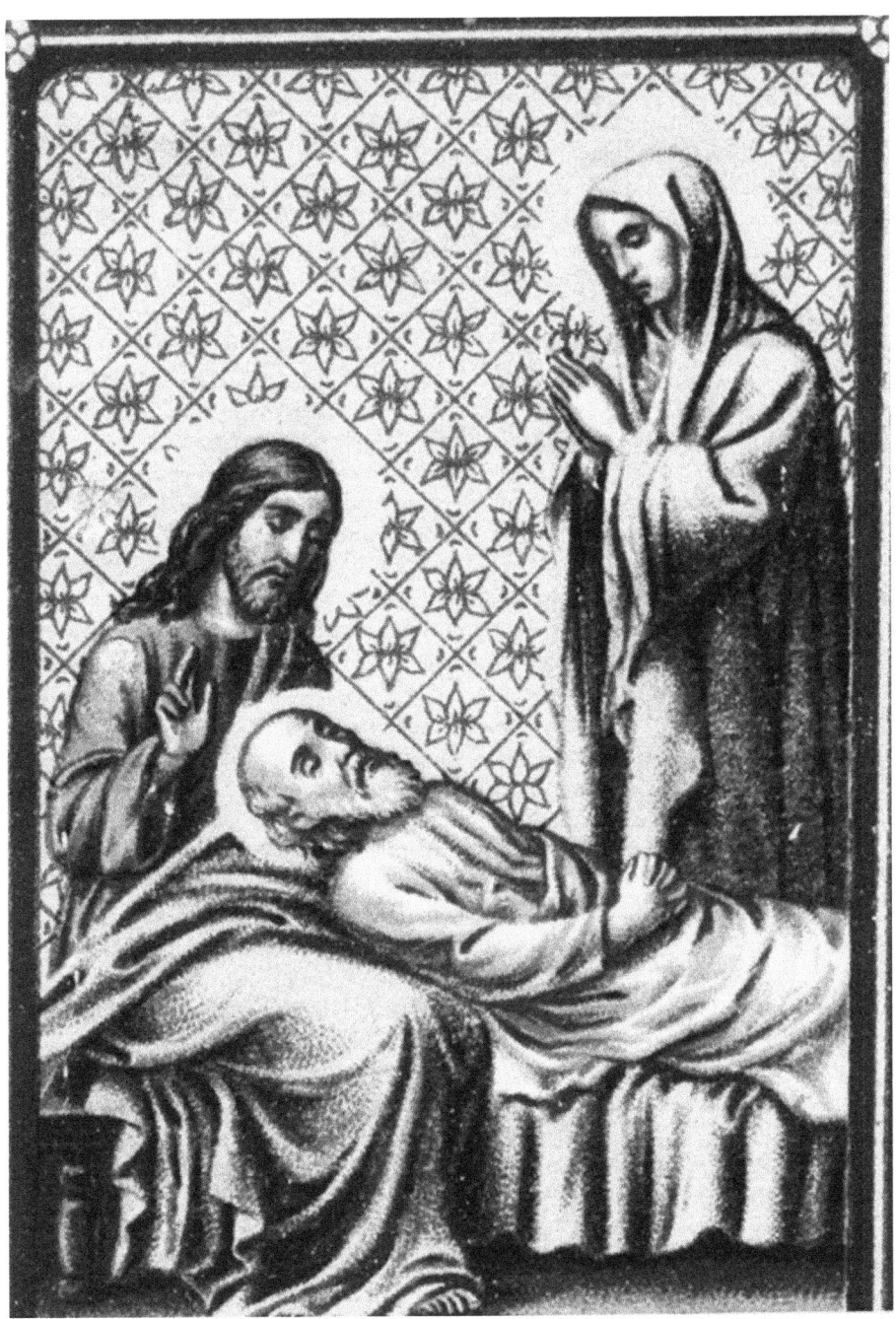

Mary and Jesus at the bedside of a dying man (courtesy Chant Art).

emphasized that there is no point—before or after death—at which the Virgin is not willing to intercede. In one seventeenth-century Belgian tale, she spares a debauched sinner from death, simply because he shows a token amount of devotion to her. According to this story, a young man returned home from a night of ribald excesses and addressed a halfhearted prayer to Mary before falling asleep. As a direct result, she spared him from the terrible death and condemnation to hell that his drinking companion met with that same night.[22]

At the time of death, she sometimes arrives personally to snatch a soul from the devil's grasp and carry it to heaven. In late medieval paintings of Judgment, she is shown tipping the balance of the scales on which a soul is being weighed. Sometimes she does this by placing her hand on the side containing good deeds, while at others she uses a Rosary or the end of her robe.[23] Less covertly, she intercedes directly with her Son, who passes judgment on the dead. When Jesus points to his wounds, claiming that sinful people deserve punishment, merciful Mary responds by indicating the womb that carried Him and the breasts that nursed Him. Ever the dutiful son, Jesus cannot refuse.[24]

Hamington writes that it was generally believed that out of love and gratitude for her being His mother during His time on earth, Jesus would refuse Mary no request.[25] She frequently turned aside the wrath of her Son by emphasizing her maternal role in a very direct and distinctly female way—she showed her breasts, reminding Him that she cared for Him when he was a helpless human infant. Mary Condren explains that just as the ancient goddesses calmed the anger of warriors by showing their bare breasts, so too Mary could be counted upon to dissolve Jesus' fury by reminding Him that she had once nursed Him.[26] When she did this, Christ could not find it in His heart to refuse His Mother. Even Marina Warner, who finds Marian devotion so ideologically revolting, argues that the Virgin's intervention, "transforms [Jesus] ... from the God of justice to the God of mercy."[27] Because of this, quite understandably, many women in the Middle Ages chose to pray to Mary, the "merciful mother," for their salvation, instead of the more judgmental, intimidating male Deity.

Even those who are already in hell are not necessarily lost forever, if Mary intercedes on their behalf. In one ninth-century tale, the Virgin restored a condemned deacon named Adelman to life, allowing him to properly atone for his sins and go to heaven. Another popular story is about a Christian from the time of the Roman Empire who had not been able to confess his sins to a priest before death. Because he never received final absolution, he was sent to endure the torments of hell. Moved by his unfortunate plight centuries later, Mary reanimated his skeleton, so he was able to obtain the needed holy sacraments posthumously.[28]

According to Irish legend, Judas himself is given a periodic reprieve from hell due to Mary's intercession. St. Brandon found the traitorous apostle sitting comfortably on a rock in the Atlantic Ocean and, in amazement, asked what he was doing there. Judas explained that Mary allowed him a rest from his

The Virgin Mary guides a recently deceased woman to heaven (courtesy Chant Art).

Mary intercedes with Jesus on the behalf of sinners condemned to hell. Note the angel bringing a Rosary to one (courtesy Chant Art).

eternal suffering on weekends, from Christmas to Epiphany, from Easter to Whitsun, and on two feast days of the Virgin. For such acts of mercy, she is seen as the particular opponent of the devil, who is frequently portrayed in literature filled with wrath at her for cheating him of sinners' souls.[29]

The medieval predilection for thinking of Mary as a merciful intercessor on the behalf of mankind rapidly led to a popular conception of her as a human, approachable figure. In *The Devotion to Our Lady*, Hilda Graef writes of the Virgin in the Middle Ages:

> Mary was becoming more "human," inasmuch as she was seen as a woman sharing all the joys and sufferings of women. God, even the incarnate God, her Son, was still felt to be in some way remote from humankind, because he was a Divine Person. Mary, however, was entirely human, wholly a mother, usually shown smiling down at her baby or weeping over him when he died.[30]

According to *Mother of God* by Lawrence Cunningham, art in public spaces, such as churches, reflected this late medieval shift in perception. Gone was Byzantine era tendency to portray her as the lofty "queen of heaven." Instead, there was a much more accessible version of her in art, where she was portrayed as human and motherly. Cunningham states that in medieval art, "We find human and palpable figures of the Virgin: a real woman who has just given birth, or a real mother, struck dumb with grief, standing near her dead son, who has been horribly executed."[31]

One cannot underestimate the influence of such visual images on the medieval woman's mind. Most people during this era were illiterate, unable to read the stories in the Bible (or the Apocrypha) for themselves. Many also attended church services that were performed entirely in Latin, a language which they usually did not understand. It is little wonder, then, that medieval churches and other public spaces were profusely decorated with religious art. It was the only real way in which the messages of Christianity could be transmitted to a largely uneducated populace. Most medieval women were entirely dependent on media such as public art and the easily accessible mystery plays performed in many churches for any understanding of their own religion.

Artists of the late medieval and early Renaissance era depicted scenes featuring Mary that would be familiar to all women, such as her weaving at a loom while Jesus takes some of his first steps in a baby walker. Medieval women also believed that Mary was close to the women in her own earthly family. She is sometimes shown in art visiting with her mother, the elderly Saint Anne. Another frequently repeated image of the day portrays her assisting at the birth of John the Baptist, the child of her cousin, Elizabeth. Nearly endless pieces of art depict the Virgin Mary nursing. According to Marina Warner, such images of "Maria Lactans" were particularly representative of the very human Mary, presenting her as an earthly mother and the Incarnation as a "gentle domestic drama."[32]

In the fourteenth and fifteenth centuries, the Black Plague was sweeping through Europe, and the movement to humanize the Virgin truly reached epic proportions. As the disease gruesomely carried off nearly a fifth of Europe's population, many lost their entire families in only a few months' time. It was regarded as the retribution of an angry God for mankind's wickedness. Chastised by their God, people desperately needed to believe that someone "up there" felt sympathy for them. Mary was the obvious choice, especially for women, who had already been taught to appeal to her in any difficulty. Particularly in Italy, prayers to abate the horrors of the plague were almost always specifically directed to Mary, and any improvement in the health of the population was credited to her. Fearful that Jesus was too angry to have pity on suffering humanity, the Virgin was their only hope. In Siena, after the pestilence had claimed sixty-five thousand people out of a population of eighty thousand, the chapel of the Palazzo Publico was dedicated to her, in gratitude for sparing anyone at all.[33] One Italian company of Flagellants, a sect that brutally whipped themselves to mollify God's anger, claimed that they possessed a letter from Mary herself, absolving them of all their sins in exchange for their painful efforts.[34]

The effort to humanize the Virgin began manifesting itself particularly strongly in the cult of Mater Dolorosa (Mother of Sorrows). The Mary who wept over the body of her dead Son had much in common with the grieving women who lived during the Black Plague, when practically everyone they knew died. Art of the time frequently depicted the traditional sorrows of Mary, including a prominent representation of her heart pierced with a sword. According to Lawrence Cunningham, the seven sorrows are: 1. Mary presents the infant Jesus at the temple and the prophet Simeon predicts that her heart will be pierced with a sword. 2. She is forced to flee to Egypt with her husband and Child to escape the murderous wrath of Herod. 3. She loses her Son at the temple in Jerusalem. 4. The Virgin sees Jesus crushed and bruised by the weight of the Cross. 5. Mary stands vigil at the Cross as Christ suffers and dies. 6. The dead body of Jesus is laid in her arms. 7. She follows His body and watches as it is put into the grave and the tomb is sealed.[35] Marina Warner argues that people felt that because Mary had suffered, she could empathize more with the misery of humans on earth. She states:

> The cult of the Mater Dolorosa stressed her participation in mankind's ordinary, painful lot, and so although the Black Death restored a degree of majesty and terror to the personality of Christ the Judge, the Virgin herself retained the common touch. Her sorrows became a commonplace of medieval preoccupations.[36]

Despite all the emphasis on the Virgin's humble humanity and her role as a merciful, approachable mediatrix, medieval women simultaneously maintained a strong belief in her role as the exalted queen of heaven and earth. This was at least partly because of the influence of the wildly popular medieval bestseller *The Golden Legend*, by Jacobus de Voragine. It was familiar even to illiterate women because it was so frequently read out loud. According to this book, the Virgin was richly rewarded for her earthly suffering by God. Jesus heaped honor after honor upon His mother in her old age and after her death, eventually culminating in crowning her queen and having her rule beside Him. Because she was crowned by Jesus and given a place beside Him on the celestial throne, she was simultaneously seen as an earthly mother and a Being second only to God. It is partly this duality which has always made the Virgin so appealing to believing women. She is somehow both human and divine, both a virgin and a mother. Yet she is also female like them.

Many considered Mary's first reward to be a personal visit from her Son after his resurrection. One scholar in the Middle Ages, Maria de Agreda de Jesus, argued that this visit was an extraordinary honor because during it, Christ united so closely with his mother that He penetrated into her body and she into His.[37] *The Golden Legend* vividly recounted this visit for thousands of medieval readers. De Voragine claimed that the resurrected Jesus' love for his mother was so great that He appeared to her before anyone else. He states:

> It is the common belief that Our Lord appeared first of all to the Virgin Mary. The Evangelists, it is true, do not speak of this; but if we were to take their silence for a denial, we should have to conclude that the risen Christ did not once appear to his mother.[38]

It should be noted that de Voragine claimed that, even at such an emotional time, Mary made sure her Son took care of other women's needs. When this meeting occurred, she supposedly requested that Jesus visit Mary Magdalene to reassure her He was not really dead. Another honor that medieval people commonly thought Mary had been given while she was still on earth was that, along with the apostles, the Holy Spirit descended upon her on Pentecost. Marina Warner comments about the recurring Pentecostal depiction of Mary in art. "In iconography of medieval Christendom ... she often holds center stage ... at the gift of tongues; a towering figure, she becomes the very embodiment of Mater Ecclesia, brimming over with grace and power of the Spirit, and before whom the apostles sometimes kneel in awe."[39] Finally, perhaps again because of de Voragine's influence, it was believed that God sent an angel to tell Mary of her own impending death. According to *The Golden Legend*, the angel greeted her with reverence and said, "Three days hence thou shalt be called forth from the body, because thy Son awaits thee, His venerable mother!"[40]

These, however, were only small rewards, compared with what people of the Middle Ages believed she was given by Jesus after her death. It was generally thought that Mary, like Christ, was bodily assumed into heaven after she died. According to Hamington, this was based on the idea that because her body was not corrupted by original sin, it also could not be corrupted by decay. Her purity had disassociated her from the material world to such an extent that even her body was not subject to its natural laws.[41]

Hilda Graef states that an eleventh- or twelfth-century treatise attributed to St. Augustine supported the idea of Mary's assumption. In this work, it is argued that since Jesus had honored His mother by preserving her virginity in His conception, it was logical to believe that He would save her body from decay.[42] De Voragine wrote that Christ summoned her from her tomb by saying, "As thou hast not felt the plague of sin in carnal dealings, so thou mayst not suffer the corruption of the body in the grave."[43] He adds that St. Thomas, who had previously doubted that Jesus had risen from the dead, also refused to believe that Mary had been bodily assumed into heaven. She therefore appeared to Thomas, and just as Christ had, she supplied him with physical evidence to assuage his doubts. In her case, she gave him her girdle, instead of having him touch her bodily. De Voragine states, "Suddenly the girdle wherewith her body had been begirt fell unopened into [St. Thomas'] hands, that so he might understand she had been assumed entire."[44]

The next honor bestowed on Mary is her coronation in heaven. Her coronation was certainly accepted as fact by most medieval theologians. They repeatedly referred to her in terms of royalty. According to Hilda Graef, medieval Biblical scholar Godfrey of Admont called her "the mistress of the world, the queen of heaven and the empress of the angels."[45] Twelfth-century theologian Rupert of Deutz believed that passages in the Song of Songs name Mary "queen of the saints in heaven as well as of kingdoms of the earth, possessing by right the whole kingdom of her Son."[46] In the same century, William of Newburgh argued for Mary's right to be crowned with Jesus because she shared in His labors and suffered with Him.

After Mary was crowned, it was thought that Jesus enthroned her next to Him to rule. The somewhat erotic imagery inherent in the portrayal of Mary and Jesus in heaven beside each other was certainly not missed by medieval scholars. It was commonly held that the Song of Songs designated her the Bride of Christ and the spouse of Jesus. Also remarked upon was the question of whether her position at the right hand of Christ was meant to imply that Mary had become the equal of her Son after her death. Hilda Graef states that many theologians did not feel this was likely, including the significant thirteenth-century scholar Albert the Great. Nonetheless, he believed it was proper to venerate her as a queen. According to Albert, "every knee, of those that are in heaven, on earth, and under the earth bows before her."[47] On the other hand, Graef adds, the medieval theologian Eadmer believed that such equality was indeed a possibility. She paraphrases: "[Eadmer] asks himself how Christ could bear to go to heaven first and leave His mother behind; perhaps, He thinks, because the heavenly court would not have known who to greet first."[48]

Despite some disagreement on this matter, however, at least one thing was certain in the medieval mind. Honors were given to Mary because of her exceptional purity and goodness during her life on earth. Despite the somewhat heavy-handed message to women to "behave," so that they too could be rewarded after their deaths, medieval women loved the idea that someone of their own gender was seated at the right hand of Jesus and could, even if arguably, be perceived as equal to Him.

Of course, there can be no escaping the fact that Mary was considered a model of behavior to aspire to in the Middle Ages. Throughout history, her

Coronation of the Virgin in heaven (courtesy Chant Art).

sinlessness has always been strongly emphasized. Somewhat astonishingly, it was commonly believed that of all women since the beginning of the human race, only Mary truly pleased God. It is this, perhaps more than any other aspect of contemporary Marian Christianity, that feminists today find objectionable. But even the most progressive women in medieval times did not regard Mary's perpetual virginity as something negative or off-putting.

In the Middle Ages, Mary was thought to have two primary virtues—her obedience to the will of God and her lifelong virginity. In this era, it was not enough simply to believe in the miraculous conception of Jesus; people also bore a strong conviction that Mary remained a virgin all her life, despite being married. Marina Warner states that it was generally believed at this time that Joseph was chosen by God to be Mary's husband partly because he was too old to have intercourse with her.[49] Joseph was supposedly so aged he felt reluctant to marry the teenaged Virgin. De Voragine states that "to [Joseph] it did not seem fitting that a man of his years should take so young a maid to wife."[50]

Other popular images of the time showed Mary holding the infant Jesus in the company of her mother (St. Anne), her two half-sisters (also named Mary) and their children. Although this artistic phenomenon does not, at first glance, seem to refer to the purity of Mary, it is actually a subtle defense of her perpetual sinlessness. The Gospels of Matthew, Mark and Luke all contain references to the "brethren" of Jesus, which caused some doubt about his mother's virginity after His birth. To keep these passages from discrediting her purity, it was sometimes argued that Biblical mentions of Christ's brethren referred to the cousins that were depicted with him in such pieces. According to *The Golden Legend*, "St. Anne, the mother of the Virgin Mary, was married twice before she married Joachim, Mary's father, and by each of her former husbands had a daughter called Mary. These other Marys, the sisters of the Virgin, in turn had children, who were Jesus' 'brethren.'"[51]

Another frequent portrayal of Mary from that time period shows her in a "garden enclosed," or a garden with some sort of wall around it. The inspiration for this metaphorical imagery came from the Song of Songs. According to Buck, both St. Jerome and Epiphanius in the fourth century argued that Canticle 4:12 of the Song of Songs referred to the lifelong virginity of the Mother of God.[52] According to Buck, St. Jerome comments on Cant. 4:12 ("My sister, my spouse, is a garden enclosed, a fountain sealed up.") that because it is closed and sealed, it has a likeness to the Mother of the Lord, both mother and virgin. Epiphanius quotes the same text when he addresses Mary in a homily, "Hail Mary, full of grace, gate of heaven of which the prophet Ezekiel declared, 'This gate shall remain shut.'"[53]

Mary was widely regarded as "a second Eve" in the Middle Ages. According to Marina Warner, this was because St. Paul had declared Jesus the new Adam. Later theologians simply took this one step further, arguing that the Virgin could be considered the "new Eve" and could undo the damage to the world that the original sinful woman had done.[54] This idea was especially popular with female scholars, perhaps because they sought an alternative to Eve as a paradigm of womanhood. The remarkable Hroswitha of Gandersheim, a tenth-century Benedictine nun, referred to Mary as "the one hope of the world, the glorious mistress of heaven, who restores to the world the life the virgin Eve had lost."[55] In the later fourteenth century, St. Birgitta of Sweden, speaking as Mary, wrote, "As Adam and Eve sold the world for one apple, so my Son and I have redeemed the world as it were with one heart."[56]

Unlike contemporary women, those who lived during medieval times were not at all discouraged or disgusted by being offered Mary as their behavioral ideal. As they were told repeatedly that they could not cast off the sinful nature they had inherited from Eve, Mary provided them with an alternative, as well as an ideal to strive toward. Her being both a perpetual virgin and a mother gave them a unique choice—both a life of virginity and the path of motherhood were honorable.

Some medieval women chose to renounce worldly ways as much as possible in order to become more like the Virgin Mary. They took vows of chastity, entering convents as nuns and emulating her life as a virgin. This freed them from the rule of husbands, the dangers of childbirth, and the demands of children. It also provided them with opportunities for solitude and solitary pursuits, which were difficult, if not impossible, to attain in a typical crowded medieval household. In this environment, they could be educated, and some became scholars in their own right. Mary's purity ultimately led to her being crowned as queen of heaven and earth. Remaining a virgin also allowed women of the Middle Ages to have a path to power. Elizabeth Abbott writes, "From [virginity] flowed consequential benefits [for women]—liberation from husbands in particular and men in general; access to prohibited professions and scholarship and knowledge; recognition as holy women; self-actualization and direction."[57]

In debates about whether or not Mary had remained perpetually a virgin, female Biblical scholars, such as nuns and abbesses, vehemently defended the idea of her lifelong virginity. For the famous abbess Hildegard of Bingen, Mary's virginity was as central to God's purpose as the Cross. She believed that the Incarnation of Jesus from a virgin mother would have happened even if humanity had not sinned, since it was the very purpose of God's creation of the world.[58] Hildegard, who wrote many fantastically beautiful songs in praise of Mary, regarded both the Blessed Mother and Mother Church as holy—specifically because they were symbols of virginity. She considered nuns to be virgin brides like Mary and always thought of chastity as a state of freedom and joy. She designed special white habits with elaborate headdresses, similar to tiaras, for her community of nuns to wear, since she believed that virgins in heaven dressed like this.[59]

Though not considered as holy as the occupation of nuns, the work of lay women was also considered highly honorable, largely because of the Virgin Mary's example. With the arrival of the humanization movement, lay women frequently saw images of Mary, the most ideal woman, performing domestic duties just as they themselves did. Especially prevalent in art was the depiction of Mary nursing her baby with an expression of motherly love on her face. For the first time since classical antiquity, women who became mothers could feel that their life choice was not only acceptable to God, but in its own way, a path to higher spirituality. Marilyn Yalom explains:

> From the fourteenth to the sixteenth centuries, the nursing Madonna was the prototype of female divinity. Pressing her breast with two fingers so as to facilitate the flow of milk, smiling serenely at the baby held in her arms, she infused holiness in the common maternal act.... The *Virgo lactans* made ... breastfeeding a sacred occupation.[60]

This increased Mary's appeal for late medieval and early modern lay women. She was an infinitely powerful saint, sometimes considered the equal of Jesus, who could relate to the sorrows and joys of daily family life. Johnson argues that a large part of why Mary was so appealing was that she had actually taken on the traditional attributes and functions of pagan goddesses, as well as many borrowed from the Holy Trinity itself.[61]

By the fifteenth century, lay women identified so strongly with the Virgin Mary that they frequently began having personal visions of her. They saw themselves interacting with her or even playing the role of the mother of the infant Jesus. Gail McMurray Gibson recounts the Marian vision of Margery Kempe, the famous Norfolk burgess's wife who penned the first autobiography in the English language. According to Gibson, Kempe wrote in detail about a vision in which Mary gave her the Christ Child's swaddling clothes and allowed her to dress Him.[62] The extent to which a visionary woman's experiences were accepted by Church authorities often determined the course of her life. Was she dismissed as a misguided madwoman, deceived by demonic forces, or honored as a true vessel for the Grace of God? Regardless of whether such visionary women were considered saints or witches, their stories caught the popular imagination. Tales of ordinary people who have encountered the mysterious and unexplainable have been popular throughout all of history.

When thinking about what the Virgin Mary has signified to women, contemporary researchers must remember that, prior to the past century, few women could read. Lay women's perceptions of her were highly influenced by popular legends, the religious artwork they saw in churches, and the sermons of clergymen. However, most of these had at least some basis in Biblical sources. It is important to be able to distinguish what is truly in the New Testament about Mary from widely believed apocrypha. Only then can we examine the Marian literature and images that were subsequently created, in order to gain some understanding of what was believed about her at a particular point in time.

2

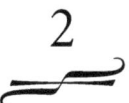

Beginnings

Mary in the Bible

Before embarking on any analysis of Mariology over the centuries, it is advisable to go to its original source—the Bible. Perhaps the first thing any Marianist who examines Biblical references to her notices is a dearth of information. Jaroslav Pelikan states on this subject, "Anyone who comes to the study of later development of devotion to her and doctrine about her ... must be surprised or even shocked to discover how sparse [biblical mentions of Mary] are."[1] There is even a book of scholarly commentary (by Beverly Roberts Gaventa) about the Virgin's New Testament appearances which makes reference to their scarcity in its title—*Mary: Glimpses of the Mother of Jesus*.

Marina Warner mentions that even when the Virgin is in a Biblical story, she is usually silent. She does not say anything at all in the Gospels of Matthew or Mark. She is at her most verbose in Luke, and even there speaks only four times.[2] It is likely that many legends and apocryphal tales were created about Jesus' mother simply to fill in the missing information. Sally Cunneen points out that many of the Marian stories she had always assumed were included in the Bible were, in fact, apocryphal. She was particularly surprised to find no mention of Mary's mother, St. Anne, nor of Jesus' appearance to the Virgin after His Resurrection.[3] There is also no chronicle of Mary's dedication at the Temple as a child, St. Joseph's courtship of her, their marriage, or her heavenly Assumption and Coronation.

Historians generally agree that the letters of St. Paul predated the four Gospels, so it is almost certain that the first non-allegorical reference to the Virgin appeared in his Epistle to the Galatians. In it, he mentions almost offhandedly that Jesus was "made of a woman."[4] The phrase was probably included in this letter to emphasize that He was, in fact, a human being. Temporally speaking, the next person to include her in his writing is the New Testament author Mark. His Gospel was quite likely written before the other three. He mentions her only twice, in the course of stories about Jesus.

The other three Gospels contain more significant amounts of Marian narrative, and she appears once in the Acts of the Apostles. In addition, many Christian theologians have argued that the Woman Clothed with the Sun in Revelation is, at the very least, an allegorical representation of the Virgin Mary. It is commonly believed, particularly among Roman Catholics, that the Bride in the Song of Songs symbolizes her, as well. However, Luke's work is clearly the standout for Marian information among the four New Testament Gospels. Catholic scholars have even postulated that his writings were based on an account from her own lips. Indeed, it has been commonly believed that a particularly close relationship existed between Luke and the Virgin. One tradition holds that St. Luke painted her portrait, and several Mediterranean towns still claim to possess an original Icon of the Virgin created by him.[5]

Even Luke, however, does not begin his writings with Mary. Instead, he starts with a formal preface establishing his credibility, a common narrative device among historians of the time. He then continues with the angel Gabriel's announcement of an entirely different pregnancy made possible by divine intervention. Mary's childless cousin Elizabeth was thought to be too old to have a baby, but her husband Zechariah was told by angelic messenger that she had conceived a son, John the Baptist. Subsequently, Gabriel did not appear to Mary until her kinswoman was six months pregnant.[6]

The interaction that followed, simply referred to as the Annunciation, is one of the best known and most frequently artistically represented stories in history. Some contemporary scholars have emphasized the contrast between the two announcements of Gabriel. Zechariah, who is a priest, came upon the angel when he entered "the temple of the Lord." Gabriel, however, visited Mary, a simple young girl, in her own home. According to Jean Galot, this signifies that, in a departure from God's ways in the Old Testament, when people had to seek Him in sacred temples, He "intends to come to men as He had never come before."[7] John McHugh points out that the divinity of Jesus is emphasized by the contrast between the two angelic announcements. Gabriel said of John the Baptist that "he [would] be great before the Lord," but Mary was told that Jesus, simply, would be "great."[8]

Since the fourth century, Mary's initial response to Gabriel, "How can this be, since I do not know man?" has been frequently interpreted as more than just a statement of her current virginity. Theologians have also taken it as a declaration that she has already made a vow of perpetual virginity. She did not, in fact, intend to "know man," despite her engagement to Joseph.[9] Galot, however, theorizes that Mary only came to understand that God intended a life of virginity for her when her pregnancy was announced.[10] By contrast, some Protestant scholars, who believe that Mary had sexual relations with her husband after Jesus was born, reject the notion that she made such a vow at any time.

The Virgin's other significant utterance to Gabriel was her assent to bear the Son of God. However, its specific form, "Behold the handmaid of the Lord!" followed by "Let it be done to me according to your word," contains connotations of womanly obedience to male authority. This is an aspect of Christianity that has troubled feminists for centuries. Warner seems scarcely able to conceal her anger when she writes, "Mary's act of acceptance came to epitomize a restricted moral notion quite unworthy of the term: that of feminine submissiveness."[11] Beverly Roberts Gaventa, however, plainly disagrees with such sentiments, stating:

> Some traditional interpretations of Mary see in these words the emergence of Mary as a model for all women, but it is difficult to find anything in the text that suggests such an identification between Mary and women in general. With her words of compliance Mary becomes not a model female but a model disciple who consents to what is not fully understood.[12]

According to the Gospel of Luke, soon after the Annunciation took place, the Virgin set off to visit her pregnant cousin, Elizabeth. When her cousin greeted Mary with great joy, she responded with the Magnificat, her longest utterance in the Bible. Unfortunately for Marianists, understandably eager for the Virgin to express herself in her own words, most contemporary Biblical scholars attribute the Magnificat to Luke. Brown writes in *Mary in the New Testament*, "Did Mary herself compose the Magnificat? It may surprise some readers to learn that today one would be hard pressed to find any critical Biblical scholar who would answer in the affirmative."[13]

The Catholic priest Jean Galot, however, believes that the Virgin's poetic answer to Elizabeth should be attributed to Mary herself. He states, "[The Magnificat] is [the Virgin Mary's] hymn of gratitude, which bursts forth from her lips at the moment, but which had doubtless taken shape in her mind along the way."[14] So perhaps there is more disagreement among exegesists about the Magnificat's origins than Brown acknowledges. At different points in history, Biblical scholars have commonly believed one of the three main theories about its creation. There is the "ancient" one, which assumes that the Virgin herself truly composed this speech. A more modern idea attributes it to St. Luke, who intended it primarily as a means of allowing Mary to show her gratitude and humility. The most recent theory is that Luke adapted a previous composition, possibly a hymn from the earliest years of Christianity.[15] Similarly, Sally Cunneen argues that St. Luke "pieced together a mosaic of phrases from the Hebrew Scriptures" in order to conflate the Virgin Mary with the nation of Israel.[16]

For Biblical scholars who accepted Marian authorship of the Magnificat, another contentious point has been how to interpret her own self-description as "lowly." This is largely because Martin Luther, one of the early Protestants, used the idea of Mary's humility to minimize her theological importance. Arguing that with the Magnificat, the Virgin "thrust mankind's esteem from her," he emphasized her role as a simple housewife. Other important Protestant Reformers, such as Calvin and Zwingli, followed suit, insisting that Mary was humble, never claiming the roles of Intercessor or Co-Redeemer for herself.[17] Thus, one of the fundamental differences between Catholics and Protestants was established.

Even today, Catholic scholars tend to disagree with this interpretation of "lowliness," seeing it as a reference to worldly poverty. Cunneen writes, "When [Mary] mentions her 'lowliness' in the Magnificat, however, she is speaking about her social condition, not her personal attitude."[18] She adds that the Virgin's intent was to speak as a representative of those who struggled against conventional power and the domination of wealth.[19] Similarly, Galot theorizes that the Magnificat was Mary's means of aligning herself with the poor.[20] Catholic theologians throughout the centuries have argued that the Virgin's calling attention to her own poverty was a means of emphasizing God's favor for the oppressed.[21]

The "poverty theory" seems to be borne out in the Nativity story which follows. Mary was forced to leave her home and travel to Bethlehem due to the census, so she gave birth to her child in a stable, underscoring her lack of material possessions.[22] St. Luke also makes a point of Mary's wrapping Jesus in swaddling, rather than a blanket of sumptuous purple material, as a queen's son would have had. This emphasizes that the Son of God assumed poverty, as well as mortality, when he took on human form.[23] Yet, Galot claims, "It is very evident that it was Mary who suffered most from the circumstances of [Jesus'] birth ... in the sacrifice of being destitute and homeless."[24]

In the Marian cycle, Luke's Nativity story is also remarkable for her silence. The Virgin speaks little or not at all throughout the entire Gospels of Matthew, Mark and John. However, she is interactive at the beginning of Luke's version, verbally engaging with Gabriel and Elizabeth. During the Nativity cycle, however, she "ponders things in her heart," connoting a sense of secrecy and isolation. Even when the shepherds come on the scene after Jesus is born, uttering cries of amazement, confusion, and exaltation, Mary is silent.[25]

According to Luke, the shepherds were actually the only visitors to the stable. The coming of the Magi, as well as the Holy Family's subsequent flight into Egypt, so prominent in Matthew's Gospel, are entirely absent from Luke's account. Sally Cunneen points out, "Believers have taken bits of Matthew and added them to Luke to make one Nativity story. Never mind that the pieces cannot be reconciled factually; they have entered the human imagination together."[26] Since this is the case, it is necessary to examine Mary's place in this part of the story here, despite the fact that it is not part of Luke's account. In both the Visit of the Magi and the Flight into Egypt sequences, the Virgin is also silent. Although she is obviously present, the reader is offered no insight into her reactions to these events. Gaventa points out that in Matthew's infancy cycle, "Mary almost fades from view ... she speaks not a single word and is the subject of an active verb only as she gives birth."[27]

Just as Luke's Gospel, overall, is a Marian piece, Matthew's focus in the Infancy Cycle is on Joseph. This is particularly obvious when attention is drawn to the idea of the angelic visit. Luke offers the reader a detailed account of the Annunciation. In Matthew's Gospel, however, the angel appears to Joseph, urging him not to "put Mary aside" for what is presumed to be her pregnancy by another man. In Matthew, the Virgin's overall role is to serve as an endangered figure, whom her husband must protect. Gaventa writes, "We learn nothing of her own thoughts, opinions, judgments, actions, desires; all we know of Mary is that she remains under threat of destruction."[28]

Despite the Virgin's lack of centrality in the Bible during the Visit of the Magi sequence, iconographic art has nonetheless assigned her that role. In the fifth century, she was frequently portrayed in rich gems and royal robes, receiving the gifts of the three kings in a kind of imperial audience. Such imagery was largely politically motivated. Church leaders at this time were actively promoting the idea that they had an authority that surpassed all earthly kings, particularly when those rulers stubbornly clung to pagan ways. In such depictions, Mary should be viewed as the personification of the Church, receiving her rightful tribute from the leaders of foreign, barbaric realms.[29]

Returning to Luke's account, however, the next event to take place after the Nativity is the Presentation at the Temple. This sequence is particularly important for traditional Catholic Marianist scholars, since it raises several theological questions about her. The first is why Mary took her Son to the temple at all. The traditional reason for this ceremony, performed in accordance with Jewish law, is to make a ritual offering, compensating for the sexual sin inherent in reproduction. Because of Jesus' virginal conception, Mary was technically exempt from this requirement. However, "in the eyes of men and Jewish society," it was right for her to undergo Purification. Many traditional theologians have argued that she did so in the spirit of humility and respect for the law. In addition, she wished to take Jesus to the Temple in order to formally offer Him to God. Galot states, "Purification for her who was pure meant relinquishing her son by consecrating Him to the Most High."[30]

In addition to the issue of Mary's decision to submit to purification, there is the dark and mysterious prophecy of Simeon. The priest at this temple told Mary that her soul would be pierced with a sword, so that the thoughts of many hearts could be revealed. According to traditional Marian theology, this was meant to signify her unique association with Jesus' self-sacrifice at the Crucifixion. Because of this, it was believed that she shared in her Son's suffering, as well as His part in human redemption. Galot writes:

> The episode of the presentation of Jesus in the Temple shows clearly the role assigned to Mary in the drama of redemption. It is of the closest association with the Savior in the suffering which is to merit salvation. Mary's suffering is merged in Jesus' and is ordained to the same end: the "rise" or "resurrection" of many, who will be led to reveal the thoughts of their hearts.[31]

John McHugh explains that there is an alternate, more contemporary interpretation of Simeon's prophecy. It could possibly have been referring to Mary not as an individual, but as the personification of Israel. In this case, the sword symbolism would connote Jesus' ministry separating Israelites who believed him from those who did not.[32] McHugh asserts that there is a means of reconciling the traditional and contemporary explanations of this prophecy. Mary's pain, particularly during the Crucifixion, stemmed from two sources. Most obviously, she suffered because her Son was being mocked and tortured. However, she also had to bear the sorrow that most people had rejected Jesus' message of salvation.[33]

The final scene in what has come to be referred to as the "Infancy Narrative" of Luke actually took place when Jesus was twelve years old. In this story, Jesus' family traveled to the Temple in Jerusalem to celebrate Passover. When they set off for home after the ceremonies, it was discovered that Jesus was not among his kin. After much searching, Mary and Joseph discovered that he had never left the Temple. The Virgin mildly rebuked him, saying that they had been looking for him for three days with great anxiety. Jesus, however, brushed off her worry, asking, "Why have you been searching for me? Did you not know that I had to be in my Father's house?"

In the chronology of Jesus' life, this tale is the first of many in which He repudiates his earthly family in favor of God the Father.[34] Throughout His entire ministry, He exempted Himself from the filial relations and responsibilities normally accepted at the time. Jesus brushed aside anyone else's mention of His expected role in an earthly family, emphasizing instead His relationship with God and the community of new Christians. He did this repeatedly in all four of the Gospels, despite the fact that, as it is explicitly stated in the Bible, Mary did not understand the meaning of her Son's words. This surely reinforced the wedge that He had already driven between them when he remained behind at the Temple.[35] However, just as she did when the shepherds visited, the Virgin struggled against her confusion, pondering the meaning of Jesus' words in her heart.

Many traditional Marianist theologians have interpreted the Temple incident, when perceived from the Virgin's point of view, as a prefiguration of her part in the Crucifixion and Resurrection. Both times, the Virgin mourned Jesus for three days before he was ultimately restored to her, and she was able to rejoice once more. Particularly in recent Biblical scholarship, however, feminists have pointed out Jesus' repeated indifference toward his mother. Galot attempts to soften it, explaining, "Unless we sense this cooperation in the drama of redemption, Jesus' behavior toward his mother would seem too cruel."[36] Marina Warner, however, remains unconvinced. As if responding to such apologetics about the Temple story, she writes, "For Catholics and especially for devotees of Mary, the passage, however symbolic, remains disturbing."[37]

Following the chronology of the Virgin's life, her next appearance in the Bible occurs in the Gospel of John. She is portrayed here sitting beside her Son, a guest at a wedding feast in Cana. Unlike Matthew and Luke, who generally use Mary's name when writing about her, John always refers to her as "the mother of Jesus." According to Gaventa, it is primarily because this Evangelist wished to call attention to Christ's humanity — obviously, He was a man, since He had an earthly mother.[38] McHugh emphasizes that John did not mean to diminish her importance with this form of identification. He points out that Arabic people still refer to a woman respectfully as a certain man's mother, especially if her son is famous.[39]

At this wedding feast, the hosts ran out of wine, and she urged her Son to remedy the situation, saying, "They have no wine." Somewhat surprisingly, he strongly resisted her implied request, saying, "Woman, what have I to do with thee? Mine hour is not yet come." Nonetheless, she told the waiters to do whatever Jesus said, and, however reluctantly, he transformed water into the needed wine. One of only two Biblically recorded conversations between Jesus and His mother, this exchange seems so strange that scholars have disagreed about its interpretation for centuries.

The traditional Catholic explanation is provided by Galot, who points out that Mary merely implied her request for a miracle. The subtle phrasing of it, "They have no wine," allowed Him ample freedom to refuse it.[40] Cunneen also underscores the Virgin's lack of demand, writing, "At Cana, Mary neither yielded her own opinion nor judged her son's; she did not impose a decision, but rather helped him make one."[41] On the surface, Mary seems to be asking for miraculous intervention for something frivolous. Unlike most of her Son's later miracles, no one here was sick, permanently maimed or in danger. The provision of wine was merely to spare the hosts of the feast embarrassment. Traditionally, Christian preachers have used this story as a means of demonstrating that the Virgin has motherly concern for young couples' happiness.[42]

Nonetheless, Galot argues, when she made this request, she was very much aware that she was asking for something more than wine. Up until this time, Jesus had never performed any sort of miraculous act. This theologian states, "Fundamentally, she is asking Jesus to deign to manifest himself at last as the savior of men, by becoming the savior of this wedding through a miracle."[43] Marina Warner concurs, writing, "Out of kindliness at Cana, she had prompted her son to change water into wine so that their hosts should not be shamed; but at a deeper level she had ... instigated the first miracle, which ... revealed the divinity of her son."[44]

Warner adds that this tale has been used to demonstrate how efficiently Mary is able to intercede with her Son — she is able to prompt Him to perform a miracle even when He is reluctant to do so.[45] Galot takes this assertion a step further, arguing that Jesus' response implied that God had originally intended His Son to perform His first miracle under different circumstances. Mary, however, understood that it would reveal Jesus as he wished to be perceived — benevolent, sympathetic, and generous to the lowly.[46] The hosts, after all, were so poor that they could not provide adequate wine for their guests. So the Virgin, in her own quiet way, was actually able to subvert God's divine plan, to some extent.

The question remains, however, of what Jesus' brusque response to Mary truly revealed about His intentions, as well as their relationship. Cunneen theorizes that He once again wanted to put some distance between them, separating His divine mission from her expectations.[47] However unsettling this idea may be to Mariologists, it is logical in the context of the other Gospels. In the work of Pere F.M. Braun, Jesus' response at Cana is also interpreted as distancing himself somewhat from Mary. He feels that Christ was telling His mother He could not obey her any longer, since He had to begin the work of God. However, as a sort of consolation, He acceded to change the water to wine. Jesus honored one last request for Mary before He had to separate from her until they could be reunited in heaven. Once there, He could listen to her requests as her obedient son once more.[48]

John McHugh offers an alternate explanation of Jesus' response to the Virgin, arguing that He wished to downplay the importance of the miracle itself. Throughout His ministry, Jesus criticized those who needed to witness His supernatural abilities in order to believe His message. He emphasized that people should not focus on the miracles themselves, but on the spiritual truths they symbolized and revealed.[49] According to McHugh, Jesus was not offering the consolation of "one more miracle for the road" but rather warning beforehand that the deed itself should not be the witnesses' focus.

Despite such mitigating explanations, it is impossible to entirely discount the idea that Jesus wished to repudiate his familial association with Mary. Mark's first Marian reference occurs when she and Christ's "brethren" stood outside of where he was teaching. Their presence there prompted His comment that whoever did the will of God was, in fact, His brother, sister or mother. Later, when Jesus returned to Nazareth after an absence, the genuinely puzzled local townsfolk asked each other if this was not the son of Mary.[50] These events, substantiated by the Gospels of Matthew and Luke, generally serve as a kind of contrast. While the general public was quick to place Jesus in the context of His earthly family, He identified Himself as the Son of God.

His most deliberate disassociation from His mother appears in the Gospel of Luke, the most Marian of the four. Here, an unnamed woman in the crowd that Jesus was preaching to called out to Him, "Blessed is the womb that bore you and the breasts that nursed you!" Jesus responded with, "Blessed rather are those who hear the word of God and obey it." Gaventa points out that due to the ambiguity of Christ's response, it is impossible to know His true meaning. It is simply unclear whether He intended to include Mary in His group of people who heard and kept the word of God.[51]

Theologians have argued for over a millennium about whether, in this instance, Jesus was praising His mother as a disciple or discounting her role in

His life. Cunneen comes down in favor of the theory that Christ was, in fact, blessing the Virgin here. The author argues that the fact that the story appears in Luke's Gospel is telling. She explains, "Luke has always made Mary first among those who hear."[52] Marina Warner, however, writes that Jesus' reply "rings harshly" and has "apparent hard-heartedness."[53] She adds that Catholic authorities have always disagreed with assessments like hers of this event. In 1974, Pope Paul VI urged all Christians to follow the Biblical woman's example in praising Mary as the mother of God. The pope claimed that Jesus was merely rephrasing the woman's accolade, emphasizing the spiritual motherhood of the Church and its prefiguration by His own mother.

Mary's final appearance in John's Gospel is a brief, though extremely memorable one, and like the Annunciation, it has been portrayed in art thousands of times. She stood at the foot of her Son's cross, alongside "the disciple Jesus loved," someone generally accepted for centuries as Christ's apostle John. Shortly before His death, Jesus called out to her, probably indicating John, "Woman, behold your son!" To his beloved disciple, He then said, "Behold your mother!"

A multitude of theories have been proposed about the significance of this scene. In fact, it is probably the most frequently debated aspect of Mariology. Its interpretation by the Franciscans in the thirteenth century, which cast Mary as the Mother of Sorrows, was probably the most visceral and least esoteric. For this reason, the Franciscan inspired cult of the Mater Dolorosa has been enthusiastically embraced by lay people. It required no complicated interpretation of typology but could be understood on a strictly emotional level. Marina Warner writes:

> Through [Mary's] sorrow, the man or woman in prayer could feel the stab of loss and agony. The Virgin was the instrument mediating bafflement at the mystery of the Redemption into emotional understanding. She made the sacrifice on Golgotha seem real, for she focused human feeling in a comprehensible and accessible way.[54]

In the seventeenth century, however, a controversy arose about whether the Virgin had, in fact, felt such agonizing loss over her Son's death at all. St. Francis de Sales argued that because Mary never doubted that Jesus would rise again, she could not have grieved over His death.[55] This called all of the moving "Mother of Sorrows" imagery into question. Interpretations of her role at the Crucifixion in subsequent centuries seemed to assign her an increasingly symbolic, less basically human function.

Most of the scholarship approved by the Catholic Church in the first half of the twentieth century focused, not on her suffering at Cavalry, but on her becoming the Mother of Christians there. According to this ideology, when Jesus told Mary and John to regard each other as mother and son, He was offering her a maternal role over all His disciples. This applied figuratively to all those who subsequently came to love Jesus—the Christians. So, as mother,

her function would be to protect her "children," keeping them united with her Son.[56] According to Galot, Christ's act of making Mary and John mother and son to each other should be viewed as the basis of modern Marian piety. He explains:

> To show devotion to Mary is first of all to fulfill the will of the Savior and to try to enter fully into the execution of His plan of salvation.... The honor which was granted to the beloved disciple to represent Christ, in a certain way, in the eyes of Mary is an honor granted to every Christian.... To take Mary to his own is part of the ideal of the life of a Christian.[57]

Some Protestant theologians have interpreted the symbolic significance of this scene entirely differently. One theory is that Mary personifies Jewish Christianity, which Gentile Christianity, symbolized by John, must honor as its true mother.[58] A more contemporary Catholic metaphorical explanation works outside of gender roles. Mary is seen primarily as a model for the disciples of Jesus, rather than their mother. Because she was present both at Cana, where Jesus' ministry began, as well as at His Crucifixion, McHugh calls the Virgin "the prototype and exemplar of faith."[59] He believes that in John's account, she is primarily meant to show readers what Christian faith really involves—believing persistently in Jesus even when evil seems to be triumphant.

Contemporary scholarship by women about Mary at the Crucifixion diverges somewhat from all of these interpretations. Sally Cunneen's is probably the most similar to McHugh's analysis, perhaps because they are both self-identified Catholics. She writes that the Virgin's presence at Cavalry indicates her role as a symbolic witness to all those who continue to believe in Christ, despite their unanswered questions and doubts.[60] However, Beverly Roberts Gaventa, a Protestant, argues that Mary at the cross emphasized Jesus' continued connection to His life on earth. When He consigned her to John's care, Christ was, in fact, removing Himself from earthly existence, in order to be reunited with His heavenly Father.[61] The separation from His mother that Jesus had been striving for, since the time when He was lost at the Temple, was truly complete at the Crucifixion.

The last undisputed appearance of Mary in the New Testament occurs in Acts, which was also authored by Luke. It is mentioned here that she was among those gathered together when the Holy Spirit descended upon them at Pentecost. According to traditional Catholic scholarship, she was there because of her role as a collaborator in God's plan of salvation. Galot explains that her involvement was necessary to ensure the Holy Spirit's intervention in the creation of the Church, as it had been with her at Christ's conception. Her mission of redemptive maternity made her the mother of Jesus, the apostles (both present and future), and the Church itself.[62] Certainly, this role would explain the iconographic depictions of Pentecost described by Marina Warner, where she becomes, "a towering figure ... the very embodiment of Mater Ecclesia, before whom the apostles sometimes kneel in awe."[63]

More recent ecumenical scholarship has tended to view her presence there as an affirmation of her work as a disciple. Protestants have tended to emphasize the disciple role for both the Virgin and Mary Magdalene. This could be attributed to a desire to establish that women and men have the same position in the Church. Brown states that Luke's inclusion of the Virgin in the Pentecost story shows her to be "of one accord with those who would constitute the nascent Church."[64] She declared herself the "handmaid of the Lord" at the Annunciation, and she still hadn't changed her mind, despite all the hardships it brought her. According to Protestant theory, Luke's primary purpose in focusing on Mary was to show that she remained steadfast in her decision to be a disciple. She refused to be dissuaded by her inability to truly understand Jesus.[65]

It is possible that there is another appearance of Mary in the New Testament, though it is, at best, both a debatable and allegorical one. The Woman Clothed with the Sun, a figure that gives birth while being threatened by a dragon, is in the Revelations of John. Rescued by God, she has been strongly associated with the Virgin since the first half of the sixth century. Many theologians, however, have strongly denied that this figure was ever meant to signify Mary. McHugh states, "To the best of my knowledge, all those who stand outside the Roman or Anglo-Catholic tradition take the woman to be a symbol of the people of God ... or a figure representing the Church ... or as a symbol of both — but certainly not as representing in any way the Blessed Virgin Mary."[66] Even Galot, normally the champion of traditional Catholic scholarship, equivocates on this issue. His work states that, strictly speaking, the woman in the Apocalypse of John is not really Mary.[67]

Nonetheless, the idea gained increased significance in the public consciousness toward the middle of the twentieth century. Pope Pius XII cited Mary's appearance in Revelations as evidence for her assumption into heaven, which he proclaimed as dogma in 1950. Many Catholic theologians of the time produced articles arguing in favor of this interpretation, in order to substantiate the pope's claims. Riani argues that the conclusion that can be drawn from Revelations is that "God wants His Church to be a double of His mother."[68] Satan perpetually does all in his power to destroy the Woman Clothed with the Sun, while the faithful feel ever-strengthening devotion to her. McHugh makes this somewhat complicated argument in favor of the theory:

> When we read chapter 12 of the Apocalypse, and see in the woman clothed with the sun a symbol of that faithful remnant of Zion which became the nucleus of the Christian Church, may we not reverse the identification made by St. Ambrose, and say that Mary was in history the living personification of the woman seen on Patmos [by St. John]?[69]

Another possible allegorical representation of the Virgin Mary occurs in the Old Testament. It is possible that she is the Bride in a book of the Bible known as the Song of Solomon, the Song of Songs, Canticle of Canticles or Ecclesiastises. Like the Woman Clothed with the Sun, the Bride is not necessarily the

Virgin Mary. Compelling arguments against the Marian interpretation have been made, especially by Jewish and Protestant authorities. Many theologians have viewed the Bride as Ecclesia, the personification of the Church, and it has even been proposed that she is Mary Magdalene.

Charlene Spretnak theorizes that the Song of Songs, with all its rich erotic imagery, may have grown out of an oral tradition that existed before 200 B.C. Its true roots might lie in the devotions commonly spoken to a Canaanite fertility goddess that predated Christianity, called Ashtoreh or Inanna. Probably because it was an appropriate outlet for celibate clergymen's sublimated desires, it became the most frequently commented on book of the Bible during the twelfth and thirteenth centuries. The language and imagery of the Canticle of Canticles contributed to the medieval tradition of troubadours' songs which celebrated the Virgin Mary.[70] In medieval times, miracle-working Black Madonna statues were given increased credibility because of the line that the Bride was "black, but lovely." These icons became so famous for performing miracles that Madonna statues were sometimes painted black, in the hopes that they would work similar wonders.[71]

Probably the first theologian to use imagery from the Song of Solomon to describe the Virgin Mary, despite the book's Jewish origins, was the ninth-century monk Paschasius Radbertus, who included it in his treatise, *Cogitis Me* (You Compel Me). The history of this work is somewhat convoluted. Radbertus actually wrote it for two nuns dedicated to Mary called Theodrada and Irma, who had taken him in as a baby left on the doorstep of their abbey. However, utilizing a common medieval literary device, the author disassociated himself from his own work. He claimed that it was actually a letter he found, written by St. Jerome to his friends Paula and Eustochium, nuns in Bethlehem. Thus, *Cogitis Me* was erroneously believed throughout the Middle Ages to be the work of Jerome.[72]

In this treatise, Radbertus (as Jerome) held up the Virgin as a spiritual model for nuns to follow. He praised her perpetual virginity with the "garden enclosed, fountain sealed up" allegory for sexual purity from the Song of Songs.[73] In the twelfth century, St. Bernard of Clairvaux, a Cistercian monk who was intensely devoted to the Virgin Mary, further popularized the Marian garden allegory. He also utilized other metaphors from the Canticle of Canticles which reinforced the sensual pleasures of her appearance and scent. It was commonly believed that sinners, because of their future destinies as rotting corpses, smelled like putrefaction. Bernard claimed that because she had conquered sin, the Virgin smelled ambrosial, like Solomon's bride.[74]

Also in the early twelfth century, though after St. Bernard, the theologian Rupert of Deutz interpreted the entire Song of Solomon from the viewpoint of Mary's historical relationship to Christ. Rupert claimed that it was meant as a prophecy, actualized by the Virgin. Supposedly, it retells the story of Mary's life four times in four different ways.[75] Rupert correlated the Bride's ardor for her lover with the Virgin's emotional intimacy with God at the Annunciation. In another comparison, he related the Bride's breasts with those of the nursing Madonna.[76] In the second half of the twelfth century, Alain de Lille expanded upon Rupert's argument. Their writings were so complementary that they became interrelated in the minds of medieval readers. Scholars in subsequent centuries nearly always discussed their work in the same paragraph, almost interchangeably.[77]

Interpreting the Bible to view the Virgin Mary in such romantic terms probably led to the creation of new legends about her, in which she was further idealized. During the medieval era, an abundance of Marian "miracle tales" were written — legends about mortal people's interactions with her. *The Golden Legend*, the ultimate medieval compilation of these stories, became one of the biggest bestsellers of the era. Although it contained stories about many saints, some of the most cherished ones were about encounters with the Virgin Mary. In some tales, people interact with her directly, often receiving her intercession to help them avoid or repent from a terrible sin. In others, however, a particularly devout person is able to bring about his or her own salvation through use of a Marian devotional object, such as the Rosary or a prayerbook called the Book of Hours. It is with just such a legend, in fact, that the next chapter begins.

3

Devotional Objects

I Carry Her with Me Always

There was a young noblewoman whose parents died, and as she was their only child, she inherited all their riches and lands. She had no one to depend upon for help or advice other than Jesus and Mary, so she promised that in return for their protection, she would always remain a virgin. As proof of her piety, she read her Book of Hours out loud every day. Despite her goodness, however, her cousins, knowing she had no man to defend her, began to steal from her. This lady knew a local knight, whom she appealed to for help for friendship's sake. He replied that mere friendship was not enough, and that he would only aid her if she would "give him her love." Having sworn to remain a virgin, she naturally refused. He continued to persuade her to repudiate her vow of chastity, telling her that her refusal made him so miserable he wished to die.

In desperation, she at last gave in to the knight and agreed to meet him secretly after nightfall in her orchard. However, he did not arrive at the appointed hour, and she grew impatient with waiting for him. She took up her Book of Hours, went into her little chapel, and began to recite the Hours of the Dead. The knight came upon her while she was reading aloud. Much to his amazement, he saw many shining ghosts who had risen from their graves to kneel beside her and cry to her for mercy. When she finished the Hours of the Dead with the words "rest in peace," the ghosts bowed down to her in thanks and slipped silently away. She then recited the Hours of the Virgin. As soon as she began, Mary was carried into the little chapel on a throne borne by angels. When the young woman ended this prayer with "Hail Mary," all the angels joined her in praising the Mother of God, then carried the throne away.

It was only afterwards that the young woman looked up, seeing the knight there, and he fell at her feet to beg forgiveness. She looked confused, and he told her of all the miracles he had seen that night. Much surprised, she swore she had not been aware of any unearthly visitors. The knight then vowed that he would fight her cousins without further demands. He also said that that when all her lands were returned to her, she should build a nunnery upon them and take vows. As for himself, he promised the lady that when he got back what was rightfully hers, he himself would become a chaste hermit, serving the Virgin Mary all the days of his life. All of this came to pass, and the lady renewed her vow of chastity. Stories of her great holiness traveled throughout the land and won many souls for God.[1]

This miracle tale shows what great power Books of Hours were thought to have for those people, particularly women, who believed in them. Simply by saying the prayers contained in her book, the holy young woman in this story was able to contact the dead, angels, and the Virgin Mary herself. She was also ultimately empowered to change her own fortune for the better. What were these powerful prayerbooks known as Books of Hours and where did they come from? Their predecessors were the excessively ostentatious prayerbooks, called Breviaries, which were often owned by clergy members. Many wealthy, secular people who had received some basic schooling and learned how to read began to desire a prayerbook of their own. Educated people were eager to integrate devotional reading into their daily lives, as most monks, priests, and even nuns did, so that they, too, could cultivate a more direct, intimate relationship with God. The prospect of possessing their own prayerbooks for the first time was exciting because it would allow them to pray and meditate without clerical intervention. In response to the spiritual needs of such people, the Catholic Church sanctified a book of psalms, known as the Psalter, for lay use.

By the late fourteenth century, however, the Psalter had largely been replaced by the Book of Hours, which was significantly different in content. John Harthan writes that, beginning in the fourteenth century, the basic text which appeared in lay prayerbooks was the "Little Office of Our Lady," a short service in honor of the Virgin Mary. The "Little Office" had previously been attached to the Psalter as a kind of appendix, but over time it became a separate, more commonly used, prayerbook of its own.[2] In addition to the "Little Office," Books of Hours also contained various collections of Biblical and apocryphal material, as well as stories of saints' lives.

Medieval people simply could not get enough Books of Hours, and demand for them was unparalleled. More were created from the late thirteenth to the early sixteenth century than any other type of book, including the Bible.[3] Lawrence R. Poos comments, "For the first time since classical antiquity, the most common book being produced was intended to remain in non-clerical hands."[4] The Book of Hours would be the preferred prayerbook of lay people for over 250 years, and its influence would continue to resonate for centuries. It has even been theorized that all subsequent lay prayerbooks have been derived from Hours.[5]

Even today, hundreds of years after Books of Hours have ceased to be bestsellers, it is obvious that most of them were highly valued by their owners.

Woman with devotional reading (courtesy Chant Art).

Laymen fortunate enough to possess these devotional works usually took excellent care of them. An ingenious fine leather or silk covering for Hours called a chemisette was developed, in order to keep the books' pages clean when they were being read.[6] Ladies who owned richly illustrated prayerbooks sometimes stored them with their most valuable jewelry and only took them out to use on special occasions.[7]

Owners of Books of Hours also wanted to be sure that the volumes they treasured would be appreciated and cared for by their heirs. They often left careful instructions in their wills about what should be done with their Hours.[8] Concern over this matter among book owners was so prevalent that the volumes least likely to be left out of medieval wills were devotional works. Intriguingly, many medieval ladies wanted to leave their Hours only to other women. Most frequently, daughters would be named their heirs, but if a mother had only sons surviving her, one of her daughters-in-law would often be chosen to inherit. Occasionally, the owner would write such a bequest in the Book of Hours itself, so that there would be no mistake about her wishes after death.[9]

Although these prayerbooks were owned by both men and women, most contemporary scholars would agree with Penkneth's statement that "a special association existed between women and Books of Hours."[10] Upper-class ladies were unlikely to be without at least one copy. In Susan Groag Bell's essay "Medieval Women Book Owners: Arbiters of Lay Piety and Ambassadors of Culture," she states why Hours may have especially appealed to women:

> It is clear that Books of Hours were much more than simple prayerbooks. They could bring spiritual consolation, edification, and perhaps peace of mind; they could also instruct, distract, and amuse. To dismiss women's devotional books merely as books of piety would demonstrate a misunderstanding both of medieval women's need for spiritual nourishment and of the richly varied contents of their books of devotion.[11]

Medieval and early modern women's reasons for owning Books of Hours were as varied as the works themselves. It has certainly been suggested that some ladies wanted to possess elaborately illuminated Hours primarily so that the books could be brought to church as vain, showy fashion accessories. Penkneth cites Eustace Deschamps' fourteenth-century satirical poem about such women:

> A Book of Hours, too, must be mine,
> Where subtle workmanship will shine,
> Of gold and azure, rich and smart,
> Arranged and painted with great art,
> Covered with fine brocade of gold;
> And there must be, so as to hold
> The pages closed, two golden clasps.[12]

John Harthan, however, warns that the contemporary scholar should not judge medieval book patrons harshly for their ostentation, stating, "With piety often went display; luxury cannot be kept out of religion."[13] Susan Groag Bell offers a more intriguing justification for women who could not resist elaborate Hours. She argues that because medieval ladies were prohibited from touching most of the artistic treasures used during liturgical rituals, they may have wanted the one item of devotion permitted to them to be as beautiful as possible.[14]

It cannot be denied, however, that some of the uses women found for their Books of Hours seem somewhat frivolous to modern thinkers. It became fashionable for ladies to seek out uncommon prayers to be inserted into their Hours. Some women in the Middle Ages even went so far as to pay priests to write unusual prayers for them. Henk van Os states, "Prayers that were out of the ordinary were eagerly collected, just as cooks collect recipes today."[15] Owners also sometimes used their Books of Hours as albums in which to keep the pilgrims' badges and other religious knickknacks they acquired on their travels.[16] An obvious contemporary parallel for this practice is the current vogue among young girls for collecting stickers or trading cards to be displayed in albums.

Ladies also employed their Hours as fetishistic talismans to ward off ill health. Many lay people felt these prayerbooks could preserve them from sickness if always carried somewhere on their bodies. It was also believed that certain prayers contained within Books of Hours would protect women from childbirth complications if placed above their heads while they were in labor.[17] An obscure martyr, Apollonia of Alexandria, appeared frequently in these prayerbooks because she was considered the patron saint of those suffering from toothache.[18]

Although women sometimes found uses for their Books of Hours that seem frivolous or strange to contemporary people, it must be remembered that these books primarily existed as expressions of their owners' most deeply held spiritual beliefs. It has frequently been mentioned by historians that commissioning Books of Hours allowed laymen to express their own spiritual convictions, since the Church permitted them to personalize these books greatly. Bell argues, "It seems likely that the laywoman would be even more interested in this escape from church control, which provided for private devotional reading."[19]

Many also owned devotional works for more intellectual reasons. Women who lived during the Middle Ages were often responsible for the education of their children, especially their daughters, and Hours served as textbooks. Penkneth writes, "Books of Hours were frequently employed as 'first reading books.' Some even contain the laboured A's and B's of someone learning to write."[20] It was generally considered important that girls first read devotional texts. Many theologians, such as St. Jerome, believed that the primary reason to educate females at all was to distract them from their own vain or sexual thoughts.[21] The Virgin Mary was frequently depicted reading in medieval art partly to show that she kept her mind too occupied to think of sinful things.

The respected late medieval female writer Christine de Pizan, who penned the famous women's advice manual, *The Treasury of the City of Ladies*, considered saying Hours important for young girls' moral development. She recommended that they do so every morning immediately after getting dressed.[22] De Pizan also emphasized the importance of exposing girls to such devotional literature early, stating:

> When the princess's daughter has reached a suitable age, she will be taught to read and thereafter to learn her Hours and her prayers.... She will not be allowed to read of vain things, folly or loose living. No such books will be permitted in her presence, for a child's learning and what is taught to her in her early youth remains with her throughout life.[23]

Just as new husbands sometimes commissioned Hours for their brides that illustrated how to be a good wife, mothers chose images for their children's prayerbooks which incorporated the values they wished to impart. Books of Hours used as first reading texts for girls frequently contained touching, intimate images of the Virgin Mary as a child being taught to read by her mother, St. Anne. Women who commissioned such pictures for their daughters probably wished to remind them that learning to read could be a pleasurable bonding experience. Bell comments:

> It is important to consider as well the power and influence that women, as commissioners of educational volumes, were able to exercise in their choice of subject matter. By commissioning books and instructing children they were able to influence both artistic and ideological developments.... A patron could decide ... whether, for example, to include the story of Solomon's judgment between the two mothers (emphasizing maternal unselfishness) or whether to include the story of Salome and the beheading of John the Baptist (demonstrating female power).[24]

Women's mothers may have been as likely as their new husbands to commission Books of Hours for them when they married. Most of these devotional works would probably have been more to their owners' tastes. Although many medieval mothers would have had their own agendas, it seems likely that they would have been at least somewhat familiar with their daughters' preferences in art and religious matters. Most prospective husbands, however, would have had little contact with their brides before the wedding. At best, they would have tried to guess what their new wives might have wanted. At worst, they would have commissioned devotional works intended to frighten their brides into "proper behavior." However, almost all women owned more than one Book of Hours, and the bride herself would have been free to commission one that was more to her liking after she married.

According to Wieck, perhaps the most important reason for the incredible popularity of these lay prayerbooks was that they "offered the medieval reader an intimate conversation with one of the most important people in his or her life: the Virgin Mary."[25] It certainly stands to reason that women brought up in the highly patriarchal medieval Catholic Church would particularly like a book which helped them get closer to the most powerful and revered female in popular religious belief. Harthan concurs with this argument, stating:

> [Mary] became, through the mystery of the Incarnation, the central figure in an unprecedented devotion in which many of the deepest emotions of men and women were involved.... Through the intensity of her cult she became the most popular expression of faith and devotion in the Middle Ages.... For the devout laity her image was always before them in their Books of Hours.[26]

Henk van Os points out that it was considered extremely important to form a clear mental image of the saint whom a medieval devotee was addressing when she prayed because "an image not only represented the person of the saint, but in a sense was that person."[27] It was precisely this sort of sentiment which iconoclastic Protestants would find particularly objectionable during the sixteenth-century Reformation. Medieval Catholics, however, believed that a strong internal image achieved through meditation could become more powerful than the "real" images of things that existed in the material world. The pious felt that with the help of such a strong visualization of the supernatural, it could become possible to "transcend visible reality and gain admission to Heaven."[28] Books of Hours were thought to be essential tools for helping their owners achieve such clear mental pictures of their favorite saints, especially Mary.

Sandra Penkneth discusses the famous patron portrait page included in the Hours of Mary of Burgundy, where the owner is shown simultaneously reading her prayerbook and appearing before the Virgin. Penkneth states that what is being depicted is not the owner having an actual vision in which the Virgin appears to her. Instead, what the artist has painted here should be seen as a "visualization of the prayer [Mary of Burgundy] reads, an attempt to create — by some empathetic turn of the imagination — an exact replica of the words she looks at."[29] A similar portrait page is included in the Hours of Catherine of Cleves, where the artist accomplishes the complex task of painting a picture of the owner conjuring up a mental image. He shows Catherine's visualization of the Virgin Mary as she meditates.[30]

In these examples, however, the Virgin in each miniature is either enormous or distant from the devotee. Other female owners of Hours chose to envision Mary in a more intimate manner. The anonymous woman who originally owned the Buves Hours has been portrayed imagining herself actually present at the Annunciation. The owner and the Virgin have been painted the same size and are juxtaposed near each other. The Angel Gabriel, who will momentarily greet Mary, stands behind the unknown lady, placing his hand on her shoulder encouragingly as she says her Hours. All of these elements in the miniature promote the feeling that the book owner is witnessing the Annunciation personally. Penkneth states "the extreme empathetic nature of this visualization creates an atmosphere of the utmost intimacy, an intimacy necessary to facilitate true and effective dialogue between the devotee and the Virgin."[31] Such desire to actively take part in events described in the New Testament was encouraged by devotional writers during the late medieval period. Sally Cunneen comments that *Meditations on the Life of Christ*, a popular medieval devotional text by an unknown Franciscan friar, urged its readers in a section on the Nativity to "pick up the child [Jesus], kiss him, and if possible help the mother."[32]

Yet another level of communion with the divine was available to those who owned Books of Hours. Similar to those who believed they brought themselves closer to Jesus by following the path of "imitato Christi" (imitation of Christ), devotees of Mary could actually identify themselves with her. They tried to become part of the Annunciation or the Nativity, actually experiencing the event from the Virgin's point of view. In some Annunciation scenes Mary holds a book which displays the opening words of the Hours of the Virgin, which could then be repeated aloud by readers. Thus, they could say their Hours along with her and "become inwardly absorbed in Mary, to whom an angel appeared after long and intense prayer."[33] Henk van Os states:

> The faithful were given the opportunity of having the Christ Child born in their own hearts. In those days that was experienced far more realistically than we can imagine. Like Mary, who became anxious and searched for Jesus high and low when he was disputing with the Doctors in the Temple, believers could also lose Christ and find him again. Empathizing with Mary, you could share her feelings of guilt, and wonder whether you were taking proper care of him.[34]

Women who lived in the fourteenth, fifteenth and sixteenth centuries identified with the Virgin so strongly that it is not surprising that they wanted her portrayed in ways they could relate to in their Books of Hours. Female patrons of Hours had her shown engaged in activities that they themselves did, feeling emotions that they felt. Occasionally, a lady would even have herself painted in her own devotional text as the Virgin. Susan Groag Bell points out that as lay women read more, demand arose for art that showed Mary reading in Books of Hours:

> Artists' insistence on portraying the most significant medieval female ideal, the Virgin Mary, as a constant reader was surely based on the reality of their patrons' lives. It suggests that women were not only acquiring books but spending much of their time perusing them. The developing association of the Virgin with books in fact coincides with the rise in numbers of women book owners during the fourteenth and fifteenth centuries.... This symbolism showing the Virgin as a constant reader in turn added respectability to laywomen occupying themselves with books.[35]

John Harthan discusses one example of a Book of Hours in which the woman who owned it was portrayed as the Virgin — the *Hours of Mary of Guelders*. In this early fifteenth-century manuscript, the patron has been painted as Mary in an Annunciation scene, wearing her blue robes and standing in an enclosed garden. The setting is a reference to one of the Virgin's titles derived from the Biblical Song of Solomon, the Garden Enclosed, which points out her perpetual virginity. The owner of this Book of Hours, Marie d'Harcourt, chose to have herself painted as the Virgin in part because she too was named Mary. Her primary motivation for having herself depicted in this seemingly irreverent way, however, had to do with the fact that she had borne no children during her ten-year marriage to the Duke of Guelders. Marie was still hoping for what would have seemed to be, after ten years of barrenness, the miraculous conception of a child. Although many women of the late Middle Ages who had no sons appealed to the Virgin Mother in their Books of Hours, Marie "went a stage further" in actually identifying herself with Mary so directly.[36]

Through church rituals, their own visions, and devotional aids such as rosaries and Books of Hours, women not only communicated with Mary, but also tried to see the events of the New Testament through her eyes. It is not surprising, then, that women wanted to see reflections of themselves when they viewed images of the Virgin created by artists of their time. Throughout history, Mary has frequently been depicted in art wearing the current fashions of the day. It has also been common to show scenes from her life taking place amidst the most contemporary architecture of the time. Perhaps women who commissioned artists to paint the Virgin wanted to see something of themselves and their lives in images of her so that they, in turn, could see this powerful, holy woman as a part of themselves.

Each Book of Hours is still unique, beautiful, and fascinating in its own way. However, there are two in particular that, even centuries later, clearly express their female patrons' ideas about the Virgin Mary. The books are the *Rohan Hours*, created in the 1420s, and the 1501 manuscript the *Hours of Anne of Brittany*. Their patronesses were both remarkable French queens—Yolanda of Aragon and Anne of Brittany. By the time they commissioned these spectacular works, both women had gained solid reputations in aristocratic society for being book art connoisseurs. They had already commissioned many Books of Hours particularly noteworthy for their beauty and artistic merit. Like many wealthy bibliophiles of that era, they ordered large devotional volumes to keep in their libraries, small, more portable ones to carry around with them, and several others that they gave as gifts.

However, the *Rohan Hours*, commissioned by Yolanda, and the *Hours of Anne of Brittany*, named for its patron, are probably the most lasting legacies of these great book art collectors. Even when compared to the many elaborate manuscripts ordered by other nobles who were their contemporaries, the *Rohan Hours* and the *Hours of Anne of Brittany* are outstanding. John Harthan calls Yolanda of Aragon's manuscript "one of the most ... forceful in religious expression of all Books of Hours."[37] Anne of Brittany's devotional text is at least as impressive. According to David MacGibbon, the goal of Anne's manuscript artist, Jean Bourdichon, was to make it the most elaborate Book of Hours ever created. Anne had instructed him to "employ all means in his power to make it a work worthy of a Queen who was a patroness of the Arts."[38]

Both the *Rohan Hours* and the *Hours of Anne of Brittany* contain many images of the Virgin Mary. Under Yolanda's direction, the artist most often represented the Virgin as otherworldly and powerful. In the Rohan manuscript, Mary is shown communicating directly with God the Father while she is on earth, and she is often surrounded by angels, who make obeisance to her. Anne of Brittany's Virgin, by contrast, seems to be simply a woman who has to exist in the ordinary world like any other mortal. She is not shown attended by angels but instead is often surrounded by members of her earthly family, such as her husband, mother and sisters.

The differences inherent in the two manuscripts' images of the Virgin Mary partially stem from the fact that Catholic theologians changed what they told the faithful about her in each century. According to Marina Warner, the image of the Virgin who was an ordinary wife and mother was first encouraged around 1414 by Jean Gerson, the chancellor of Paris, when he was writing sermons about the Holy Family.[39] During Yolanda of Aragon's lifetime, Gerson's ideas about the Virgin Mary would have been new and somewhat radical. She almost certainly imagined Mary as the regal Queen of Heaven, who, crowned and enthroned, was featured in French cathedral sculpture as early as the twelfth century. Intriguingly, however, Yolanda's manuscript contains several paintings of the Virgin in which she seems entirely human, indicating that the patroness may have heard of Gerson's theological theories and approved of them. Conversely, Queen Anne's Book of Hours includes a few images of Mary as a powerful, even awe-inspiring, regal figure, which seems to show that the concept of the Virgin Mary as a queen did not entirely die out after Gerson's cult of the Holy Family took hold.

It cannot be proven that Yolanda and Anne specifically requested certain images of the Virgin, instead of leaving choices about how she was portrayed up to the male artists they hired. However, many historians have emphasized that one reason Books of Hours were so popular in the late medieval and early modern eras was because the Church allowed patrons to personalize them. Certainly both women ordered the artists in their employ to do some specific things. Porcher comments that Yolanda of Aragon instructed the Rohan Master to base his work on the *Belles Heures* manuscript that she had acquired from the Duc de Berry.[40] According to Butler, Queen Anne was particularly fond of the *Hours of Anne of Brittany* because it contained paintings of the flora and fauna native to her homeland, which she probably requested Bourdichon to include.[41] It also seems likely that Anne would have been interested in how Mary was portrayed, since she felt a particular devotion to the Virgin. Butler writes that when Anne's second husband recovered from a life-threatening illness in 1505, she made a five-month pilgrimage to the Marian sanctuary Notre Dame de Folgoat in Brittany to give thanks and donate funds.[42] It therefore seems likely that both women would have been directly involved in making decisions about these visual images of the Virgin Mary.

It is certainly true that both Yolanda of Aragon and Anne of Brittany were very influenced by the perceptions of Mary popular in their day when they chose images for their Books of Hours. However, neither woman limited herself to only the most commonly held views. Yolanda was aware that the Virgin was beginning to be seen as not just an otherworldly queen, but also as a real woman who raised a child and watched Him be executed. Conversely, most people in the sixteenth century saw Mary as merely a humble wife and mother. Despite this, Anne felt free to commission images that reminded her of the transformation of Mary from an ordinary mortal woman into the awe-inspiring Queen of Heaven. Most intriguingly, each of these patronesses did not hesitate to use familiar Marian imagery as a means of advancing their own earthly agendas.

Surprisingly, in the *Rohan Hours*, no miniature represents either the Nativity or the Adoration of the Magi, two of the most touching scenes in the Bible. Instead of including an actual Nativity scene, Yolanda of Aragon chose to have the artist paint Eve, dressed in the Virgin's traditional veil and robes, maternally cuddling a nude baby Cain. The idea of conflating Mary with Eve was old, even in the fifteenth century. According to the *Dictionary of Mary*, Saint Irenaeus first pronounced Mary the New Eve in the second century, stating that just as Adam was redeemed through Christ, the new Adam, so Eve was saved through the grace of Mary.[43] This particular image in the *Rohan Hours* is still remarkable, however, because although Mary had sometimes been portrayed in medieval art with some of Eve's attributes, such as the apple, it was rare for Eve to be painted as the Virgin. Through this seemingly simple image, it is quite possible that Yolanda of Aragon wished to express a radical idea. Henry Kraus states that in the Middle Ages, ordinary women were always associated with Eve, not Mary. They were sometimes referred to as Daughters of Eve, and many men held them in disgrace for bringing about man's fall in the Garden of Eden.[44] Yolanda probably wished to suggest that even mortal women who were not free from sin, such as herself, could nonetheless emulate the immaculate Virgin.

Perhaps the most interesting Marian image in the *Hours of Anne of Brittany* seems, at first glance, not to be one at all. Close examination of the calendar page for April, however, reveals that it is actually a subtle portrait of Queen Anne as the Virgin. Butler identifies the woman in this miniature, who is being offered a bowl of strawberries as she sits in an enclosed garden, as Anne of Brittany.[45] The enclosed garden itself was one of the most recognizable visual metaphors for Mary in existence during the early modern era. This setting emphasizes Mary's purity. The woman kneeling before Anne is in the pose the angel Gabriel is shown assuming in most iconographic Annunciation scenes. She offers the queen fruit, which has symbolized human fertility since ancient times.

Anne's choice to portray herself as the Virgin Mary at the Annunciation may at first seem irreverent or even blasphemous. However, she probably considered the painting a means of appealing to the Virgin for a son. At the time when she commissioned her Book of Hours, Anne had only managed to bear one child to her husband (King Louis XII) who survived. That child was a girl, prohibited by law from inheriting the throne, so it would have been extremely important to Anne to have a son.

It cannot be explained precisely what combination of factors caused Books of Hours to catch hold of medieval women's imaginations so strongly and hold on for so long. Women during this time had a wide variety of reasons for owning Hours. It was impossible to tell if a woman longed for a sublime, mystical understanding of the Virgin or simply wanted to follow the fashions of the day. It is true, however, that even the most frivolous lady most likely felt some attachment to Mary, and even the most crude copy of the beloved medieval prayerbook contained emotionally powerful representations of the Virgin. Whether she is portrayed as a sweet child in St. Anne's embrace, a loving, affectionate mother to the infant Jesus or a powerful queen protecting her followers, images of Mary can often move even contemporary skeptics who do not believe in her. To women who lived during a time when no one openly questioned the Virgin Mary's daily benign presence, there can be no doubt that gazing on such pictures daily helped them feel closer to the female face of God.

One of the most striking things about Books of Hours is that they come only in two basic sizes. There is the enormous version, so large that it was obviously meant never to leave the library where it was kept, often attached to a wall or table with a chain, discouraging invaders from making off with it. Thieves such as Vikings were almost never interested in Books of Hours for their spiritual value, but they were quite keen to have the precious jewels embedded in their ornate bindings.

The other size that Hours came in was very small, almost minuscule. These books were also meant to be on a chain, but such chains would have been tiny and delicate, worn on the belts of women's dresses. Medieval women usually carried a few essential objects on their belts, such as keys to all the doors in their homes. It is intriguing how (somewhat literally) attached these women must have been to their Books of Hours to actually carry them like this everywhere they went. There was a strong desire among such women to ensure that their prayerbooks would always be at hand, as close to them as possible, almost directly on their bodies.

The only other Marian devotional object that was meant to be always worn on the body was the Rosary, a necklace of beads still in use today by many Catholics, especially women. Unlike Books of Hours, Rosaries are still a common sight. There are a lot of similarities between the private devotions associated with the Book of Hours and the Rosary. The inevitable question connected with this is: Why do women no longer have Books of Hours, while the Rosary is still in fairly frequent use? (Admittedly, there is room for debate about how widespread this practice is.) Like the Book of Hours, in medieval times, the Rosary had popular legends and even songs associated with it. One of the most interesting, because of its strong resemblance to the fairy tales of later centuries, is that of Mary, the Charcoaler's Daughter.

There was a pious and hardworking girl named Mary, who was the daughter of a charcoaler. She devotedly helped him in this dirty and difficult work. When she was a very small child, her mother taught her to pray the Rosary, so she always kept her beads attached to her belt as she worked. After each task, Mary would recite the Lord's Prayer and ten Hail Marys, so her work and prayers were never separated.

Once or twice a week, Mary would bring a load of her father's charcoal to the castle of the king, and one day his son, the prince, took notice of her praying. Curious about her piety, he asked her name and what prayer she was saying. She answered his questions courteously. After that, whenever she came to court to deliver the charcoal, he would stop whatever he was doing to speak with her. In time, he began to like Mary well enough that he encouraged her to spend time with his sisters, enjoying herself. She always refused, however, because she did not want to waste time in idleness.

Finally, one day soon after this prince had become king, he went hunting in the woods near Mary's family's cottage. He stopped by the little house to gain the consent of her astonished parents for their daughter to become his wife. They gladly agreed. But even as she was swept away in the royal carriage, wearing a fine new dress the king had brought her, her father was gathering up her old clothes, which were as black as night from charcoal. He knew in his heart that Mary would soon need them again.

While Mary the charcoaler's daughter reigned as queen, there was no war in the land. She saved the poor from the greedy clutches of unjust nobles, and she replaced corrupt government officials with good and pious ones. However, the selfish lords of the land, angry at having their money and high positions taken from them, threatened to kill the king if he did not renounce his lowborn wife. Seeing no alternative, the sorrowing king summoned her before him, stripped off her beautiful dress, and commanded her to leave the palace with only her shift to cover her. Having nowhere else to turn, she went back to her father's house. As soon as he saw her, her father ran out of the little cottage to return her old dress, so that she could clothe herself again.

For a time Mary remained in her father's house, but with her gone, all the lords of the land began to quarrel among themselves and make war upon each other. The king prayed to the Virgin for help in ending this constant strife. The Mother of God, who loved the charcoaler's daughter well, appeared to him. She said that he would never have peace in his lands until he restored Mary to her rightful position as queen. He hastened to do as the Virgin instructed, reclaiming his wife from her father's house, and peace returned to the land. The queen became a special patroness of the clergy, monasteries, hospitals, and churches, as well as a beloved protector of the poor. Throughout the rest of her days, she continued to pray the Rosary, and she instructed all her servants to do so as well. If she found out that anyone wished to pray the Rosary that did not have one, she would generously give him or her a fine set of beads.[46]

This very Cinderella-like story is truly remarkable because it portrays the Rosary as the source of an indigent woman's rise to power and prosperity. According to this legend, in addition to all the Rosary's spiritual rewards, it could actually raise you from rags to riches overnight. Credited with such abilities, it is certainly understandable why so many people in the medieval era, especially women, would turn to the Rosary in droves. Indeed, few in contemporary times would be able to resist such a devotional object, if they believed it could change their lives in this way.

The history of the Rosary is difficult to decisively write about because its true origins have always been shrouded in mystery. According to the spiritual writer John D. Miller, many pious Catholics today still attribute its introduction into the Christian world to St. Dominic (1172–1221). According to popular legend, this saint was trying to convert the heretical Cathars who lived in the south of France. They were members of an influential sect of the time which denied the humanity of Jesus. Dominic was initially quite unsuccessful in his attempt to convert them to a more orthodox form of Catholicism, and he retreated to a nearby cave to fast, pray, and generally regroup his thoughts for a second try. Here, the Blessed Virgin appeared to him and, in a gesture of support for his work, quenched his thirst with milk from her own breast. She then told him that his current methods would never be effective in winning over the Cathars. Instead, she said, giving him the first holy circlet of beads, use this Rosary to do your work. She then taught him the proper prayers to say with each bead. Armed with the new Rosary and the counsel of the Virgin herself, Dominic once again went out to work on converting the heretics. This time, of course, he was successful. The Rosary prayer "Hail Mary" included the phrase "Blessed is the fruit of thy womb," and for some reason, this was enough to convince the Cathars that Jesus was a real man, born of a real woman.[47]

Many scholars today have written this story off as a mere legend propagated by Alanus de Rupe, the fifteenth-century theologian. De Rupe, in trying to promote the Rosary, wanted to lend it a sense of authenticity by claiming that it had divine origins. He also said that he himself had received recurring visions of Mary, in which she urged him to get people to pray the Rosary as she had taught St. Dominic.[48] Despite the dubiousness of the traditional St. Dominic story, however, numerous Popes throughout the ages have attested to its authenticity. The Pope most famous for endorsing the tale, however, was Leo XIII, who set off a new wave of devotion to the Rosary in the nineteenth century with his ardent encouragement of it.[49] Indeed, in spite of much historical evidence to the contrary, many Catholics today would be horrified and

St. Dominic receives the Rosary directly from Mary's hand (courtesy Chant Art).

even offended at the intimation that the St. Dominic story is not completely factual.

Some scholars who are dubious about this legendary origin, though, claim that the Rosary was actually introduced to Europe in the twelfth century by crusaders. These men made the arduous journey to Jerusalem to attempt to wrest control of the Holy Land from Muslims. Some of the fortunate ones who survived both the travel and the battles returned home with chains of Muslim prayer beads.[50] By the time of the Crusades, praying with beads had already been a common part of Islamic religious culture for hundreds of years. They had used beads for counting prayers as early as the ninth century, when chains of 99 beads were used as a memory aid for reciting the 99 names of Allah. The medieval explorer Marco Polo reported that the king of the Middle Eastern country of Malabar wore a chain of gems, which he used as an aid for reciting his morning and evening prayers.[51] Once the idea of praying with beads was introduced to Europe by the crusaders, some contemporary historians believe that the idea took on a life of its own for Catholics.

While more objectively credible than the St. Dominic tale, the theory that crusaders brought the Rosary into common usage in Europe has some flaws. Evidence exists of prayer beads being used in Europe well before the return of the crusaders. In England during the eleventh century, the same Lady Godiva who is now (somewhat wrongfully) infamous for public nudity left very specific instructions in her will for the disposition of her "prayer beads." She stated that after her death, they should be used to adorn the Madonna statue at the monastery church at Coventry, which she had founded with her husband.[52] It is also possible, though less well documented, that even as early as the sixth century, the Irish saint Brigid of Kildare was using strings of wooden beads to aid in her prayers. This claim is somewhat dubious, however, since the historian who made it could have been confusing St. Brigid of Kildare with the much later St. Birgitta of Sweden.[53]

Though the true origins of the Rosary remain unknown, certainly there is no doubt about its tremendous popularity during the Middle Ages. It was originally intended as a tool to help the wearer keep track of how many "Our Father" and especially "Hail Mary" prayers she said. Saying the Rosary was considered the common person's equivalent of reciting the clergy's daily prayer, the Divine Office. The key difference was that using a Rosary for one's religious devotions did not require literacy. As a result, it was more accessible to a wide range of people. To say the Rosary, you merely had to recite a memorized set of simple prayers, called a decade. A decade consisted of an "Our Father," ten "Hail Marys" and a "Glory Be to the Father." Decades were recited over and over until one reached the end of a string of Rosary beads. The beads, of course, were used for keeping track of what prayer you were on and how many you had said. One Rosary consisted of five groups of decades, but in order to truly say an "entire" Rosary, the person praying had to make her way through the full set of beads three times.

Medieval women soon began to love this Marian devotional object. Anne Winston-Allen writes that during the Middle Ages "it was not uncommon for people to sleep with a rosary around the neck so as not to be taken by death in the night without this vital link to the Virgin."[54] It was certainly a factor in its popularity that, essentially, the Rosary was a lovely piece of jewelry that even the most pious could wear without being accused of vanity.

Like Books of Hours, Rosaries grew more fashionable over time, and for some women, a certain amount of worldliness became associated with the practice of wearing them. Some particularly frivolous sets of Rosary beads actually had a pomander (a receptacle for holding perfume) attached to them.[55] Enough women in the fifteenth century became ostentatious in their choice of rosary beads that, in the city of Nuremberg, an ordinance was passed stipulating that no woman could wear a Rosary valued in excess of twenty guelders. Those who violated this law were fined the amount of money that the offending beads exceeded the stipulated limit.[56]

By the late Middle Ages, however, it definitely was not only the wealthy and fashionable who wore Rosaries daily. According to Bridgett, "in the fourteenth and fifteenth centuries the use of the beads in England was universal; it was common to kings and nobles, to churchmen and to soldiers, to the most learned and the most ignorant, to old age and to youth."[57] Even poor peasants could fashion Rosaries out of cheap, common materials such as clay or wood, while the wealthy opted for gold and gemstones. Chaucer's prioress, who was portrayed in *The Canterbury Tales* as tasteful and not overly worldly, wore Rosary beads made of coral. In the sixteenth century, Richard Patten, the father of a bishop, was artistically portrayed in his son's church carrying a purse, a dagger, and a Rosary, so that he might be prepared for every possible emergency.[58]

The Rosary has always been particularly associated with common women's piety, at least in part because using it did not take up too much time and could be done at home. Ever busy, just as most of their female descendants are today, these time-pressed women of the Middle Ages wanted a devotion that could be performed while doing more practical tasks at the same time. It was quite possible to say one's Rosary while simultaneously cooking or doing laundry, which made it attractive to both the women themselves and their husbands. Men during this time sometimes feared that if their wives became too religious, they would get so busy with spiritual matters that they would neglect their housework.[59]

The obvious importance of the Rosary in women's lives was further emphasized by the fact that, much as wealthy women did with their Books of Hours, women of all classes frequently left specific instructions in their wills about what was to be done with their Rosaries. An example of this practice is in the will of Eleanor, Duchess of Gloucester, who left two coral Rosaries to her mother in 1399. Isabel Wilton, a far less exalted woman than the Duchess, specified in 1486 that her daughter Marion was to inherit her beads. In 1498, the will of Anne, Lady Scrope, specified somewhat unusually that her particularly magnificent rosary was to be divided up and given to several famous statues of saints to wear. Her Marian proclivities were revealed by the fact that Our Lady of Walsingham and Our Lady of Westminster both received some of the jewels.[60]

Many women were, of course, attracted to the Rosary because of its strong association with the Virgin Mary. In England, the formal blessing routinely performed over Rosaries by Catholic clergy specifically spelled out the beads' direct connection to Mary. According to Bridgett, part of this standard prayer was, "And whoever endeavours by means of these [beads] to honour by holy service the most Blessed Mary, Mother of God, may her Son our Lord Jesus Christ return him great things for small; may He accept his devotion, forgive his sins, fill him with faith, indulgently succour him, mercifully protect him, destroy whatever is adverse to him, and grant him what is prosperous...."[61] According to this prayer, impressively powerful blessings were supposed to be available to those who just spent a little time every day reciting Rosary prayers.

Even more overtly Marian were the "mysteries," or scenes from the lives of Mary and Jesus, that pious people were supposed to meditate on while they counted out their prayers on Rosaries. Set forth by theologian Jakob Sprenger in the 1470s, the idea of the mysteries is still used by those who pray with the Rosary today. Sprenger's ideas were widely accepted because Emperor Frederick III endorsed them, which, due to the somewhat complex politics of the day, soon led to Papal support.[62] Sprenger espoused fifteen mysteries to think about, and these were grouped in sets of five. The first set centered around the joyful moments Mary experienced while on earth (the Joyful Mysteries). The second focused on her unhappiness during the Passion and death of Jesus (the Sorrowful Mysteries). The third was about the joys associated with her death and subsequent bodily assumption into heaven (the Glorious Mysteries).

Sally Cunneen, the contemporary spiritual writer, states, "The use of the rosary was similar to that of devotional art: to help the praying one think and act as Mary did."[63] Jakob Sprenger himself still further associated the Rosary with Mary when he set an old thirteenth-century legend down in print. This story was about a man who was visited by the Virgin Mary while saying his Rosary prayers. She miraculously pulled a rose from his mouth as he said each "Hail Mary" and wove it into a crown of flowers for herself.[64] When he had finished praying, she placed the crown on her head and returned to heaven. Because of the popularity of this tale, people who regularly said Rosary devotions came to believe that their prayers were making a beautiful, very tangible gift for their beloved Virgin.

In the late fifteenth century, Alanus de Rupe and Jakob Sprenger, both famous proponents of the Rosary, founded societies in which people pledged to pray regularly using the beads. Members of these organizations, known as Rosary confraternities, prayed on behalf of themselves and also (more importantly) for dead people who were thought to be suffering in purgatory. The Pope actively encouraged this practice by offering indulgences (official assurances of reduced

The "mysteries" of the Rosary (courtesy Chant Art).

Mary's blessings as roses (courtesy Chant Art).

time in purgatory) in exchange for saying the Rosary a certain number of predetermined times. Popular songs of the day were composed to emphasize and glorify the Rosary's power to liberate the souls of the dead from purgatorial tortures.

Rosary confraternities were credited not only with the ability to alleviate the suffering of the dead but also with some earthly miracles as well. In 1573, Pope Pius V instituted the feast of Our Lady of Victory, which commemorated the defeat of the Turks at the Battle of Lepanto. This battle was particularly important to the Christian world of the time because it broke the power of the Turks in the Mediterranean. Pius declared that the victory was the direct result of Marian intercession, which had been obtained by the prayers of Rosary confraternity members in Rome.[65]

Such power was probably intensely attractive to most lay people, who often felt more like observers than participants in religious masses. Active involvement in spiritual life was, for the most part, limited to the clergy. Miller states, "[The Rosary confraternities'] greatest strength was that they were open to all, men and women, rich and poor, clerics and lay people."[66] They also required no formal vows and (perhaps most importantly) did not cost anything to join. Of course, all of these aspects also made them particularly attractive to women. Although women were interested in joining because of their strong Marian affiliations, it was also exciting for them to be allowed membership in any sort of organized society at all. Women were routinely excluded from most other formal groups, both religious and secular. They responded to the unusual openness of this society by joining in droves. Soon, female participants became the overwhelming majority in such groups. In some Italian Rosary confraternities, women outnumbered men nearly four to one, and they frequently served as officers.

The importance of such organizations became increasingly apparent over time. Somewhat incredibly, they even continued on in sixteenth-century England, where they were unequivocally banned. During the strongly Protestant Tudor era, membership in a Rosary confraternity became a political act. Due to the sweeping religious reform ushered in by the very worldly King Henry VIII, continued allegiance to the Catholic Church and its Rosary was considered treasonous and punishable by death. Even under such dangerous circumstances, staunch believers continued to pray with the beads, which they referred to as "the badge of the Catholics." Confraternities, with their largely female membership, continued behind closed doors. Miller writes that in the late sixteenth century, at great personal risk, Father Henry Garnet illegally wrote, printed and distributed a Rosary handbook which encouraged people to continue their devotions. In a letter to his sister, he explained that he considered the prayers of the confraternities to be essential because "[praying the Rosary together] allowed English Catholics to follow in spirit the calendar of the Roman Church, even though they were so often deprived of Mass."[67]

The more such societies were declared illegal by the government of England, the more people resisted disbanding them. Indeed, it was in part precisely because the Rosary was so strictly forbidden in countries declared officially Protestant that the practice has persisted so strongly to this day. So why did devotion to the Rosary continue, while the use of Books of Hours died out over time? Government officials took less notice of people who continued to pray with their Books of Hours, since they were in much more limited circulation. Only those with enough money and literacy to make use of Hours even owned them. Protestant religious authorities also found more effective ways of countering some people's attachment to their Books of Hours. The Book of Common Prayer was introduced during the seventeenth century, essentially as a kind of substitute. Protestant clergy encouraged their literate parishioners to read this new book, as well as the Bible itself, rather than resorting to other religious writings.

Nothing was offered as a substitute for the Rosary, yet Queen Elizabeth I felt particularly strongly that it must be eradicated. Under her rule, punishments such as death or imprisonment were not uncommon for those who stubbornly insisted on keeping up with their devotions. The Rosary, however, was incredibly widespread, so it was particularly difficult to get rid of. According to Lisa McClain's book, *Lest We Be Damned*, Catholics in Elizabethan England who wanted them had many options for obtaining the illegal beads. Priests often kept a secret cache of them, which they distributed to the faithful. They were also frequently left to family members in Catholic wills. Rosaries could be brought back from the continent by travelers or sent through the mail. A devoted Catholic could even make her own set of beads, or if all else failed, use a picture of the Rosary to aid her prayers.[68] People at all economic levels could afford them, and no literacy was required to use them.

Loyal Catholics kept them as a means of protesting against government policies that they found unacceptable. As it became increasingly politicized over the centuries, use continued. Warner writes, "Devotion to the Rosary rises when the Church feels weak and insecure; the prayer, therefore, often indicates an embattled mood among Catholics."[69] Mary, Queen of Scots, used a Rosary when she was imprisoned by Elizabeth. In an impressively dramatic gesture, the Jesuit John Olgilvie flung a set of Rosary beads from the scaffold just before he was executed for treason.[70]

Under attack, English Catholics needed to feel a strong sense of spiritual protection against the Protestants who persecuted them. As a result, the Virgin Mary took on a new role in their lives—that of protector and warrior queen. Mary was given a new title—"Mother of Power"—and she was no longer portrayed in Catholic art accompanied by an honor guard of warrior saints, as she had been in previous centuries. This new, fierce Mary was perfectly capable of protecting herself. Lisa McClain writes, "English priests presented Mary as accessed through the Rosary as a warrior, defending English Catholics and their souls."[71] The beads began to be thought of as a sort of holy weapon, which faithful Catholics could use to call upon her aid in times of trouble. According to theologians of the time, her formidable presence could set the Church's adversaries and their "Satanical Armies" to flight.[72] This English Catholic concept of the Mother of Power differed sharply from the version of her commonly accepted by Protestants, as well as the Catholics of continental Europe. These Christians, by contrast, were not constantly vulnerable to a hostile government and society. Among them, she was generally thought of as a "meek, self-sacrificing humble servant of God and role model for Catholic female docility."[73]

In Ireland, however, struggles against invasions of English and Scottish Protestants have marked much of its history. Miller argues, "The Rosary has been dubbed the 'Irish catechism,' suggesting that it was of considerable importance to the people of Ireland during the troubles of the Reformation period, when the Catholic faith was under attack."[74] The battle between devoted Catholics and English monarchs became particularly extreme, even for Ireland, in the seventeenth century. In 1639, it was decreed by the English that all statues of the Virgin in Ireland should be destroyed, and in 1658, an "oath of abjuration" was required for all Irish citizens. In it, they were required to swear that they rejected all devotion to the Virgin Mary: "I firmly believe and avow that no reverence is due to the Virgin Mary or to any other saint in heaven, and that no petition or adoration can be addressed to them without idolatry."[75] The Irish people, of course, rebelled all the more fiercely after these laws had been passed. Frequently, those captured went to prison clutching their Rosaries. In the mid 1700s, the growth of Rosary confraternities in this country exploded, directly as a result of much despised laws prohibiting them.

In the nineteenth and twentieth centuries, praying the Rosary was no longer proscribed in England, though Protestants still regarded it as an outmoded form of credulous superstition. Admittedly, popular devotion to the Rosary among Victorian-era Catholics seems to have included ideas and practices that would not have seemed out of place in medieval times. Rosary confraternities became popular again, and groups consisting of fifteen people known as the "living rosary" commonly met each month to recite an entire set of beads together.[76] In 1870, the poem "A Legend of the Rosary" was required reading for students at the Catholic school St. Leonards-on-Sea. Like a medieval cautionary tale from *The Golden Legend*, it relates the purportedly true story of a pious orphan girl who once forgot to say her Rosary. Because of this unfortunate mistake, she received a personal visitation from the Virgin Mary, who strongly reprimanded her. The child died later that same day.[77] As late as 1919, copies of a spurious document entitled "The Revelations of St. Bridget" were in common circulation. It promised, among other benefits resulting from a daily recitation of the Rosary, that practitioners would be safe from crime, sudden death, childbirth complications, and illness. In addition, a visit from the Virgin Mary was guaranteed three days before death.[78]

Catholic reluctance to allow any objective research to displace their beloved traditions was perhaps most strongly demonstrated in 1901. In that year, a series of articles by Herbert Thurston appeared in the popular periodical *Month*, in which he published his discovery that Rosary devotion had not, in fact, originated with St. Dominic. However well documented, his assertions were met with a flurry of horrified letters from all levels of the Catholic community. Some of his detractors, such as historian and future cardinal Aiden Gasquet, actually admitted the literal truth of Thurston's theories. Gasquet, however, still objected to "the general principle of knocking traditions on the head."[79] One nun from the Convent of the Holy Sepulchre admitted her suspicions, long privately held, that St. Dominic had not begun the Rosary. Nonetheless, reading Thurston's articles had instilled her with a sense of "terror that the secret locked up in [her] heart would be divulged to the world."[80]

Unlike previous eras, widespread devotion to the Rosary among English Victorian Catholics was not attributable to persecution or even any political movement. Instead, it occurred largely because the beads received a particularly ringing endorsement. According to the reports of thousands of witnesses, the Virgin Mary herself began appearing at sites all over Europe, encouraging the faithful to pray with Rosaries. Today, the Catholic Church has officially accepted some of these occurrences as true miracles, setting off a flood of pilgrimages to sanctioned sites that has not been equaled since the Middle Ages.

In 1858, in the first of these Marian visions, the Virgin appeared to the peasant girl Bernadette Soubirous, holding out the beads. When the girl responded to this apparition by praying her own Rosary, Mary instructed her to come closer. Only a little more than twenty years later, in Pontmain, France, an invading Prussian army was supposedly deterred when villagers recited the Rosary prayers to an apparition of the Virgin. The most unmistakable supernatural endorsement, however, occurred in Fatima, Portugal, in 1917. This time, Mary appeared to three children named Lucia, Jacinta, and Francisco. She held out a white Rosary made of pearls. In this incarnation, she repeatedly urged them to say the Rosary prayers in order to avoid going to hell. Then, perhaps as a strong warning, she displayed to them a detailed vision of hell in its full horror. When Lucia asked her if the three of them would go to heaven when they died, she responded that they would, but that Francisco would first have to say many Rosaries. In her final interaction with the children, she declared herself the Lady of the Rosary and informed them that she wanted a church built at the site of her appearances. She also stipulated that at this church, the Rosary was to be said in its entirety every day.[81]

Although this is certainly the most overtly Rosary-oriented Marian apparition of recent times, it is not currently the most well known one. Without question, that distinction belongs to the Marian vision of six teenagers at Medjugorje, Yugoslavia, in 1981. Mary appeared to these young people multiple times, urging them to pray with the beads every day as a group. Though not yet officially acknowledged as the site of a miracle by the Pope, popular belief in this particular apparition is truly astonishing. Each year, thousands of people, especially women, flock to Medjugorje, despite local political upheaval, in the hopes of directly encountering the Virgin Mary.

The self-described former skeptic Beverly Donofrio is an example of someone who has attested that visiting this site changed her life. As a young woman, she openly expressed her disgust with all things Marian by dumping potato peels on top of an image of the Virgin. Yet even she was won over by the magic of Medjugorje. After a long physical and mental journey in search of Mary, she returned from Yugoslavia, finding herself handing out Rosaries to other women and struggling to keep from proselytizing. When she gave out one set of these beads to her female friends, she said, "These were blessed by Mary. I know, I know — it's hard to believe. But they have power. Just keep [them] near you. Put them under your pillow."[82] Later, she found unexplainable little miracles springing up around the necklaces she gave away. One woman she offered a set to exclaimed in surprise that she had just looked up how to say the Rosary on the internet the day before. The woman had then said to Mary that if she was supposed to pray, the Virgin should give her a sign by making a Rosary appear. Another mystified recipient claimed that she had just said a "Hail Mary" that morning for the first time in twenty years. Finally, when Donofrio gave one to a friend, the woman informed her that she had recently been to mass after her father died, and as she sat in church, she wished for a Rosary.[83]

Perhaps the most intriguing evidence of this devotional object's enduring emotional hold on women is in a tiny book written by Rosemary Haughton. It was printed in 1976, a year marked by overwhelming mass rejection of the Virgin Mary by women. Somewhat surprisingly, the book is called *Feminine Spirituality: Reflections on the Mysteries of the Rosary*. In it, Haughton relates her personal story about pumping water by hand into the pipes of a trailer, where she had to live while a more permanent home was being built for her. Of her own accord, she came to the realization that praying the Rosary while pumping water made the tedious task bearable. So she began working "with a Rosary in one hand and the pump handle in the other,"[84] for all the world like a medieval woman in a confraternity. Even in the 1970s, when any pro–Marian sentiment by a woman was astonishing, it seems that the practice of doing household tasks while praying the Rosary had not entirely vanished.

In every era since the Middle Ages, there have been at least a few women for whom the Rosary has added a spiritual dimension to the tedium of chores. It seems that women's devotion to this practice may wax and wane over the centuries, but it will never entirely vanish. Conversely, Books of Hours are no longer intrinsic parts of women's spiritual lives, but as long as some copies these magnificent books exist, there is the possibility that their significance may be rediscovered.

4

Marian Places

The Virgin at Home and Abroad

It seems puzzling at first that any connection could exist between medieval women's devotional objects, such as the Book of Hours and the Rosary, and Marian gardens. However, many Hours prominently feature flowers in their marginal illustrations, as well as depictions of the Annunciation taking place in a garden. In a fifteenth-century French Book of Hours, an illustration of the Immaculate Conception includes floral emblems and biblical phrases such as, "A Lily Among Thorns," "Rose Plant" and "Fair Olive Tree." There is also a similar volume of Hours which is even more direct in its Marian floral symbolism. Its image of the Annunciation includes columbine, representing espousal of the holy spirit, a white lily for purity, a red rose for the incarnation, myrtle for virginity, and a violet for humility.[1]

Even in the early years of Catholicism, theologians used flowers and gardens as allegories for the Virgin Mary, especially roses. During the fourth century, Saint Ambrose referred to Mary as "the rose of modesty." She became so strongly associated with this flower that, in the twelfth century, a legend about them springing up everywhere she rested during the Flight into Egypt became popular.[2] During this same era, Rosary beads were carved to resemble roses. According to Krymow, "The word 'rosary' originally meant a rose garden and later referred to a garland of roses. The devotion known as the rosary [was] a garland of prayers in honor of Mary."[3]

The rose, however, was only the beginning of the abundantly lush floral symbolism that came to be associated with the Virgin. Roses and lilies both played a prominent part in an apocryphal, yet widely believed, medieval story about the Assumption of the Virgin. When ever-doubting St. Thomas opened Mary's tomb to seek proof that her body was truly gone, he found only these flowers. The metaphor of the lily probably originated with Saint Bede in the eighth century, who wrote that its petals symbolized her pure body and the gold anthers her soul.[4] By the Renaissance era, the Madonna Lily had become

Mary as the "Mystical Rose" (courtesy Chant Art).

Mary's conflation with rose symbolism (courtesy Chant Art).

so strongly associated with Mary's virginity that Church authorities actually instructed Italian artists to always portray Gabriel holding it in depictions of the Annunciation.[5] Such flower symbolism lingered in the thoughts and writings of theologians for hundreds of years. As late as the fifteenth century, Jean Gerson included it in his invocation of the Blessed Virgin, "Beautiful Rose and more comely than the rose, you are a unique rose. For you are the only rose who is also called lily and violet, sweet and full of honey."[6]

Medieval scholars did not have to look any further than the Bible itself to find floral imagery used to symbolize all that was considered ideal in women. This naturally became conflated with Marian piety, since the Virgin was considered the perfect example of womanhood. The Song of Songs, traditionally believed to refer to Mary, used the metaphor of an enclosed garden for the chaste female body. Similar references to it as "the rose of Sharon, the lily of the valley" are also included. According to Church teachings of the time, Mary's seat in heaven was a throne in a walled garden, reminiscent of Eden. This association was further reinforced by the idea that she was thought of as the New Eve, bringing redemption in the heavenly garden of paradise.[7]

As strongly as both Books of Hours and Rosaries were associated with women's devotion to the Virgin, records of Mary gardens in spaces set aside for medieval women are remarkably rare. The first Mary garden in history was created by the patron saint of gardening, an Irish man called Fiacre. In the seventh century, he planted it at his hospice for the poor and infirm. There are, however, notable exceptions to this rule, such as the delightful description from the thirteenth century of a garden at Wherwell Benedictine nunnery in England. The abbess, Euphemia, "built a place set apart for the refreshment of the soul, namely a chapel of the Blessed Virgin, which she adorned on the north side with pleasant vines and trees."[8]

Contemporary Mary gardens seem to be almost exclusively associated with women. The few books in existence about them have been written by female authors. Newspaper and magazine articles about Mary gardens are almost invariably filled with interviews of only female gardeners. Nan Sears, founder of a particularly well known one at St. Mary's Catholic Church in Annapolis, Maryland, stated to the *Baltimore Sun*, "I don't ever walk through a garden that I haven't thought of [Mary]. I feel she is there, part of everything beautiful in the outdoors. I wanted a Mary Garden as a tribute to her." Sears's fellow garden worker, Laura Van Geffen, was considerably more rueful, saying, "I feel as if I've been tricked. I'm Catholic, but I never understood the veneration of Mary. I used to pray, 'I don't get it. Show me how to love your mother.' Then this fell in my lap ... I would have preferred a revelation to years of backbreaking work."[9]

Even the famously lapsed Catholic Beverly Donofrio found her way to Mary while concurrently discovering of her own love of gardening, though she did not set out to create a Marian garden. When she accidentally made a shrine

Mary with lilies symbolizing her purity. From a holy card created in the 1920s (courtesy Chant Art).

66　　　　　　　　　　4. Marian Places

The heart of the Virgin Mary covered with lilies. From a 1931 holy card (courtesy Chant Art).

The "Queen of Maidens" offers the lily of virginity to a young girl (courtesy Chant Art).

of her house, the Virgin came in, knowing a good opportunity when she saw one. She states:

> While my house continued to fill with Mary [images] ... I dug a garden along the back fence and a plot twenty feet by six in the lawn.... After a full day's gardening, [I] stood at the bathroom sink to wash my hands. I glanced at my face in the mirror and noticed for the first time it was next to Mary's face on the varnished print. It looked like we were standing next to each other ... but beautiful pink roses made a ring around [her heart]."[10]

Despite the strong association of the Virgin with roses and lilies, the first recorded flower named after her is the marigold. Referred to as "seint mary gouldes," it appeared in a 1373 recipe for a potion supposedly useful for warding off the plague. Originally called "Mary Gold" because it bloomed during important medieval feast days of the Virgin Mary, the flowers were frequently used to decorate churches in her honor. Popular tales during this time associated these plants with the coins in the Virgin's purse. It was said that when the Holy Family was robbed, all the bandits found in her purse were marigolds. They were frequently left at the feet of Madonna statues in place of coins, particularly by the poor.[11]

The contemporary Marian gardener, however, has an abundance of flowers and plants to choose from when planning her garden. There are over a thousand flowers and herbs with some Marian association, each with its own unique medieval legend. The aster is "Mary's Star," baby's breath "Mary's veil," the daffodil "Our Lady's Easter bells," the cornflower "Mary's crown," and fuschia "Our Lady's earrings."[12] Just about every possible aspect of her body, clothing and life has been manifested in floral form. Everything from her hair and fingers to her nightcap, purse, candlestick, and even cheese has a flower to represent it.

The ability to create a Marian space close to home with gardening has sometimes not been enough for women strongly devoted to the Virgin. At times, both contemporary and medieval women have wanted to seek out someplace uniquely dedicated to her — ideally, one which has been officially recognized by the Catholic Church. This has frequently meant a long and arduous journey. For centuries, such faith-based travel has been called a pilgrimage and those who undertake it, pilgrims. The devotion of female pilgrims to Mary during medieval times is typified by two characters in Chaucer's *Canterbury Tales*. Both the prioress and nun speak about Mary at great length when they amuse their fellow pilgrims with stories. The prioress's tale involves a miracle in which the Virgin restores the life of a pious child slain by Jews, while the nun prays extensively to Mary before beginning her story of St. Cecile.

Setting out to visit a Marian shrine traditionally required a great deal of courage, as well as faith in God's protection. Travel during the Middle Ages was dangerous for everyone, but especially for women, who risked being robbed, raped, and even murdered on the road. Medieval literature abounds with stories of women who met a bad end while on pilgrimage, though at least in part, these were probably cautionary tales used to frighten women into staying at home, where they supposedly belonged. It was often feared that nuns would be violating the ideology of remaining cloistered by undertaking a journey, while secular women's chastity could be lost on the trip, due to rape or sinfulness. In the popular French legend "Floire et Blanchefloir," a young widowed noblewoman traveling with her father is captured by the Saracens.[13] The biography of Altmann, bishop of Passau, includes a purportedly true tale of a young abbess, also seized by the Saracens, who was raped repeatedly by her captors until she died.[14]

A woman would not attempt such a dangerous, morally dubious journey unless she had powerful motivation for doing so. Often, this was an illness that she feared could be cured only with the Virgin Mary's divine intervention. During the Middle Ages, it was commonly believed that touching or kissing a blessed Marian relic such as a piece of her robe, or phials containing her tears or breast milk, would bring about a miraculous healing. Everything from leprosy to toothache was supposedly cured at Marian shrines. Those who were genuinely sick, as well as people suffering from psychosomatic ailments, often went on pilgrimage to be made well.

If a cure for a particular body part was sought, such as a leg afflicted with swelling or a rash, a wax image of it would often be left at a shrine. In this way, the diseased limb could be handed over for the Virgin to handle. Similarly, such effigies were also frequently left at shrines in thanksgiving for a healing already accomplished.[15] Occasionally, a donation of wax equal to the weight of the sick person would be substituted. In the hopes of obtaining miraculous cures or other favors, offerings of jewels were also frequently made at Marian shrines.

The idea behind the practice of offering jewelry was that it represented a bargain or a pledge that the Virgin Mary could not honorably refuse. The shrine of Our Lady of Walsingham "dripped jewels and shone with the glow of candlelight on plate," while the statue of the Virgin at the Church of the Holy Trinity in Suffolk "was festooned with votive offerings, including rings, enameled and bejeweled girdles, rosaries of silver, coral and jet, brooches and buckles set with precious stones, and velvet, satin, and damask vestments."[16] It was not unusual for a wealthy woman to leave some offering to a Marian shrine in her will, especially if she believed that her prior pilgrimage to it had been of benefit to her. In 1360, Elizabeth de Burgh, Lady Clare, bequeathed to Walsingham four pounds in pence, two cloths of gold and a silver and enamel cup. Over a century later, Lady Elizabeth Andrew left Our Lady of Walsingham a ring with diamonds.[17]

Understandably, this practice of paying for the favors of the Virgin Mary and other saints came under fire. In the twelfth century, Bernard of Clairvaux criticized the Church for blatant profiteering, while Christine de Pizan wrote in her famous behavioral handbook for ladies that money expended on pilgrimages could be put to better use.[18] After a trip to Our Lady of Walsingham, Erasmus described feeling uneasy because of the close watch the shrine's attendants kept on its visitors, to prevent theft of expensive offerings and possibly as a means of encouraging more generous giving.[19]

Pilgrims to Marian shrines constantly had to be on guard against scheming churchmen who wished to make a profit at their expense. In addition to financial gain from direct offerings, those who were in charge of shrines could sell indulgences and sacred objects. Much to the consternation of the truly pious, in exchange for a sum of money, priests at holy sites would issue documents stating that the purchaser had been freed from a fixed amount of time in purgatory.

Water in which objects belonging to the Virgin Mary had been powdered or immersed was considered particularly curative.[20] At Our Lady of Walsingham, two holy wells were purported to contain water that could cure headaches and stomach aches, as well as grant wishes. Pilgrims commonly purchased some to take back home with them. It was sold bottled in small lead flasks, with the letter "W" stamped on their sides to show that they genuinely came from Walsingham. Pregnant women particularly valued these small vials of holy water, which they would wear around their necks as a means of ensuring health for themselves and their babies.[21]

A far more dubious business transaction regularly took place at the priory of Bromholm. A holy girdle which adorned the waist of its Madonna statue was purported to have miraculous powers, helping pregnant women who came into contact with it to have safe deliveries. For the right price, it could be rented out by wealthy women to wear during their confinements. Seemingly a harmless practice at first glance, it unfortunately kept the holy relic out of the reach of less influential women. They frequently made the journey to Bromholm simply to touch or kiss the girdle, only to find out when they arrived that it was unavailable. Denied the assistance of Bromholm's miraculous relic, they often had to settle instead for pilgrims' badges from Walsingham depicting the Madonna and Child.[22]

Desire for profit, however, was not the worst thing that the founders of a sacred site could be guilty of. Particularly during the medieval era, when religious toleration was practically nonexistent, misplaced Marian devotion could transform a holy place into something entirely more sinister. Perhaps the most infamous example of this occurrence took place in Regensburg, Germany in 1519, when a Marian shrine became a site for anti–Jewish propaganda, fuelling hatred and violence against the Jews. Regensburg was already virulently anti–Semitic before it became a Marian pilgrimage site. An official proclamation which formally expelled Jews from the city was accompanied by the communal destruction of their temple by Christians. When stonemason Jacob Kern was injured while helping with the demolition, his wife prayed to the Virgin Mary to save his life. He made a seemingly miraculous recovery. As a result, the City Council established a chapel on the synagogue site dedicated to The Beautiful Virgin Mary of Regensburg.

As increasing numbers of miracles were reported there, pilgrims began to pour in by the thousands to visit it. Many local Catholics soon came to believe that the shrine's miracles were meant to signify that Mary was anti–Jewish. It had already been commonly thought that the Virgin resented the Jewish belief that she was a mere carpenter's wife whose premarital pregnancy had resulted from sin. Catholics reasoned that violence against and expulsion of any remaining Jews in Regensburg was entirely justified. After all, if the Virgin Mary herself hated them, how could good Christians possibly have any empathy for their suffering? Anti-Jewish violence increased to an even greater level.[23] As the hate-fueled fervor continued to rise, Catholic pilgrims frequently took part in frenzied behavior, such as dancing, speaking in tongues and pronouncing prophecies of the Apocalypse. Ironically, Protestants subsequently attributed this to the demonic influence that the Jews supposedly exercised over their former holy site.

Tragically, such thinking was common during the Middle Ages. Chaucer referred to it in the *Canterbury Tales*, though scholars still debate about how anti–Semitic the medieval author actually was himself. His character the prioress is strongly identified with Mary—even her name, Eglantyne, is derived from a flower associated with the Virgin. The tale she tells the company of pilgrims places the Holy Mother in direct opposition to the Jews. In it, a Jew is so angered by a seven-year-old boy's singing of the Marian hymn "Alma Redemptoris" that he kidnaps the little Christian and slits his throat. The Virgin subsequently comes through for the pious child, bringing him back to life through the agency of a magical grain of wheat. In a warning to any Jews who might be overhearing her story, the prioress cautions her audience that Mary will not allow them to get away with evil.

Despite such rampant profiteering and anti–Semitism, medieval women sometimes chose to become pilgrims, with or without the motivation of illness. There were probably nearly as many reasons for a woman to go on a Marian pilgrimage as there were female pilgrims. Some genuinely had a desire to foster a closer relationship with God through the Virgin. In her book, *To Be a Pilgrim: The Medieval Pilgrimage Experience*, Sarah Hopper writes, "The great prestige and spiritual virtuosity of a venerated figure were felt to be most readily experienced by visiting their shrine."[24] In the fifteenth century, theologian Antoninus of Florence lent respectability to the practice by asserting that Mary herself had gone on a pilgrimage after Christ's Assumption, visiting all the places where he had done important works.[25] That women who wished to venerate her would do the same is a logical extension of this idea. Others wanted to rid their souls of the burden of their sins and believed that a pilgrimage would help them to find forgiveness.

Visiting a Marian shrine was thought to be especially helpful for those who wanted divine assistance with some problem related to childbearing.

Everything from conception to safe labor to milk production could be dealt with by taking a trip to a sanctioned pilgrimage site. Midwives often encouraged their patients to visit a Marian shrine or two while pregnant. Many male authorities, though, believed this custom to be far too dangerous, and the sixteenth-century bishop of Salisbury, Nicholas Shaxton, chastised midwives for encouraging it.

Sometimes a pilgrimage was undertaken as the result of a vow made during a particularly difficult childbirth. The woman in labor would promise Mary that if she preserved her life, a journey would be made to a particular shrine in exchange. If the woman was subsequently unable to go (usually for reasons related to ill health), a papal dispensation would be required. She would then have to send money, gifts, or a proxy to the specified shrine instead. In one recorded instance, a French woman whose life was saved during a difficult birth commuted her vow because she was pregnant every year thereafter and unfit to travel.

Many pilgrims, however, did not have such noble motives for their decisions to visit a holy site. Often begun in the spring, when the weather for traveling was at its finest, a pilgrimage could be an appealing vacation. Minstrels and dancers frequently traveled with bands of pilgrims, providing entertainment during the journey. Especially for women, whose home lives frequently offered little but a repetitive routine of domestic responsibilities, the prospect of getting out and seeing the world could be incredibly tempting.

It is well known that vacations are times when many contemporary people indulge in hedonistic behavior. The popular advertising campaign, "What happens in Vegas stays in Vegas," is based on this idea. Medieval women also sometimes undertook supposedly holy journeys in order to pursue sexual conquests. As early as the eighth century, St. Boniface criticized women for sacrificing their virtue while on pilgrimage. Around 1175, Etienne de Fougeres, the Bishop of Rennes, warned that a married woman could arrange an assignation with her lover by feigning sickness and getting a pilgrimage prescribed as a cure.[26] During the Tudor era, Thomas More wrote against women who sang bawdy songs while traveling to holy sites. A bestselling book of the fifteenth century by Arnold von Harff contained a list of useful phrases for pilgrims, including several to use when propositioning fellow travelers.[27]

Certainly Chaucer's Wife of Bath, who might more accurately have been described as the "Widow of Bath," is a well known literary example of a female pilgrim whose overt sexuality caused consternation. Notably, she is the only woman among Chaucer's pilgrims who is not a member of a celibate religious order. Boldly setting out on a pilgrimage unaccompanied by any male protector, she flies in the face of the predominant sexual morality of the day. Her clothing choices immediately identify her to medieval readers as a woman of dubious virtue. She wears red stockings and a flamboyant hat, despite her status as a recent widow.[28] She also speaks openly and frankly about her previous marital sexual relations, which were somewhat scandalous for being both frequent and motivated primarily by lust.[29]

Sometimes, the decision to undertake a journey had to do with what pilgrims were leaving behind. Escape from various troubles was sometimes a strong motivator for going on a pilgrimage. An anonymous writer of the medieval era said that three things drove a man from his home: a quarrelsome wife, a smoking fireplace and a leaking roof.[30] Sometimes the trip was a means of getting out of an area where the harvest had been scarce or the plague was spreading. Criminals could even go on a pilgrimage to escape punishment. Anyone wearing the sacred pilgrim's cross was exempt from being arrested or taken to civil court. The offender could still be tried in an Ecclesiastical court if the nature of her crime was religious, however.[31]

Once past all the dangers of travel, women who had arrived at their destinations frequently had to face gender-specific difficulties about gaining access to shrines. Acknowledged holy sites were sometimes located in monastic churches, where the brothers took vows to live entirely secluded from women. According to Diana Webb's work, *Pilgrimage in Medieval England*, "The need to make special provision for female pilgrims who desired to venerate the Virgin at the churches of strictly enclosed monastic orders" had to be addressed.[32]

In 1244, Eleanor, the countess of Leicester, obtained an indulgence from the pope allowing her to make offerings at a Cistercian abbey for monks.[33] A more encompassing solution was offered in 1399, when Pope Boniface IX offered special dispensation for women who wished to visit a Carthusian church on any of the major feasts of the Virgin. This sort of exemption from normal monastic rules was encouraged in the fifteenth century by King Edward IV's pious mother, Cecily, Duchess of York. However, not all orders of monks were willing to be accommodating. The "no women" rule was strictly observed at St. Cuthbert's shrine in Durham and at the Chapel of St. John the Baptist in St. John Lateran.[34]

Partly as a means of setting aside some Marian spaces for women, a few orders of medieval nuns applied to the pope for official sanction of their churches as pilgrimage sites. The nuns of St. Mary Clerkenwell wrote to him in 1476 to inform him that the Virgin had been performing miracles at their Muswell Chapel. They requested permission to claim it as an official Marian shrine, which they received.[35]

The most famous Marian pilgrimage site in England, that of Our Lady of Walsingham, was established in the eleventh century by a woman, the aristocratic widow Richeldis de Favershes. She claimed to have experienced a vision in which she specifically received the Virgin Mary's request to build it.[36] According to Richeldis, Walsingham is a replica of the house where the Annunciation took place and where Jesus lived as a child. Almost immediately upon its completion, legends sprung up that the Virgin had physically relocated the original building there.

The original "Slipper Chapel" associated with this shrine, where particularly pious or desperate pilgrims could remove their shoes and approach the holy site barefoot, is still used today by Catholics as a sacred Marian site. Perhaps because the building itself has always been so unassuming, it escaped the destruction wrought by Henry VIII when he decided to eliminate the shrine. Its status as a pilgrimage site was only fully restored in 1934, when a new statue was created for it, based on the image on the seal of Walsingham's medieval priory.

The shrine's revival was largely due to the prolonged efforts of two clergymen, Fr. Philip Fletcher and Revd. Arthur Hope Patten. Since before the turn of the twentieth century, these two men had worked toward bringing about a sort of Marian revival movement.[37] Patten, particularly, wished to restore English spiritual life to the condition it would have been in if Henry VIII had never broken from the Roman Catholic Church. Many aspects of the devotion he fostered at Walsingham were strongly influenced by his particular brand of medievalism, recalling, in rather idealized form, pre–Tudor era Marianism. Members of the Society of Our Lady of Walsingham, which he established in 1926, were instructed to wear a form of monastic scapular known as "the livery of Our Lady," in order to "recall the age of chivalry." Their names were entered in a richly illuminated manuscript book, much like those produced during the Middle Ages. Priests wore elaborate robes embroidered with heraldic insignia, and coats of arms were emblazoned in the official church of Walsingham's shrine.[38]

There are many other Marian shrines which are popular with contemporary women. Medjugorje, Fatima, and Guadalupe are world famous sites where the Virgin Mary is said to have appeared to her chosen visionaries. The most frequently visited Marian pilgrimage site since the nineteenth century, however, is probably Lourdes, France. Like Walsingham, Lourdes was created due to the Marian vision of a woman. It is probably more accurate, however, to refer to this visionary, Bernadette Soubirous, as a girl at the time when she had her mystical experiences. At the age of fourteen, this barely literate peasant had a series of visions in 1858 that became one of the most universally accepted Marian encounters in history.

Doubters have long maintained that Bernadette was so widely believed because her visions confirmed recently proclaimed Catholic dogma. In 1854, Pope Pius IX had declared that the Virgin Mary was "the Immaculate Conception," the only human being free from all taint of original sin. According to this dogma, Mary had not only conceived Jesus without sex, but also she herself had also been created asexually in the womb of her mother, St. Anne. When Bernadette asked the woman in her visions to reveal her identity, she replied "I am the Immaculate Conception."[39]

It is difficult to find a biography of Bernadette Soubirous, now canonized as St. Bernadette, that is not filled with superlatives about what an exceptionally good, simple girl she was. Catholic literature seems to promote the idea

The Virgin appears to Bernadette Soubirous. Both Mary and the future saint are holding Rosaries (courtesy Chant Art).

that she was practically faultless before, during and after the visions that made her internationally famous. In a book entitled *The True Story of St. Bernadette* (emphasizing an intent of objectivity), Fr. Henry Petitot writes, "As a child, a noteworthy characteristic of Bernadette was her anxiety about upright conduct, and even her premature concern to practice virtue and make others do so."[40] He later adds that enumerating all her virtues would be impossible, but the most important ones were her fortitude, her disinterest in any profit from her visions, her lack of vanity, and her piety.[41]

Although contemporary women can travel to Lourdes on airplanes that lack few high-tech conveniences, much has remained the same about Marian pilgrimages since the Middle Ages. As at medieval pilgrimage sites, a tremendous amount of commercialism has sprung up around Lourdes—supposedly a place for spiritual enlightenment. Like Walsingham, holy water from Lourdes has been bottled and sold to the faithful for over 150 years. In the late nineteenth century, a female pilgrim complained in a letter to the shrine that selling the water for an exorbitant price of five francs per liter was serving to "destroy the name of Our Mother."[42] Far from being deterred by this sort of outcry, however, the clergy at Lourdes began a profitable mail order business that shipped holy water directly to people's homes.[43]

As early as 1893, articles appeared in magazines criticizing the absurdity of the objects sold by the French clergy at the sanctuary. They included scapulars, rosaries, medals, Bearnaise waffles, Saint Mary vanilla cookies, Lourdes lozenges, and Virgins, Christs and saints covered in chocolate or barley sugar. All of these objects, it was pointed out, were specifically blessed before being sold.[44] Somewhat unfortunately, it seems that this practice never waned over the course of the twentieth century.

In 1958, two articles in *Time Magazine* decried the excess of commercialism at Lourdes, listing for sale, "alarm clocks that tinkle 'Ave Maria,' cellophane bags of throat lozenges made from 'Genuine Lourdes Water,' neckties, corkscrews, fountain pens and egg timers."[45] In 1976, Marina Warner also had a list of ridiculous souvenirs from the shrine: "piles of tinsel and plastic amulets, the dross of holy water bottles shaped like the Virgin (her crown the stopper), cocoa bean rosaries, grottoes in snowstorm globes, Bernadettes wreathed in roses that light up." Readers can easily sense the frustration in her words, "It is undeniable that the souvenir shops and bric-a-brac undermine the spiritual experience to be expected from the greatest Marian shrine in the world."[46]

Another particularly notable similarity between the contemporary pilgrimage and that of the Middle Ages is an officially sanctioned emphasis on the shrines' ability to cure women's illnesses, no matter how great or small. Of course, the curative powers of Marian shrines, both medieval and modern, have never been limited to women. One of the most famous of the documented cures at Lourdes is that of Pierre de Rudder, a Belgian workman. His broken leg bone, visible through a constantly open sore, would not heal for eight years.

Lourdes, France (courtesy Chant Art).

After a visit to Lourdes, however, he was miraculously completely restored to health.[47]

Yet it is impossible to overlook the fact that the majority of those cured of every conceivable ailment at Marian shrines have always been women. Dr. Boissarie, head of the Medical Authentication Bureau at Lourdes, lists women cured of sores, breast cancer, tuberculosis, paralysis, epilepsy, and diseases of the eyes and nerves. He offers detailed accounts of each one's suffering before her pilgrimage to the holy site, the failure of conventional medicine to heal her, and her subsequent miraculous cure at the shrine. These accounts, however remarkable, make for somewhat dry reading, due to their inevitable medical nature. Meant to convince the skeptic with scientific evidence, they distance the lay reader with the discourse of medical biology.

Much more personally affecting, however, are descriptions that female believers themselves have written of their own cures. In *Lourdes, Body and Spirit in the Secular Age*, Ruth Harris comments on them, "They frequently did not see their transformations just in terms of their own cure, but as part of the Virgin's plans for mankind."[48] It was a common belief among those cured that the Blessed Mother herself had made them endure their illnesses and bodily suffering, in order to increase their faith subsequently through the agency of miracles. Many of the earliest of this sort of first-person narrative, written toward the beginning of the Lourdes shrine's existence, were created because of a parade.

The year 1897 marked the 25th anniversary of the Lourdes shrine, and the Church decided to organize a procession of hundreds of pilgrims who had been cured at the site. This was meant to both reaffirm the belief of the faithful and to provide incontrovertible proof for those who scorned the miraculous powers of the shrine. To select those who would be included in the procession, a request was extended by the Assumptionist order for healed pilgrims, called miracules, to submit succinct written accounts of their experiences. Hundreds of women responded to the call, attracted by the idea that, based on their cures, they would be treated as "important individuals, worthy of celebration." If selected for inclusion in the procession, they would be given special privileges, including permanent access to the Lourdes grotto. Ultimately, 117 female applicants were chosen, and the accounts of their miraculous experiences were permanently archived at the shrine.[49]

During the first half of the twentieth century, many popular American periodicals featured firsthand descriptions of women's travels to Lourdes. At this time in history, however, most people concurred with the societal belief that "Catholics were in significant ways different from other Americans."[50] In order to be more appealing to a broad readership, these articles were usually written by Protestant women. They were meant to provide those who did not believe in the miraculous cures with perspectives penned by objective observers. In 1939, Margaret Gray Blanton stated in an article entitled "A Protestant Looks at

Lourdes" that the most remarkable things there were the positive atmosphere, the kindness of the visitors toward each other, and the resultant serenity of the sick pilgrims. In 1934, H. Flanders Dunbar, a prominent female physician, argued in the *Forum* that even if the healing at Lourdes was psychosomatic, it "clarifies the power of human emotions and the connection between mind and body."[51]

Despite some undeniable similarities between medieval and contemporary pilgrimages, without a doubt, there are also vast differences. People in the modern world are certainly more aware of scientific explanations for what once seemed like miraculous phenomena. So, the overarching question remains— what could inspire a contemporary woman to go on a Marian pilgrimage, as millions have done? This question is particularly relevant in the twenty-first century, when, as Paolo Apolito points out in *The Internet and the Madonna*, extensive web sites are available for every major Marian shrine.[52] These frequently feature digital photographs of significant aspects of the pilgrimage experience, offering the armchair explorer something that amounts to a "virtual voyage."

It is impossible to truly understand this worldwide phenomenon without once again resorting to the discourse of the suffering female body—illness and health. Since the earliest days of the Lourdes shrine, women have always been by far the majority of miracle recipients. Only ten men were included in the famous jubilee procession of 127 people miraculously cured at Lourdes. Women also served as the primary caretakers of the sick at shrines. Most of the lay women who did not come to Lourdes seeking a cure arrived to nurse, feed, and comfort the thousands of sick, frequently infectious, pilgrims who poured into the site.

The debilitating illness of many Lourdes pilgrims, who frequently suffered from tuberculosis and deforming lupus, was often distressing for the sheltered Victorian-era ladies who attended them. Healthy young women under the age of twenty-five were prevented from seeing the sick unless accompanied by their mothers. Despite this, even upper-class women, who had never done dirty work before in their lives, frequently volunteered to serve as caretakers of the sick at Lourdes.[53] Similarly, today, the world wide web abounds with sites featuring women telling stories of illness and healing at Marian shrines. These are generally of two types—either the women are joyously expounding on their experiences of being cured or they emphasize the feeling of being transformed through helping the sick there.

In her intriguing article, "Rachel's Tomb and the Milk Grotto of the Virgin Mary," Susan Starr Sered proposes that a "successful women's shrine should (a) offer concrete help for the real and serious problems faced by many women and (b) provide space where women can feel a sense of belonging, but where their presence does not threaten their already precarious position in patriarchal society."[54]

She then proceeds to argue that, by this standard, Rachel's Tomb is successful. It offers a spiritual solution to the problem of infertility, and it provides a comfortably furnished space that only women are permitted to enter. By contrast, at the Milk Grotto of the Virgin Mary, emphasis is placed on the less serious problem of lactation, and women are both guided and guarded by a male Franciscan who accompanies them everywhere on their visit. Although it could be argued that, as a Jew, Sered cannot escape her bias in this matter, it does not invalidate her argument.

If the Milk Grotto fails to satisfy these requirements, certainly Marian shrines such as Lourdes, Fatima and Medjugorje, famous for the Virgin's miraculous cures, nicely fit the bill. They offer concrete help for a serious problem — physiological illness of one sort of another. As for providing a place of belonging that does not threaten patriarchal society, Ruth Harris provides a lengthy discussion of this phenomenon at Lourdes. She states:

> The experience of women in the history of Lourdes suggests that the calls of feminism went unheeded not because the Church sought to block women's aspirations, but because it was so effective at channeling them in spiritual and practical directions outside the republican mainstream.... The Church did encourage the subordination of women; at the same time, however, it offered them a world of opportunity and found a means of cultivating their loyalty and energies.[55]

Traditionally, leaders of the Catholic Church have believed in keeping lay women busy with many different forms of "women's work." Some feminists today hold the somewhat cynical view that if Catholic wives and mothers are not too preoccupied with housework and children to notice inequality with men, at the very least, they are too tired to protest. Since ancient times, the religious holidays present in every society's calendar have been a source of additional work for women. Almost invariably, these annual events require a great deal of cleaning and food preparation, as family members come together to celebrate. There is also usually a strong emphasis on activities for children, for whom women have traditionally had the primary responsibility. Particularly in the medieval era, the year prominently featured several Marian holidays which were celebrated with all of the enthusiasm now associated with Christmas. Despite the additional work these may have caused, women have clamored to keep them when religious forces such as Protestantism have threatened such holidays with extinction.

5

Marian Times

Days, Months and Life Passages

Even today, certain times have been set aside by the Catholic Church to honor the Virgin Mary, though they are not as widely and enthusiastically celebrated as they were during the medieval era. There is a Marian day of the week (Saturday), a month of Mary (May) and various Marian feasts that occur throughout the liturgical year. Some of these are solemn, others joyous, and most have folk customs associated with them. The Council at Vatican II called for decreased emphasis on all things Marian, but her holidays are still very much a part of how people in many cultures measure time. Especially in regions such as Southern Italy and the Philippines, where the Virgin is still highly venerated, Marian celebrations are important community events.

The practice of dedicating Saturday to Mary can be largely attributed to the eighth-century Benedictine monk, Alcuin, who held a position at the court of Charlemagne equivalent to the modern Minister of Education. He composed six devotional masses for each day of the week, excepting Sunday. For Saturday, he created two masses in honor of the Blessed Virgin. His choice of Saturday for the Marian masses was due to an apocryphal, yet widely believed story. On the Saturday after Christ's death, all of his disciples supposedly lost faith in his divinity, but Mary still believed. As a result, Jesus appeared only to her on that day. The *Dictionary of Mary* claims that "the liturgical reform of Vatican II did not abolish this traditional practice."[1] In *Mary's Day—Saturday*, author Mark G. Boyer recommends setting aside Saturday each week as a time "to give reverence to the Blessed Virgin, who waited for Christ's resurrection with full faith and hope."[2]

Sources disagree about how May became associated with her. According to the *Dictionary of Mary*, the practice of dedicating this month to her arose at the end of the thirteenth century, as a means of Christianizing popular pagan spring festivals. By the sixteenth century, books were published in which celebrations in May honoring Mary were encouraged. The practice became particularly popular among the Jesuits and, by 1700, was regularly observed by their students at Roman College.³

However, Marina Warner, in *Alone of All Her Sex*, claims that May only began to be set aside for the Virgin in the eighteenth century. Begun in Naples, Italy, the practice was supposedly meant as a replacement for the licentious pagan holiday of Ludi Floreales. In this traditional fertility festival, men and women pelted each other with flowers to honor Flora, the Roman goddess of fruitfulness.⁴ Although there are no officially recognized Marian prayers or rites for May, many churches honor her during that month with daily rosary recitations or the crowning of a Madonna statue. By the mid-twentieth century, several editions had been published of *The Golden Wreath for the Month of Mary*, a book of Marian meditations for each day in May.

There is also little collusion among authors about how many Marian holidays are actually present in the liturgical year. *The Dictionary of Mary* lists twenty specifically Marian celebrations, enough that most months include more than one. Francis X. Weisner, who mentions only five in his *Handbook of Christian Feasts and Customs*, seems almost stingy by comparison. His accounting is probably more realistic, however, in terms of the number of feasts which are actively celebrated in most places. In the *Journal for Mary*, Sister M. Marguerite Andrew enumerates thirty-one, including those which are honored only regionally. She writes, "Holy Mother Church does not leave us long without a liturgical feast of Mary. Indeed, it would seem that Our Lady herself has seen to it that her children ... should have many reminders of her."⁵

The five which all sources agree upon, however, are Candlemas (February 2), the Annunciation (March 25), the Assumption of the Virgin (August 15), the Birth of Mary (September 8), and the Immaculate Conception (December 8). Admittedly, it is impossible to celebrate many other important days in the liturgical calendar, particularly Christmas, without at least some reference to the Virgin. However, on these five feast days, the focus is on her alone. There is a significant feast of Mary for each season of the year, with an extra one added for winter. Also, only two of these feasts—Candlemas and the Annunciation—commemorate events which actually appear in the Bible, while the rest are apocryphal. According to Warner, all of these annual festivals other than the Immaculate Conception (the most recent addition) were brought to Europe in the seventh century by monks fleeing the Moslem invasion of the Holy Land.⁶

Candlemas, the first of these feasts to occur in the calendar year, is so strongly associated with women that it seems almost required for feminist religious historians to write about it. It commemorates an event described in the Bible, in which Mary ritually presented an offering of a lamb and a pigeon at the temple. According to Jewish tradition, she could be ritually purified from uncleanness of childbirth in this way. Of course, there was some level of irony inherent in this action—as the Virgin Mother, she had experienced nothing the Jewish faith would consider defilement during the conception or birth of

Jesus. According to Catholic belief, it was only her humility which led her to follow this custom, as other women did.

Until recently, scholars believed that the feast of Candlemas, celebrated as early as the sixth century, was a Christianization of Lupercalia, a pagan festival in honor of Pan held annually on February 14 and 15. However, new research has indicated that it is more likely a transformation of a holiday honoring the nature goddess Demeter. With its emphasis on light and candles, it is probably an imitation of her search through the night for her missing daughter Persephone.[7] In folk custom, these candles were made in people's homes, preferably from expensive beeswax, then taken to church to be ritually blessed. They were subsequently used during times of sickness and storms, when strong divine protection was needed. The traditional prayer used to bless the candles included the invocation that wherever they were lit, the Devil would flee away in "fear and trembling."[8]

According to a popular Polish legend, the Virgin Mary annually makes a personal visit to all villages on Candlemas, frightening wolves away with her fearsome "thunder candle."[9] The wax from these candles was thought to have protective powers against illness and misfortune — it was ceremonially dripped on people's heads and shoulders, on the horns of cattle, and on beehives. Crosses made from it were also traced on doors and windows. In Wales, to invoke the Virgin Mary's influence, men carrying candles went from house to house on Candlemas eve, singing carols about her light.[10] In several other countries, however, it was girls wearing white veils who walked through the night in candlelit processions to dispel fearsome shadows.[11] The Catholic custom of "churching," in which women were blessed with candles after childbirth, was a sort of personalized imitation of Mary's Candlemas holiday. Over time, the churching ceremony became so important to women that they fought bitterly to retain it when Protestant leaders eliminated it from the practice of their religion.

Like Candlemas, the second Marian feast to occur in the calendar year, the Annunciation, is also a commemoration of a Biblical event. This is when the angel Gabriel appeared to Mary to inform her of the virginal conception of Jesus. Logically, this festival is celebrated annually on March 25, nine months before the birth of Christ. Its origins date back to the fifth century, and it is one of the few Catholic feasts also honored by Protestants. Sometimes called "Lady Day," it was considered a public holiday in Catholic countries until 1918, and people were routinely given the day off from work. In central Europe, it is known as the "Feast of the Swallows" and thought to be when the first swallows return from their migration.

The Annunciation has been celebrated with pageants and mystery plays since medieval times. In one traditional German performance, a young boy dressed as an angel was suspended by a rope and lowered down into the church through the "Holy Ghost Hole." This simple special effect would naturally gain the full attention of all the children in the congregation. While they were thus distracted, their mothers stealthily placed cookies and candy on the pew benches, telling the little ones afterwards that they were gifts from Gabriel's invisible companion angels. In Russia, gifts of food have also traditionally accompanied this holiday. During the church service, priests blessed large wafers of wheat flour and presented them to their congregations after the service. Small pieces were then eaten silently by all members of the family, including servants. The final remaining crumbs of "Annunciation Bread" would be buried in the fields as protection for the crops against bad weather. During the Middle Ages in Rome, the Annunciation was an occasion for gifts of an entirely more lavish kind. After mass was celebrated, the pope would distribute fifty gold pieces each to three hundred virtuous but poor girls, in order to provide them with dowries.

The Assumption of the Virgin, sometimes referred to as the "Dormition" or "Falling Asleep" as a sort of reference to death, commemorates the bodily ascension of Mary into heaven. Because of her purity and her special relationship with Jesus, He supposedly did not allow her body to decay. Instead, Catholic leaders teach that, like her Son, she ascended bodily into heaven. This event is never mentioned in the Bible but has been widely accepted as fact by Catholics since the seventh century. Not long after the initial introduction of this festival in the eighth century, it was heavily promoted by three saints— Germanus, Andrew of Crete, and John Damascene. They wanted a reaffirming holiday that would help to counteract Catholic uneasiness accompanying the Moslem invasion of the Holy Land.[12] It was, however, only actually proclaimed official dogma by the pope as late as 1950.[13]

The Feast of the Assumption is still honored throughout the world with processions in which statues of the Virgin are carried through the streets. In medieval times, it was believed that herbs harvested in August would have great healing power, and they were blessed by priests on Assumption Day. This custom has continued into contemporary times in Bavaria. The traditional French observance of this day is a sort of harvest festival, in which priests bless the standing corn.[14] Similarly, in Armenia, the first grapes are harvested and blessed on Assumption Day, and it is forbidden for good Catholics to taste them before this event. The holiday is observed with particular solemnity in this country— somewhat uniquely for a Marian festival, it is preceded by a week of fasting. The only place where a similar custom is practiced is Sicily. In honor of the Virgin, abstinence from fruit is required for pious Catholics during the first two weeks of August. A special celebratory dinner featuring fruit consecrated during the Assumption Day services is then eaten after mass. As part of the festivities, baskets of fruit are also presented to friends and family. In Portugal, this holiday is a time for blessing fishing boats and the ocean, while in Britain and Ireland, the water association is celebrated by bathing in oceans, rivers, and lakes to preserve health.

The Birth (or Nativity) of the Virgin is never specifically mentioned in the Bible, though it can, of course, be assumed that she had a birthday. Its celebration as a holiday originated in the sixth century in Syria and Palestine. By the twelfth century, however, the event was commemorated with festivities throughout Europe. Somewhat strangely, the only explanation offered for the date — September 8 — is that it coincides with the consecration of a church dedicated to her in Jerusalem. The French grape harvest has traditionally started each year on the Feast of the Nativity of the Virgin. Catholic owners of vineyards still bring their best grapes to churches to be blessed each September 8th, and some are afterwards tied to the hands of Madonna statues. When adorned in this manner, she is known as "Our Lady of the Grape Harvest." In the Alps, cattle and sheep are driven out of summer pastures, with the lead animals wearing elaborate decorations of flowers, ribbons and bells.

Intriguingly, the feast of Immaculate Conception, celebrated on December 8, does not honor the conception of Jesus, but rather that of Mary herself. Proclaimed as dogma in 1854, it has been one of the most hotly contested points of theology in the history of the Catholic Church. Both the Miraculous Medal and the visions of Bernadette Soubirous at Lourdes, France, were promoted by the Catholic Church as confirmations of this doctrine. Still, the idea that Mary was miraculously conceived without sex by her mother, St. Anne, sits uneasily with many people, including pious Catholics. If accepted as fact, it means that she is the only human in history untouched by original sin. The Immaculate Conception is the only feast of the Virgin which did not come to Europe by way of Rome. Instead, it began in southern Italy, moving through Normandy before permeating the rest of Europe. Though celebrated unofficially as early as the ninth century, it was proclaimed a holiday in 1166 by the Byzantine Emperor, Manuel Comnenus. Popes, however, refused to recognize it as a Marian feast until the eighteenth century, though it had been celebrated as a public holiday in Spain since 1644.

Spain and Spanish-speaking countries are the only places with well-established customs for this festival, since it has been celebrated there longer than in any other region of the world. There, it is commemorated with processions, and children usually make their first communions on December 8 in honor of this holiday. It is also Spanish Mother's Day, as well as a sort of homecoming day for the alumni of schools. In the northern provinces, balconies are decorated with flowers, carpets, and flags, and windows are adorned with candles. In Seville, the famous "Dance of the Six" is performed each year by six boys, attracting local folk dance fans, as well as a good crowd of tourists.

Marian feasts are generally times of celebration and eating, though her traditional Saturday observance obliquely became associated with fasting. Beginning in the second century, Christians were supposed to fast on Wednesdays, in commemoration of the betrayal of Judas, and Fridays, the day of Christ's death. Thursday was known as "the day between the fasts." These, however, were only "half fasts," and one meal a day was allowed. In 417, Pope Innocent I added Saturday as a fast day, motivated by the fact that the disciples supposedly mourned Jesus' death by abstaining from food.[15] Because of its previous Marian connotations, Saturday became known as a day to fast in honor of "Our Lady."

Of the yearly liturgical feasts, only the Assumption seems to be at all associated with any sort of voluntary privation. In medieval times, good Catholics fasted and abstained from sex during Lent and Advent, as well as all Fridays, Sundays, and Ember Days.[16] Rarely observed in contemporary society, Ember Days were proclaimed as times of abstinence by medieval Christian leaders. This was largely in reaction to pagan seasonal feasts taking place around the same times, which glorified gorging on food and sexual excess. Ember Days were solemn, and those studying to be priests traditionally took their Holy Orders during this time. Souls in purgatory were supposed to be able to show themselves to their still-living relatives and friends on Ember Days. According to tradition, they usually did this to thank the living for praying on their behalf, as well as to request prayers for others who had no one to remember them.[17]

Restrictions on sex in honor of Mary were rare but not completely unknown. During the fifth and sixth centuries, Christian women would go on a retreat away from all men during Advent. They did this in order to imitate Mary, whom they believed gave birth alone. Because these women were separated from men, abstention from sex necessarily occurred.[18] Somewhat oddly, in medieval times, couples were encouraged to abstain from sex on their wedding nights to honor the celibate marriage of Mary and Joseph. Bridegrooms who wished to disregard this stricture had to pay a fee to church authorities.[19]

Sex, or the lack of it, in large part defined women during the Middle Ages. A medieval woman was classified by society at different stages of her life according to her sexual status—virgin, wife, or widow.[20] Just as there were Marian times of the week, month and year, especially for women, certain stages of life were closely associated with the Virgin Mary. The time of marriage, however, was decidedly not associated with the Blessed Virgin. From a spiritual standpoint, getting married was particularly problematic for medieval women. With its inherent sexuality, their status as wives forever conflated them with sinful, sensual Eve, instead of the chaste Virgin Mary. Chaucer's Wife of Bath, Alisoun, was characterized as excessively sensual and meant to remind readers of the original sin of Eve.[21]

Although Mary, the ideal woman, had been a wife, particularly pious women would likely have had an abhorrence of the idea of marriage and sexual activity. In the fourth century, St. Jerome insisted that the inherent good of marriage lay only in the fact that it allowed people who would be lifelong virgins to be born.[22] Gory tales of female virgin martyrs were well known during the Middle Ages, featuring girls who nobly endured torture and execution because they resisted marriage. Popular female saints included St. Agatha, who had her breasts cut off rather than give up her virginity, and St. Apollonia, who had her teeth torn out for the same reason. St. Lucy did not even wait to be persecuted by others for her decision — she instead gouged out her own eyes because men found them attractive.

In Marian legends, the Virgin is constantly "rescuing" people who intend to marry from this unfortunate (from her point of view) choice. Medieval ambivalence toward the idea of marriage is well expressed in the Marian miracle tale, "The Dove that Returned." According to this story, as a result of black magic, a girl expecting to become a nun fell in love with a clerk. When she told her father that she wanted to marry the young man, he only agreed to her decision in order to save her from the sin of fornication. When she declared her intent to marry, he responded sorrowfully:

> I had devoted you to be a bride of Jesus Christ, that you might be of the household of the angels, and with them rejoice in the perfect love of God. But now you are inflamed with earthly passions, and desire the love of a man, which is a poor and transitory thing.[23]

Because of such legends, medieval girls were sometimes inspired by saintly examples of virginity. When they expressed a pious unwillingness to marry, however, it was often considered problematic by their families, as well as Church authorities. To overcome potential brides' objections, clergy emphasized the uniqueness of the Virgin Mary. Medieval theologian Guerric of Igny stressed the vast differences between the Holy Mother and earthly motherhood. In particular, he pointed out her exceptional humility in choosing to undergo the traditional Jewish purification ceremony after she gave birth, despite her virginal status.[24]

Most girls were encouraged to have admiration for the Virgin but not to imitate her purity, as nuns did. Particularly for peasants, it was her maternity and her association with the fertile earth that was considered significant, not her chastity. For this class of society, the most important thing about Mary's virginal status was that it led to her spiritual fertility.[25] When all else failed, frustrated family members could remind reluctant brides of Mary's obedience, emphasizing her role as the "handmaid of the Lord." Medieval theologians such as Gratian and Peter Lombard argued that Mary's vow of virginity was conditional — supposedly, she only planned to keep it if it did not go against the will of God, her parents, or her husband.[26]

In the thirteenth century, an alternative to the sensuality of married life was encouraged by Thomas Aquinas. He proposed that all marriages could be modeled on that of Mary and Joseph. Like them, both partners in a couple could please God by agreeing to practice chastity. Aquinas emphasized that such an agreement necessarily had to be mutual, since a partner who was unwillingly in a chaste marriage was likely to commit the mortal sin of adultery.[27] Such a vow was frequently undertaken only after years of marriage with sex. Both Margery Kempe and St. Birgitta of Sweden got their husbands to agree to chaste marriages after they had many children.

Marriages of lifelong chastity were not unheard of, however, and these were believed to be looked upon favorably by the Virgin Mary. There are several recorded instances of reluctant brides being convinced to marry by a visitation of the Virgin, who promised them a chaste union. At the turn of the fourteenth century, Dauphine of Puimichel received such a vision, as did Lucia Brocadelli of Narni in the sixteenth century. Both of them succeeded in preserving their virginity for life. Lucia took matters into her own hands, fleeing her husband and joining a convent, but further divine intervention preserved Dauphine's chastity. Her husband had a mystical experience on the feast of the Assumption of the Virgin, during which he lost all carnal desire.[28]

The idea of the chaste union came about largely as a result of a twelfth-century debate about what constituted marriage. Was sexual intercourse necessary before a couple could be considered married? French theologian Peter Lombard argued that only an exchange of marriage vows by the couple was required, since to believe otherwise would negate the marriage of Mary and Joseph.[29] A century later, Thomas Aquinas took up Lombard's point of view, stating that Mary and Joseph's marriage necessarily had to be considered a "true" one. He explained that they "both consented to the conjugal bond" and, despite the lack of sexual relations, had Jesus as their son. Furthermore, he asserted that Mary and Joseph's marriage was a sacrament because there was no adultery and no divorce.[30]

Perhaps in part because of such attitudes toward sexuality, marriage was generally considered a civil contract, not a sacrament, until the sixteenth century. Throughout the Middle Ages, it was believed that the partners in a marriage had the legal authority to declare their union valid without the intervention of a priest. In what was known as a "clandestine marriage," a couple could exchange vows without clerical officiation in any location they chose. By the thirteenth century, formalized church wedding ceremonies were encouraged, but those who privately married without any clergy present were still considered man and wife.[31]

Sexual activity was frequently referred to as "the marriage debt" during medieval times, since it was the obligation of each partner to render it when asked, by word or sign. Men were advised to have frequent sex with their wives to prevent them from committing adultery. There was even some debate among theologians about whether husbands' demanding "the debt" during times when sexual activity was proscribed was a sin. Such periods of Church encouraged abstinence included when a woman was menstruating or pregnant, as well as important holy times such as Lent and Advent.[32]

It was commonly believed that women who did not engage in sexual intercourse regularly would become ill. They could suffer from "uterine suffocation," leading to difficulty breathing, convulsions, fainting fits and even madness. These illnesses were generally considered a result of the noxious nature of "female seed," which had to be regularly expelled during intercourse and menstruation. Female seed was considered so inherently evil that in the thirteenth century, a theological question arose about whether Mary, the perfect woman, menstruated. Eventually, it was decided by Church authorities that she probably had.[33]

According to the popular medieval medical manual *Encyclopaedia of Bartholomew the Englishman*, menstrual blood nourished unborn children in the womb. After the birth, the blood was supposedly driven into the breast of the mother and transformed into milk.[34] It was probably due to a misunderstanding of why menstruation ceases during pregnancy that most people believed Jesus had been conceived of Mary's flesh. Aquinas wrote that the body of Christ was created directly from the Virgin Mary's "blood subjected to a certain fuller concentration by the generative capacity of the mother."[35]

Although Mary did not approve of sexual activity, the Holy Mother's love for children was well known. The collection of miracle tales from the shrine of the Virgin of Chartres is full of stories in which she spares children from horrible fates. A boy's tongue, cut out by a wicked knight, is restored, an infant who choked to death on glass is brought back to life, and drowned children are revived through her intervention.[36] One of the few references to her in any part of the wedding ceremony is the folk custom of laying the bride's bouquet at a Madonna statue's feet.[37] According to Wilson, this was done "in the hope by this gesture of obtaining fertility and happiness." He adds that in Rumania, girls' trousseaus included glass paintings of the Virgin and Child, in order to bring about fertility in marriage.[38] It was through becoming a mother, not a bride, that a woman could find the path back to Mary that had been temporarily lost with her virginity. Motherhood conflated women with the Madonna, and pregnancy was the first of her Marian life passages.

Women who wanted to get pregnant, particularly those who had difficulty, were encouraged to appeal to the Blessed Mother. Katherine of Aragon, the first wife of Henry VIII, whose inability give him a male child eventually led to her divorce, made several pilgrimages to Our Lady of Walsingham. In 1513, she sent a letter to her husband, expressing a desire for his return home from battle. With the aid of the Virgin, she believed that they would surely produce an heir if he came home to her. She wrote, "Praying God to send you home shortly, for without this no joy here can be accomplished; and for the same I pray, and now go to Our Lady of Walsingham."[39]

Walsingham was far from the only statue of Mary thought to be helpful in bringing about fertility for women. An inscription at the base of the statue of Notre Dame de Grace at Gignac recounts that after twenty-five years of barrenness, Catherine Pastourel gave birth to a son. This was supposedly the direct result of her vow to visit the shrine for three successive years on the Feast of the Virgin's Assumption. Until after World War I, childless women in Provence would climb up to the chapel of Notre Dame des Oeufs, carrying two eggs. They would consume one there at the spring festival, then bury the other in the

Mary's special relationship with children: Little girls offer flowers to a Madonna statue (courtesy Chant Art).

Mary's special relationship with children: A young girl tends to a shrine of the Virgin in her "Star of the Sea" aspect (courtesy Chant Art).

The Madonna embraces a dark-skinned child (courtesy Chant Art).

ground to be eaten the following autumn. This was believed to be a sure-fire remedy for barrenness.[40] Invoking the aid of statues of the Virgin for pregnancy, however, was thought to have its risks. Such images, after all, were lifeless, and it was possible that conceiving through their help could bring about a stillbirth. Those who hoped to become mothers in Lucania were always careful to end supplications to Madonna statues with, "Let my [baby] be fine like yours, but flesh and blood like me."[41]

When the time of childbirth arrived for medieval women, it was necessarily accompanied by a great deal of pain. At least at first glance, labor seemed to once again conflate women with Eve instead of Mary. Church theologians considered the pain of childbirth the legacy of the original sin of Eve. In Genesis, after all, God told her that she and her descendents were forever cursed to bring forth children "in sorrow." As late as the nineteenth century, there was religious hostility to the use of obstetrical anesthesia, since many believed that to give birth without pain was against the will of God.[42] According to medieval theologians, Mary's labor was painless. She escaped Eve's curse by not conceiving her child through sin. As the cult of the Mater Dolorosa grew in popularity, however, many came to believe that Mary's pains had merely been deferred to the Crucifixion, when she suffered equally with her Son.[43]

Some feminist authors have argued that pregnant women must have felt removed from the Virgin Mary because of her immunity to labor pain. Marina Warner states, "It remains ironical that that the mother who brought forth virginally and without pain should be invoked in sympathy."[44] But the great proliferation of Marian devotional objects, prayers, and art related to childbirth throughout the ages seems to contradict this idea. In the medieval era, the Magnificat, recited by the pregnant Virgin when she visited her pregnant cousin Elizabeth, was sometimes written on a prayer roll and worn during labor.[45] Henry III's queen, Eleanor, wore a girdle that supposedly belonged to the Virgin herself in order to facilitate childbirth.[46] Despite her lack of pain during the delivery of her Son, medieval women certainly considered labor a Marian life passage, as well as one in which the Blessed Mother particularly watched over them.

In an article by Marianne Elsakkers, it was stated that the Marian "peperit" (childbearing) prayer was frequently used as a sort of folk magic charm. It makes references to several miraculous conceptions and births from the Bible, ultimately highlighting the Virgin Mary's. Her lack of labor pain is emphasized in the peperit charm, implying that the pregnant woman is praying for a similar miracle — a painless and rapid delivery.[47] This prayer was meant to be written down, as well as spoken aloud, even if the woman in labor could not read. It could be inscribed on food, such as bread, butter or cheese, which was then swallowed by the mother-to-be and thus, quite literally, internalized. More prosaically, it could also be written on paper and worn on the body as an amulet. These were thought to have such powerful magical properties that birth attendants were advised to quickly remove any amulets from mothers' bodies as soon as their children were born.[48]

It was believed that the Virgin Mary sometimes personally interceded to help a pregnant woman. According to legend, the Virgin Mary of Rocamadour successfully removed a dead fetus from a woman who had been carrying it for thirty months. The aid of other female saints could also be invoked, such as St. Anne, who was Mary's mother, St. Catherine, who protected against sudden death, and St. Dorothy, who protected against miscarriage. The patron saint of childbirth, however, was St. Margaret of Antioch, ironically a virgin, who got the job by miraculously emerging unscathed from the belly of a dragon.[49] The Virgin was also known to intercede when a baby was stillborn, especially when it was brought to one of her "respite shrines." Such holy places were common — 260 of them have now been identified in France alone. At her trial, Joan of Arc made reference to a miracle in which a three-day-old stillborn baby was restored to life by Notre Dame des Ardents.[50]

Mothers of sufficient economic means were expected to have a time of rest or "lying-in" after a birth that lasted about a month. In Hungary, the bed in which a woman delivered a child was curtained off and dedicated to the Virgin Mary during her lying-in.[51] Due to this custom, many new mothers were not even present at the baptisms of their own children, which almost always took place within eight days of their deliveries. Mothers only re-emerged publicly after a birth at their "churching," a celebration eagerly anticipated by nearly all medieval women. In this religious ceremony, a new mother made an offering of candles at a local Marian altar in thanksgiving for a successful childbirth.

The churching ceremony was a direct imitation of the Virgin's festival of Candlemas. Participating in a churching was believed to be the best way for ordinary mothers to share in Mary's experience of sanctified maternity. Arguably, this event was the most direct conflation with the Virgin Mary that a lay woman could experience during her life. Most women dressed in fine clothes and jewelry for the service, and a feast or party followed. A lavish celebration was so common that St. Elizabeth of Hungary was thought to be exceptionally humble because she wore neither jewelry nor expensive clothes at her churching ceremonies.[52]

New mothers were further identified with the Madonna through the shared life passage of lactation. The importance of the medieval image of the breast-feeding Blessed Mother cannot be overemphasized. Marina Warner states, "The image of the Virgin suckling Christ represented women's humility in accepting the full human condition."[53] In the fifteenth century, John Lydgate wrote in the *Life of Our Lady* that it was Mary's milk, not Christ's body, which actually redeemed the sin of Adam. Medieval miracle legends abounded in which Mary saved her fatally ill followers with the precious gift of drops of her milk. In the thirteenth century, phials which supposedly contained a few drops of it were venerated as holy relics throughout Europe.[54]

Women during this time were exhorted to nurse their children themselves, rather than hiring wet-nurses. It was believed that the qualities of the mother or nurse were transmitted to the child through breast milk, including morality. In legends of saints, it was written that some refused to suckle after their mothers or nurses had sex.[55] Frances of Rome, the fifteenth-century saint, was considered particularly virtuous because she chose to nurse her three children herself. When she got a painful sore on her breast, the Virgin supposedly visited her and healed it with a "wonderful liquid."[56]

One particularly well documented Marian miracle related to breast milk happened to a woman named Maria Caroens, who lived in the seventeenth-century Dutch city of Gent. This woman, a poor mother of fourteen who sold waffles to help support her large family, was having trouble producing breast milk. Fearing that her youngest child would starve because it refused to eat "pap," a Renaissance-era baby food, she visited a local statue of the Virgin to pray for help. Craig Harline, who relates Maria's tale in his book, *Miracles at the Jesus Oak*, states, "Perhaps Maria was working on the common assumption that ... the Virgin was best for problems surrounding pregnancy and mothering, due to her own immaculate conception and Jesus' miraculous conception."[57] Leaving an offering of two breasts carved in wax, she asked the statue to solve her troubles. This appeal was apparently successful, since she returned home with a greater supply of breast milk than she had ever produced for any previous child.[58]

This miracle was so well documented because the Jesuits, in whose church the statue resided, were very eager to have it acknowledged by Catholic authorities. This was partly due to a rivalry with the nearby Franciscan church, which also boasted of a miracle-working Virgin statue. More importantly, however, they wished to publicize such miracles in order to contend with Protestant sects. According to Harline, "Churchmen recognized the appeal of miracles ... for Protestantism's transcendent, distant God had little to match Catholicism's God-is-with-us-and-all-around-us."[59] So anxious were the Jesuits to encourage belief in Maria's breast-milk miracle, they unwittingly caused a controversy by "elevating" the statue prematurely. The ceremony of elevation simply involved moving a miracle-working object to a more sacred and honored place. In their enthusiasm, however, they neglected to obtain permission to do so from their bishop.[60]

During the twelfth century, the state of marriage gained new respectability after it had to be defended by Church authorities against members of the heretical Cathar sect. Catharism was a political and religious movement which had taken over much of southern France and northern Italy. Although the brutal Albigensian crusade effectively neutralized its political threat, the ideology behind it proved more difficult to eradicate. The Cathars, who shocked mainstream Catholics by allowing women to become priests, believed that evil endured as a direct result of sexual reproduction. Marriage, with its inherent impetus toward the birth of children, caused pure souls to become imprisoned in fleshly bodies. Casual sex, which wasn't as likely to lead to babies, was actually thought to be a lesser evil than marital sexual relations.[61]

Forced to defend marriage against the threat of Cathar ideology, ecclesiastical respect among Catholics for the choice of marriage and motherhood increased. The idea that marriage was a difficult lifelong commitment, maintained only with the help of God, firmly took hold. In the thirteenth century, theologian Jacques de Vitry, though vowed to lifelong celibacy himself, referred to marriage as a religious order, with its own duties and obligations.[62]

In the fifteenth century, the rise of both lay and clerical devotion to St. Joseph, Mary's husband, as well as St. Anne, her mother, further dignified the married state. The Cult of the Holy Family, with its emphasis on the humanity of Mary, allowed women to see her as someone they could truly identify with at all stages of their lives. The Holy Family, after all, was made up of real people who lived together, just like earthly families did. Increasingly, the Virgin was portrayed in art not as a distant, powerful queen, but a peasant mother sitting on the ground to nurse her hungry baby.[63] In the poetry of the time, Jesus instructed His mother to "recognize in her own agony [at the Cross] the pain of every mother, to have compassion for all mothers."[64] Julian of Norwich equated the love of mothers for their children with the love Christ has for humanity. By the sixteenth century, the world was ready for the Protestant message that marriage was most people's life calling, while celibacy was only for a few exceptionally pious individuals.

Throughout history, most girls have been raised with the expectation that they will marry and have children, and the Middle Ages proved to be no exception. Despite the fact that the majority of women from this time became wives and mothers, there are remarkably few firsthand accounts of these experiences in existence today. Autobiographical descriptions of nuns' lives are far more common, despite the fact that they were a social minority. Most nuns, after all, were far more educated than the average woman, and their freedom from family responsibilities allowed them time to write. Mothers were frequently illiterate and far too busy caring for their families to have time for anything else.

Similarly, most works written by religious scholars about motherhood, Marian or otherwise, would never be encountered by a single laywoman. They were intended for monks or nuns, who were meant to spiritually "give birth" to the Lord through their piety. Clarissa Atkinson argues in *The Oldest Vocation*, "It is sometimes asserted that medieval women found strength and support through identification with the maternal status and power of the Virgin. This may be true, but it cannot be demonstrated from the writings of twelfth-century Cistercians."[65] Married women, whose inherently sexual lives precluded them from Marian identity, instead found their models in married saints, such as St. Monica, St. Birgitta of Sweden, and particularly, the Virgin's legendary mother, St. Anne.

6

Context

Relationships with St. Anne, St. Joseph, Eve, and the Devil

Throughout history, some married women have always found the Virgin Mary's inaccessible purity troubling. In part, this has been because clergy repeatedly hammered home the point that the lives of mothers and wives were inherently infused with sexuality. According to such teachings, they could never hope to be truly like the Virgin Mother. By contrast, Mary's mother, St. Anne, made a much more comprehensible role model — one of piety within the context of sexually active marriage. Catholics traditionally believed in the "Holy Kinship" — the idea that Anne was married three times and became grandmother to a large brood of children. Many of these, in turn, grew up to become disciples of her most famous grandchild, Jesus.

Mary was supposedly partial to lifelong virgins, and as a result, not generally as sympathetic to the needs of wives or husband-hunting girls, however modest their behavior. The eve of Anne's annual liturgical feast day, July 26, became the date of many customs associated with finding a husband. In England, even the official recognition of St. Anne's Day as a public holiday came about as the result of a wedding. When Anne of Bohemia married King Richard II in 1382, Pope Urban VI ordered that the feast of the new queen's name-saint be observed in the English church.[1] In subsequent centuries, girls in England often practiced divination on this day, in order to see their future husbands in dreams.[2] In royal courts and more humble homes, it became the traditional time to hold "coming out" receptions for debutantes. Both Johann Strausses composed "Anne Polkas" for newly "out" girls to dance to with eligible young men.[3]

With such an important role being fulfilled by Anne, it is little wonder that devotion to her sometimes rivaled even that accorded to her daughter.[4] Unlike the vast majority of female saints, she lived out her holiness through the marriage relationship and in loving cooperation with her husbands.[5] Reassuringly for married women, her carnality was not an impediment to sanctity. Rather, it was the vehicle through which she was able to live out her literally God-given destiny. Anne's very association with the body allowed her to take on an enhanced role in Christ's incarnation. According to late medieval theologians, Jesus' female progenitors, Mary and Anne, were responsible for His physical body and essential humanity, while God the Father was responsible for His divinity.[6]

Anne has been referred to by scholars as one of the "marrying saints," and her role as a champion for married women and mothers has been pointed out for centuries. In the visions of St. Birgitta, St. Anne identified herself as "the lady of all wedded folk" and offered intercession for those hoping for fruitful marriages.[7] In her essay, "Appropriating the Holy Kinship," Sheingorn discusses the changing nature of female sanctity in the late Middle Ages. Emphasizing that the existence of saints like Anne showed that virginity was not a prerequisite for holiness, she states:

> Marriage and motherhood were no bar to sanctity for these women, nor did they discard traditional female behavior in order to pursue the spiritual life. Rather, these female saints carried the behavior of motherhood into the spiritual realm, as, for example, when they acted as mother to a band of spiritual children.[8]

Naturally, such a disassociation of piety with virginity, particularly for women, did not enter into the public consciousness unchallenged. Those who wished to defend the sanctity of marriage and motherhood, however, could point to the story of St. Colette of Corbie. Colette was a virginal abbess who initially refused to pray to Anne because she considered her three marriages sinful. The nun then had a vision in which a richly adorned St. Anne presented her children, all renowned for their holiness. Anne declared that no one in the history of Christianity had been as honored for the sake of her children. As a result of this divine intercession, Colette recognized the error of her ways. She subsequently founded special chapels and devotions to Anne in all her convents.[9]

To counteract the idea of Anne as a sexual being, clergy during the medieval and Renaissance eras held her up as a model of female decorum, like her daughter, the Virgin Mary. According to theologians, Anne and Mary were rarely seen in public as a young girls, and they "recoiled in horror" from the typical frivolities of adolescence. Church authorities further insisted that St. Anne experienced no carnal desire during her married life. Supposedly, she took husbands only in obedience to the law and with the hope of producing good, honorable children.

In medieval France, the need to separate Anne from carnality became so extreme that a legend sprang up, asserting that both she and her father, St. Fanuel, were immaculately conceived. According to this traditional tale, Anne's grandmother got pregnant when she unknowingly picked a flower that had been seeded by the Tree of Life. This led to the birth of St. Fanuel, who, in turn, conceived Anne when he wiped the juice of an apple with miraculous healing powers on his thigh. His thigh became engorged, and much as Athena sprang from the head of Zeus, the infant Anne emerged from her father's leg.[10]

The desexualization of Anne continued in France during the Renaissance. In the early sixteenth century, the theologian Jacques Lefevre d'Etaples called into question whether she had truly married three times. Instead, he claimed that her only husband had been Joachim and her only daughter Mary. This idea found favor at the French court, largely due to the complicated politics of the day. Louise of Savoy was the mother of the heir to the French throne, Francois I. Her deceased husband, however, had not been the King of France, Louis XII, but his first cousin, Charles of Angouleme. Louise's son was heir because the king's wife, Anne of Brittany, had produced only girls—Claude and Renee. The rivalry between Louise of Savoy and Anne of Brittany was so intense that it became something of a contest to determine which woman could become most identified with St. Anne.

This competition resulted from the French belief that the terrestrial ruler was a reflection of the divine, the royal family of the Holy Family.[11] Because Anne of Brittany had been named for Saint Anne, she frequently adopted her saint's iconography. The conflation was particularly noticeable in the primer she commissioned for her daughter, Claude, in which all the St. Anne imagery could also be interpreted as Queen Anne's.[12] In response, Louise of Savoy promoted the work of Lefevre d'Etaples, because he claimed that St. Anne, like Louise, had married only once, remaining a widow when her husband died. Anne of Brittany, by contrast, had remarried after the death of her first husband.

Despite clerical fears about Anne's sexual nature, her popularity was almost universal. Men and women, young and old, all seemed to love her and want to be associated with her. She was adopted as the patron saint of woodworkers, and, in Paris, the mixture of strong glue and sawdust used to fix holes in planks was known as "St. Anne's brains."[13] Seamstresses also regarded Anne as their patron because she had created the Virgin—known as the "robe without seams" that had enveloped the incarnate Christ.[14] She was strongly associated with grapevines, since the grape has traditionally been one of the primary symbols of Christ. Wine, after all, was His blood, and Anne was often portrayed by artists in a bright red cloak to underscore this idea. In the iconographic vineyard, Mary was thought of as the flower that produced the grape.[15]

A function of St. Anne which greatly encouraged her popularity was her ability to help people out of financial difficulties. In "Saint Anne: A Holy Grandmother and her Children," Ton Brandenbarg writes, "Anne could see to prosperity and success on earth ... change poverty into riches and disgrace into honor."[16] Traditionally, one of the most widely known miracle legends about her has been the story of her restoration of prosperity to a man named Emmericus of Hungary.

Through a series of disasters, Emmericus is rendered penniless and decides to go on a pilgrimage to Santiago de Compostela, to visit the grave of his patron saint, James. On the road to this shrine, St. James appears to him as a fellow pilgrim, declaring that he is a "grandson of Mother Anne." He instructs Emmericus to make an effigy of St. Anne, to which he should light candles and say prayers each Tuesday. That day, James explains, is sacred to Anne because her birth and death, as well as the birthday of her Holy Daughter, Mary, all happened to fall on Tuesdays. The impoverished man is also encouraged to get others to perform these devotions, so that the practice of her veneration will grow. Emmericus does what St. James instructs him to do, and worship of St. Anne, indeed, becomes widespread in the area where he lives.

Several years later, he is given the task of painting a large mural of her on the highest tower in his town, so that its residents will be blessed with prosperity. Just as he completes his piece, a gust of wind blows him off the scaffolding. The image of Anne reaches out from the building to lend him her cloak, and he reaches the ground unharmed. When the king hears of this miracle, he is so impressed that he rewards Emmericus with a large sum of money, appoints him mayor of the town and makes him one of the royal counselors. In gratitude, the now wealthy man advises the king to make Anne's liturgical feast day a national holiday and to produce a large number of effigies of her. At the end of his prosperous life, the Virgin Mary appears to escort Emmericus' soul into heaven, calling herself his sister, since they are both "children of Anne."[17]

Though many legends about Anne, like this one, became popular during the medieval era, stories about her had already existed for centuries prior to this time. The first known reference to her appears in the second-century book of apocrypha, *The Protoevangelium of James*.[18] Increased interest in genealogy during the Middle Ages also played a part in St. Anne's cult. Around the turn of the first millennium, people became very interested in their own ancestry, as the custom of passing property from father to son took hold. Given the strongly religious nature of society at the time, this interest extended into a curiosity about the details of Jesus' genealogy. Concurrently, married women, such as Matilda, queen of Henry I, and Edith, wife of King Otto I, were fulfilling an increasingly important role in religious and social life. They wanted to encourage devotion to Anne, who lived "a worldly life in harmony with Christian values."[19] Her veneration was further popularized with the inclusion of her life story in the bestseller, *The Golden Legend*.

Toward the end of the medieval era, St. Anne's cult was strongly encouraged by the Carmelites, a Catholic sect which claimed descent from the prophet Elijah and his disciples, who lived on Mount Carmel. The Carmelites believed that the rain cloud described in the Bible, which miraculously appeared over Mt. Carmel to end a drought, was an allegory of the Virgin Mary. More specifically, they felt that it represented her Immaculate Conception in the womb of Anne.[20] In order to encourage acceptance of this hotly contested idea, Carmelite theologians publicized a more detailed genealogical background for the Virgin Mary. This even included the history of her grandmother, Emerentiana, a woman who reluctantly left monastic life to marry after she had a vision of her destiny as Christ's ancestress.[21]

Given the history of tremendous popular devotion to St. Anne, it seems somewhat surprising that she does not appear anywhere in the Bible. Her very existence in Christian thought probably stems from two theological questions about Mary. The first is whether the Virgin herself was immaculately conceived. The second is related to the mysterious brothers that Jesus mentions in the New Testament. The implications of their existence makes the Catholic dogma of Mary's lifelong virginity a dubious proposition. Brandenbarg asserts, "From the earliest times the devotion to Anne has always been indissolubly bound up with the veneration of her daughter Mary."[22] Francesca Sautman argues for a somewhat radical interpretation of their relationship, stating, "Anne and Mary become associated as two faces of divine womanhood, the very young and the very old, both becoming mothers by divine intervention."[23]

According to legend, St. Anne was good and pious, but she and her husband, Joachim were unhappy because they had been unable to produce any children. When he went to the temple to make an offering, the high priest there chastised him for his childlessness, asserting that it was a sign of God's displeasure. Miserable, he fled into the desert for forty days to do penance. Meanwhile, at home, St. Anne was painfully reminded of her barrenness when she saw a nest containing a mother sparrow with several babies. While both members of the couple wept, separated, angels appeared simultaneously to them, announcing that Anne would soon become pregnant. Joyously, Joachim rushed back home to his wife, who ran to meet him at the Gate of Jerusalem. They embraced, and at that moment, the Virgin Mary was conceived.[24] Although not officially accepted as dogma until the nineteenth century, this idea of the immaculate conception of Mary existed as early as the second century.

To address the theological question about Jesus' brothers, the idea that St. Anne was twice widowed and remarried was proposed in the ninth century by Haimo of Auxerre. According to his writings, Anne's second husband was called Cleophas and her third was Salome. Each of these marriages also produced a daughter named Mary. These children would grow up to be two of the women at Jesus' tomb, in the well-known scene from the New Testament. They would also become mothers to their own holy children. Anne's second daughter Mary had four sons—James the Lesser, Jude Thaddeus, Simon, and Joseph the Just, who wished to replace Judas in Jesus' company but lost the honor to Matthias. Anne's third daughter gave birth to James the Greater and John the Evangelist. According to most medieval theologians, these were the "brethren" that Jesus spoke of in the Bible. To complete the Holy Kinship of Anne's family tree,

Haimo further asserted that Anne's sister Esmeria gave birth to St. Elizabeth. This holy woman from the Bible was the Virgin Mary's cousin, as well as the mother of John the Baptist.[25]

In spite of her apocryphal origins, St. Anne was thought to share many characteristics with her oldest daughter, the Virgin. She began to take on many of her daughter's significant roles in women's lives, supplementing Mary's powers as well as complementing them. Like her daughter, St. Anne was invoked by barren women throughout Europe when they wished to conceive children. She was even known as the patron saint of infertile women. Many miracle stories attest to St. Anne's power to give children to the unhappily barren. In several such legends, her intervention causes them to give birth to triplets, since Anne herself had three children over the course of her life. In one well-known story, a wealthy, childless woman from Lorraine venerates Anne and becomes pregnant. Before the end of her term, however, she becomes negligent in her prayers, and the baby is stillborn. Miserably, the woman confesses her impiety, and St. Anne restores the child to life.[26]

Women's prayers to Saint Anne to lift the shame of infertility never ceased. In the late seventeenth century, English women commonly went to the St. Anne chapel in London's Temple Church, a site that enjoyed a good reputation for getting prayers for babies answered favorably. In France, would-be mothers quite literally "put a hat on St. Anne" to get pregnant, offering her statue their own headgear. Dramatically, a barren peasant woman in nineteenth-century Brittany visited St. Anne's shrine at Auray on foot, painstakingly dragging a cradle behind her for many miles.[27] Anne was also called upon to aid women during childbirth. In France, written or printed prayers addressed to her were often placed on the bodies of women in labor. In Corsica, knots dedicated to St. Anne were tied and untied in fabric as a means of magically facilitating delivery. Women elsewhere in Italy dressed in yellow and green, her officially recognized colors, after successfully giving birth.[28]

The practice of transforming pagan goddesses' sacred wells into sites dedicated to the Virgin Mary also carried over to St. Anne. Possibly because of the intrinsically liquid nature of nursing, both of these holy mothers were strongly associated with water. Anyone wishing to end a drought, as well as sailors hoping for safe passage, commonly addressed their prayers to Mary, Anne or both. In German tradition, water which had been consecrated to St. Anne was used to guard against mumps. In the French town of Brie, near Vitry, her sacred spring was reputed to cure fevers as well as illnesses of the eyes and throat. Pilgrims to this spring commonly timed their visits to coincide with Anne's feast day, July 26, or the nativity of the Virgin, September 8.[29]

In England, the well at Buxton in Derbyshire had been considered a holy place in pre–Christian times. In Roman-ruled England, it was a famous site for miraculously curing the sick. After Christianity took hold, it was rededicated to St. Anne. Pilgrims often left votive offerings there in hope of (or in thanksgiving for) a miraculous cure. The shrine was well known enough that it was singled out as idolatrous by Henry VIII and destroyed. Although its identity as a site of holy intervention was temporarily obliterated, it was reopened as a health spa during the reign of Elizabeth I.

By the mid-twentieth century, however, its associations with Anne and mystical healing had been restored. In 1955, a prayer was said over it at the annual Blessing of St. Anne's Well which included the invocation, "Accept our thanks for those who first found these healing waters; and grant Thy blessing to all who come to drink thereof; that being healed of their pains and infirmities, they may show forth Thy praise."[30] This event, which still takes place each June, also features a "Well Dressing," in which elaborate mosaics of Biblical scenes are created entirely from flower petals. This charming custom is strongly reminiscent of the traditional floral offerings given to statues of the Virgin during the month of May, which supposedly ensure the earth's fertility. At one point in the mid-twentieth century, the Well Dressing was considered significant enough to attract the presence of Elizabeth II, while she was still Princess of Wales.

One of the most famous shrines to Anne, however, is that of St. Anne d'Auray, in Brittany. It came into existence in a manner that distinctly echoes the origin story of many Marian holy sites. In 1623, Anne began showing herself, in a series of apparitions, to a pious peasant named Yves Nicolazic. She repeatedly demanded that he rebuild a church that had once been dedicated to her, which was destroyed in the eighth century. When he passed this request on to local Church authorities, they rebuffed him, disbelieving that his visions were true ones. In the face of such opposition, St. Anne continued to show herself to Nicolazic. She also provided him with practical support, causing money for her church to magically appear in her chosen visionary's house.

Finally, one night in 1625, St. Anne gave him a vision of where to dig to uncover a statue that depicted her and the Virgin Mary. This was particularly remarkable because the image that was found was over 900 years old. After it was uncovered, many miracles were subsequently attributed to it, ranging from bringing the dead back to life to averting shipwrecks, plagues and fires. Despite initial clerical opposition, the church was built and has continued to serve as a pilgrimage site to this day.[31] In 1954, Pope Pius XII recommended that the faithful undertake a pilgrimage there.[32]

Of all the miracles attributed to the St. Anne statue at Auray, however, one of the most intriguing is the conversion of Pierre de Keriolet, a man known as "the Devil of Kerlois." He was a seventeenth-century nobleman of Brittany who was "given to debauchery, duelling, and blasphemy, in fact ... the whole gamut of vices."[33] Because some of his companions became possessed by the devil, he appealed to St. Anne for intercession, so that he could be spared their fate. In return for her help, she made him repent of his decadent ways. Keriolet did true penance for his sins, eventually even becoming a priest. According to popular belief, when he performed one exorcism, the devil he forced out of its victim reminded him that Saint Anne had truly saved him. Emphasizing its point, it told him that there were as many devils at his heels as blades of grass where he had trod.[34]

By the seventeenth century, belief among Catholics in St. Anne's ability to aid people in attaining salvation was well established. In *Mary's Mother, St. Anne in Medieval Europe*, Virginia Nixon argues persuasively that, uniquely among the saints, Anne assimilated Mary's power to ensure her faithful believers admission into heaven. She claims that promoters of St. Anne's cult appropriated Marian tropes and motifs to emphasize her salvific abilities, which had been acquired due to her matrilineal relationship with Jesus and Mary. The author states, "Other saints, however powerful they might be, are normally spoken of as interceding for the soul before God. Anne, by contrast, is frequently presented through images that imply that she exercises salvational power."[35]

In *Saint Anne, Her Cult and Her Shrines*, a work published in 1927 which was intended to be more devotional than scholarly, author Rev. Myles V. Ronan elaborates at some length upon this concept:

> It may be reasonable ... to think that [favors and graces] shed on the daughter were communicated in some measure to the mother. If Mary's glory was incomparable in being chosen to be the Mother of God — the glory of the Son of God shed over His mother — may we not presume that Mary's glory in a somewhat similar manner was extended to her own mother? ... The fruit enriches and ennobles the tree from which it has sprung.... And since the body of the Incarnate Word has been derived from the substance of S. Anne through that of Mary, S. Anne surpasses all prophets, patriarchs, apostles, martyrs, and saints of God.[36]

Significantly, like Mary, St. Anne was frequently called upon by the dying to help them escape the clutches of the devil. Many prayers for this purpose were written during the medieval era. They often included a pleading line addressed to her, such as "in the hour of our death free us from the enemy."[37] The devil has always been an intrinsic part of St. Anne's story. According to one legend, her mother, Emerentiana, had six husbands killed by Satan before marrying Anne's father, Stollanus.[38] Particularly in Germany, much of the art depicting St. Anne in the fifteenth and early sixteenth centuries portrays her in a manner which emphasizes her role in human salvation. This was accomplished primarily by appropriating features of late medieval Marian imagery.

As the Reformation and subsequent Counter-Reformation took hold, iconography which included Satanic elements was largely replaced with depictions of St. Anne instructing the Virgin and, sometimes, her grandson Jesus. This was meant to emphasize the responsibility of good Catholic mothers to teach their children the catechism at home.[39] By contrast, in Muslim theology, Anne's adversarial relationship with the devil never ceased to be emphasized, even to the present day. Here, it is believed that directly because of Anne, Mary was spared both the devil's influence and the taint of original sin. Gerald Messadie, author of *History of the Devil*, states:

> Muhammed has Mary's mother Anne, declare during her pregnancy, 'Lord ... I dedicate to your service that which is in my womb.' Since she has been consecrated to Allah, Mary could not be subject to Satan, and she is therefore free of original sin.[40]

The association of the Immaculate Conception of Mary with her power over the devil also exists in Western thought. One artistic interpretation symbolizing the Immaculate Conception is an image of the Virgin stepping on a serpent, denoting her victory over Satan. Marina Warner states, "The image of the Immaculate Conception is still a favourite one in southern Europe, in Sicily and Spain ... where in churches and marketplaces Mary tramples the serpent's crushed head underfoot."[41]

Other connections between the defeat of the devil and the Immaculate Conception have also appeared in more recent Christian theology. In his book *Evidence of Satan in the Modern World*, Leon Cristiani claims that the devil appeared to several people at Lourdes, shortly after Bernadette Soubirous had her Marian visions. According to this author, Satan's primary motivation for these apparitions was to discredit the young mystic.[42] It is notable that the devil supposedly wished to interfere at Lourdes, since the Marian miracles there were largely responsible for reinforcing popular belief in the Immaculate Conception.

There is another case cited by Cristiani, which also takes place in mid-nineteenth century France. It concerns Iscarion, a devil who had possessed a Lyonese man named Antoine Gay. Exactly one year before the Immaculate Conception was proclaimed as dogma, the possessed man was found kneeling at the foot of a statue of the Virgin. The demon was supposedly being forced by Jesus to praise Mary. Among the proclamations made by Iscarion (through Gay's mouth) were, "Thou wast conceived without sin, thou art immaculate!" and "Thy divine Son compels me to say that [today] is the most solemn of all the [liturgical] feasts."[43]

Leon Cristiani's book is a remarkable text for its time period. Published in 1959, it nonetheless reads like the work of a medieval mind. It is filled with numerous lurid examples of demon possession and exorcism, which he claims are factual. In many of the cases cited here, the Virgin Mary intercedes directly to expel the devil from the afflicted person. In 1953, a woman referred to only as "Mme. G." was possessed by a devil who cried out (through her mouth), "I'm afraid of her, the Great Lady [Mary], of her alone, for I can do nothing against her: her will prevails."[44] Cristiani points out that Mme G.'s devil was ultimately driven out on a Saturday, the traditional day of the Virgin. When explaining her power over the devil, he quotes at length from *Concerning True Devotion to the Blessed Virgin*, a work by medieval theologian St. Grignion de Montfort. He states:

> The most terrible of the enemies of Satan created by God is Mary, his Blessed Mother.... The Devil fears her more, not only than men and angels but, in a certain sense, than God himself.... Satan, being proud, suffers infinitely more from being overcome and punished by the little, humble servant of God, her humility humiliating him more than the divine power; and secondly, because God has given Mary such great power over devils that, as they have often been obliged to admit, in spite of themselves, through the mouths of possessed persons, they are ... more daunted by a single threat from her than by all their other torments.[45]

During the Middle Ages, this direct, adversarial relationship between Mary and Satan was believed to be a fundamental truth. In both clerical sermons and popular legends, the Virgin defended those who were faithful to her against the machinations of the devil. When a sinner who had been devoted to her was condemned to hell, she would arrive to save the fortunate soul, sending Satan into paroxysms of frustration.

In one popular tale, Mary even saved both the life and the soul of an otherwise good woman who committed the sin of incest with her own son. When she had a child as a result of this union, she killed it out of shame. The devil, recognizing an opportunity to obtain a soul, disguised himself as a clerk and went to a local court of law. There, he accused the mother of this heinous crime, demanding that she be burned at the stake in punishment. She prayed to the Virgin for help, however, before she was brought to face her accuser. Once there, the devil claimed he saw no sinner or murderer, but a holy woman whom Mary supported and protected. Thus, the woman was spared, and the devil vanished with a great "reek and stink."[46]

In a more humorous story, devils tempted a knight's wife who had grown close to her confessor into lusting after him. Spurred on by the demons, she stole all of her husband's treasure and ran off with the monk she desired. When they had only been gone for a few hours, the knight returned home to find all his valuables gone and no sign of his wife. At last, one of his servants reluctantly reported what had happened. He set off in search of them and found them eating dinner in an ale house not far from town. Fortunately, he had come upon them before they had committed the sin of fornication. Furious, he clapped them into the local stocks and rode off to inform the monk's abbot. While the knight was away, the lady and the monk repented bitterly of their rash behavior. The lady, who had been taught by her confessor to pray to the Virgin twice a day, began to sincerely beg for her help.

Shortly afterward, when the knight reported the monk's behavior to his abbot, the man replied that it was impossible. The abbot asserted that he had just seen the lady's confessor in the cloister. The knight insisted that the monk be sent for, and much to his surprise, the holy man immediately answered the summons. Perplexed, he returned home to find both his wife and his treasure where he had left them. At last, greatly puzzled, the knight and the abbot rode out to the stocks. The knight was so certain that he had left his wife and her intended lover there that he required some final proof that they were not. When they arrived, they found only two devils in the stocks, one looking like a monk, the other like a lady. In all likelihood, these were the same ones who had tempted the knight's otherwise virtuous wife and her confessor in the first place. When the abbot said a prayer over them, they rose into the sky and disappeared. The two men returned to town, distressed by the cleverness of the devils, who had caused great strife with their illusions.[47]

As these stories show, it was very much accepted during medieval times that demonic forces were always actively at work in the mortal world. Any real or perceived hostility towards images of the Virgin Mary not only identified people as heretics, but also linked them with Satan. Thus, both Jews and iconoclastic Reformers were thought to be in league with the devil. In medieval legends, the devil's mother, Lilith, who was strongly associated with Jewish women, parodied Mary by singing her demonic son's praises at his throne.[48] Medieval Christians generally believed that Jews particularly despised Marian images, though there seems to be no basis in fact for this supposition.

In *The Devil and the Jews*, by Joshua Trachtenberg, a popular medieval story is recounted of a rich Jew who moved a statue of Mary into his house, then proceeded to blaspheme at it, "as if it had been the very Virgin herself." Worse, he also threw excrement on it, both day and night. When his horrified wife saw this and cleaned the statue off, he grew enraged and strangled her until she died.[49] Similarly, when Luther and other Reformers declared their opposition to the use of images, they were branded as "Jews" by Catholic authorities. When four professors of the Sorbonne were tried for heresy in 1534, one allegation against them was that they had obtained books from Germany "printed by Jews who are Lutherans."[50]

It was considered an illustration of Mary's extreme kindness that, despite the Jews' supposed hostility toward her, she sometimes personally intervened to convert them to Christianity. Medieval sermons abound with such exempla. According to them, Mary generally accomplishes the conversion by causing some miracle to happen which proves the truth of Christianity. In one such tale, a Jewish man asserted that it was impossible for a Virgin to bear a child. In response, Mary intervened so that the baby Jesus in a painted Madonna image moved to nurse at His mother's breast. The Jew was duly impressed, and declared that it was less miraculous for a virgin to conceive a child than for a painted image to move. (One inevitably wonders what this man would have thought of cartoons on television or in the movies!)[51]

However, there are other stories in which she comes to earth to intervene more directly, such as one in which she rescued a Jewish man from thieves. When he asked his benefactor who she was, the Virgin emphasized the traditional adversarial relationship between Christians and Jews, saying, "I am Mary, whom you and all your nation despise, and dispute that I ever bore God's son from my body. But nevertheless I have come to bring you out of the error that you are in."[52] She then proceeded to show him both heaven and hell and asked him, somewhat rhetorically, which he preferred. After this experience, the Jew not only converted to Christianity but remained devoted to the Virgin for the remainder of his life.

Despite widespread use of such imagery, however, it is possible that the idea of Mary as the serpent-devil's adversary could be based on an erroneous translation of the Bible. The passage containing God's words to the serpent, as translated by St. Jerome, read, "I will create enmity between you and the woman, and between your children and her children: she will crush your head, and you will stare at her heel." In the fifteenth century, however, humanists provided another interpretation of this passage, which read, "I will place enmity between you and the woman, and between your seed and her seed: it [the seed] will crush your head, and you [the serpent] will repel its heel." In other words, the descendants would be fighting the serpent, which would be fully capable of retaliation.[53]

Because of Jerome's translation, theologians assigned Mary the role of "Second Eve." John A. Phillips writes in *Eve: The History of an Idea*, "When an error in the Vulgate Bible transformed 'they' into 'she,' it was understood to mean that a human woman would come in the place of Eve and strike at the head of the serpent–Satan.... Mariologists identified the Virgin Mary ... with the woman clothed with the sun, trampling the serpent of Genesis underfoot."[54] In *Eve and Mary*, Peter Thomas Dehau emphasizes this idea, stating, "Indeed [the Virgin] does crush the head of the serpent in us all and through us all ... The fact which dominates everything is that neither man nor angel nor archangel can conquer the serpent except in Mary and through Mary."[55]

One result of this characterization has been that both Eve and Mary came to be seen as examples of what Woman is and what could be expected of her. In the second century, theologian Justin Martyr proposed the quintessential dichotomy: Eve was disobedient and sexual, while the Virgin was obedient and celibate.[56] Many Church teachings about Mary, such as the preservation of her virginity after the birth of Jesus, her own Immaculate Conception by Anne, and her Assumption into heaven stemmed from her role as the "Second Eve." The Catholic Church, however, ultimately fell short one crucial step in officially recognizing all that the role implied. In the interests of ecumenism, Vatican II downplayed the Virgin Mary's importance, instead of emphasizing it by declaring her Co-Redemptrix, the equal of Christ, who is known as the Second Adam.[57]

Throughout history, many people have been concerned or even dubious about the implications of the Mary-Eve dichotomy for Christian women. At least on the surface, it offers a characterization of Eve as temptress and Mary as paragon. How these women are truly perceived, however, is a fairly complex issue which seems to vary a great deal over the centuries. Gary Anderson offers an explanation of how the Eve-Mary dichotomy was thought of at the dawn of

Christianity in *The Genesis of Perfection: Adam and Eve in Jewish and Christian Imagination*. He states, "Eve is a Janus-faced figure for early Christian writers.... On the one hand, she is the exact opposite of Mary.... But at the same time, Eve anticipates Mary."[58]

Toward the beginning of the medieval era, there was an emphasis on what each of these women heard and what came about as a result. Eve conceived death because her ear was receptive to the Serpent's word, while the Virgin conceived the Son of God when she heard the message of the Annunciation.[59] Medieval theologians further emphasized the importance of words, both spoken and heard. They pointed out that the word "Ave," which Gabriel used to begin the Annunciation, was an exact reversal of the name, "Eva."[60] Despite the ameliorating influence of typography and wordplay, however, most male Biblical scholars during the Middle Ages regarded Mary as a completely unique entity, unlike any other woman. Most Church leaders believed that mortal women were to be equated only with sinful Eve.

Tertullian wrote love poems to the Virgin Mary but penned only scathing criticisms of earthly women, claiming they were "the gateway to the devil." Augustine, who was greatly devoted to the Virgin, stated that if women truly understood their great sin of bringing death on the human race, they would wear no color but black all their lives.[61] In such a scholastic climate, it is not surprising that the few women who did have the ability to publish their views glorified their own gender. The twelfth-century mystic, composer, and abbess Hildegard of Bingen praised the Eve-Mary relationship in the songs she wrote. Here, Mary more than compensated for Eve's sin with her sublime purity. Hildegard believed that the two women were made one through the mystery of the Incarnation. She claimed that both were "cosmic theophanies of the feminine whose purpose is to manifest God in the world."[62]

This positive outlook was carried on in Venice during the thirteenth century. According to custom, women were given their own distaffs and spindles eight days after they married. In this way, they were conflated simultaneously with Eve and Mary, who both had roles as cloth-makers for their families. The time span of eight days was associated with Adam and Eve's eviction from Eden, as well as Christ's Resurrection. In this way, Anderson states, "These newly married women, bearers of distaffs and spindles, have their wombs compared to that of the ever-virgin Mother of God."[63]

When the medieval era was succeeded by the Renaissance, the Eve-Mary dichotomy was depicted in a very important manner. Michelangelo included several visual references to this idea in his famous painting on the Sistine Chapel ceiling. In the "Creation of Eve" panel, she is shown emerging from Adam's rib. The specific imagery chosen by Michelangelo here also suggests Mary, as the personification of the Church, coming out of the crucified Christ's body. In the panel representing the Temptation, Eve's middle finger simultaneously points (directly) at her own womb and (indirectly) at Mary. The Sistine Chapel itself was subsequently dedicated in 1483 on August 15, the liturgical feast of the Virgin's Assumption into Heaven.[64]

In the nineteenth century, the Eve-Mary dichotomy began to be viewed in a more critical light, especially by women. The English poet Christina Rossetti looked to Mary as a model for her chosen life of celibacy, which she felt was conducive to spiritual growth. Still, Rossetti admitted that she considered Eve more maternal than the Virgin and thought of both as positive archetypes of womankind. During the same time period, Charlotte Brontë criticized Church teachings about Eve through her novel *Shirley*. Refusing to attend church like a good Marian girl, Brontë's main character instead chooses to stay outside, communing with Nature, like Eve. Shirley describes Eve as "a living, liberating symbol of the divine in feminine form."[65]

All of the negative potential of the Eve-Mary dichotomy for women seems to be realized in Peter Thomas Dehau's book, *Eve and Mary*, originally published in 1950 with Catholic Church sanction. Even for a work produced during an era of traditional gender roles, his writing borders on the misogynistic. He states, "Women believe the serpent more easily than men. They are more easily deceived."[66] He also argues that the primary reason why Eve sinned was because she made an important decision for herself, rather than asking her husband for advice. Dehau writes:

> The last word, the definitive judgment, was the duty of the man, husband and priest, as it continues to be the duty of the man, husband, father, or priest. If woman usurps this function of the definitive judgment in certain grave matters, everything will necessarily be awkward, unpleasant, and destructive of the order which submits her to man.[67]

Dehau's scholarship, in fact, seems to adhere closely to that of his medieval predecessors in many ways. Despite his disdain for womankind, particularly her intellect, he does accord honor to the Virgin Mary, a woman who was obedient to the will of God. He states that Mary's humility stands in contrast to the maternal pride of Eve, which he asserts is "for every woman a sensitive point."[68] He also claims that the Virgin's obedience can remedy the maladies and adversities humankind has inherited from Eve.[69]

Adding insult to injury, Dehau restates a traditional Catholic argument against the ordination of women. He writes, "Eve lost everything. She was injured even in her faith, which is why woman's role in the Church will always be so different from man's. Even consecrated virgins do not preach, do not teach...."[70] Similar reasoning was still used in 1988, when the Orthodox Church held a theological symposium at Rhodes to address why women were not ordained. According to Kyriaki Karidoyanes FitzGerald, who attended this conference, it was officially concluded that the role of women could be expressed using the typological analogy "Eve-Mary." It was also argued there that if God had intended women to be ordained, Mary, the Theotokos, would have been.[71]

In response to the council's findings, Maja Weyermann, information officer of the Church of Switzerland, wrote a dissenting article. She states, "We find questionable examples of an inappropriate application of the texts about the Adam-Christ and Eve-Mary typologies in the reports of the Inter-Orthodox Theological Consultation at Rhodes (1988) concerning the place of women in the Orthodox Church and the ordination of women."[72] Weyermann argues that the Church fathers' typologies were taken out of context at Rhodes. She believes that both Adam-Christ and Eve-Mary parallels were meant to transcend gender and apply to all of humanity. She concludes, "The maleness of Christ and the femaleness of Mary therefore have no influence on the theological significance of their types."[73]

Some contemporary women are choosing to reinterpret the roles of Eve and Mary, making them more relevant to their own lives. Christine Garside proposes a sort of compromise, "A woman is being called to create for herself the identity she wants. Most likely it will have some of Eve and some of Mary, some periods of chastity and some of sexuality, some periods of obedience and some of defiance."[74] In certain ways, female spirituality seems to be coming full circle. It is mirroring the positive associations that medieval women, such as Hildegard of Bingen, had for the Eve-Mary dichotomy. Sally Cunneen, a Catholic scholar who sees goodness in both Eve and Mary, states:

> The relationship between Eve and Mary is more continuous than oppositional. We should no longer blame Eve for the loss of a mythical Eden, nor look down on sex, the flesh, and human possibility. Seeing the continuity between Eve, Mary and ourselves, we might instead see our own responsibility for building the peaceable world their Creator desired.[75]

John Phillips believes that the Eve-Mary dichotomy could be viewed as the link between pagan and Christian belief. He states, "The divine activity of the Second Eve even redeems the mythology that underlies the characterization of the First Eve — the pagan notion of the Creatrix, the Mother Goddess."[76] Both women function as prototypical Mother Goddesses, yet unlike most pre–Christian deities, they do not abandon their offspring in order to maintain their freedom. Eve becomes the Mother of All Living when she is consigned by God to monogamy and Adam's control.[77] Mary chooses domestication of her own accord through her perpetual virginity, motherliness, and willingness to accept the authority of her husband, Joseph.

According to early Christian thought, however, it was the devil who was responsible for bringing about the Virgin's marriage to Joseph. Origen, the third-century theologian, wrote that she had to be married because it was necessary to conceal her Son's divine nature from Satan. St. Thomas Aquinas, who lived during the medieval era, agreed with Origen's ideas on the subject, stating, "The devil was to be deceived lest he harm the Child Jesus before the time permitted by God."[78] In his much more contemporary book, *Discourses on St. Joseph*, the Rev. Nicholas O'Rafferty expresses similar sentiments, "For on seeing Jesus born of a married woman instead of a virgin, [the devil] would not immediately understand that He was the promised Messias [sic] and would not begin at once to wage the fierce war against Him which he did later."[79]

O'Rafferty puts forth several other theories about why the Virgin had to be married, despite her divine conception of Jesus. He states that, according to St. Jerome, her marriage was necessary for people to know Jesus' ancestry. "For with the Jews, genealogy was always reckoned through the father ... since father and mother had to be of the same tribe and family."[80] In addition, she married so that she would not be publicly considered a sinner due to her pregnancy. In this way, she was spared from condemnation to death by stoning, as the law dictated. Finally, she took Joseph as her husband so that he could help and protect her during times of difficulty, such as the flight into Egypt.

Church teachings about the importance of St. Joseph's role have varied a great deal over the course of time. Similarly, popular veneration of him has also waxed and waned fairly dramatically throughout the centuries. Carolyn C. Wilson claims in her book *St. Joseph in Italian Renaissance Society and Art*, "Joseph attracted little in the way of a cult for more than a millennium."[81] Possibly the first influential person to encourage it was St. Bernard, a twelfth-century theologian who was fervently devoted to the Virgin Mary. He wrote that Joseph's divine grace should be recognized because he was the foreordained spouse of Mary, the recipient of God's word in dreams, and the first witness of the Incarnation. By Bernard's lifetime, parallels had been drawn in theological literature between the Virgin Mary and Ecclesia, the abstract personification of the Church. As her husband, Joseph could be said to represent a variety of male figures that were considered "spouse of the Church," including God, Christ, popes, and bishops.[82]

The idea of Joseph as the man whose duty was to protect Mary, and by extension, the Church, led to a popular perception of him as saint whose function was primarily protective. In one popular legend, a man whose house was robbed prayed to an image of St. Joseph, and his stolen money was mysteriously restored the following night.[83] By the thirteenth century, a full-blown cult of St. Joseph had developed, complete with the veneration of his relics. In 1254, the Crusader Sire de Joinville brought back a piece of cloth from the East, which he claimed was the "girdle of St. Joseph." He built a chapel in France to house the relic, which eventually became the site of a shrine so important that even Louis XIV and Cardinal Richelieu visited.[84]

During the early fifteenth century, Jean Gerson, chancellor of the University of Paris, began a letter-writing campaign to have a universal liturgical Feast of St. Joseph established on March 19. He was particularly devoted to the saint because he felt Joseph's intercession had spared his life at the time of a Parisian riot, when his house was pillaged. Partly as a result of Gerson's efforts, this day was officially declared the liturgical feast of St. Joseph by Pope Innocent VIII in the late fifteenth century. However, at least one contemporary author, Filas, believes, "The actual choice of March 19 as St. Joseph's day appears to have been made by mere coincidence and suggestion."[85] In early Christian manuscripts, that day was set aside as an annual commemoration of another Joseph, who was martyred in Antioch. Largely because they shared a name, however, the two sometimes became conflated by medieval theologians.

In 1512, the Italian city of Bergamo shut down all business on Joseph's feast day, in order for a procession to take place to obtain his protection against war and plague. In 1522, Francesco Sforza, the Duke of Milan, similarly set it aside for public processions, in thanksgiving for deliverance from both the plague and the French army.[86] After the reign of Innocent VIII, however, the next pope to publicly honor St. Joseph was Pius IX, who lived in the nineteenth century. He repeatedly expressed great personal devotion to the saint throughout his time on the papal throne. In 1865, he issued a decree that the month of March was to be dedicated to St. Joseph, as May had been set aside for Mary.[87] In 1870, he designated Joseph the Patron of the Universal Church, placing all Catholics under his protection.[88]

The story of how Joseph was chosen as the husband of Mary probably first appeared in the apocryphal Book of James. In this legend, Zacharias, the high priest in the temple where Mary was living, declared that it was time for her to be married. He ordered all of her suitors to assemble at the temple with rods in their hands, so that God could provide a sign of which man He wished to marry her. In some versions of the tale, a dove burst out of Joseph's staff and alit on his head. In others, the suitors were instructed to leave their staves at the temple overnight, and Joseph's was found the next day covered in flowers.[89]

It is commonly accepted that Joseph had to be a virtuous man in order for God to select him as Mary's spouse. However, it is also widely believed that, like St. Anne, he became truly worthy of veneration through his association with the Virgin Mary. In 1889, Pope Leo XIII claimed that because St. Joseph had married the Blessed Virgin, "there can be no doubt that more than any other person, he approached that supereminent dignity by which the Mother of God is raised far above all created natures."[90] O'Rafferty writes, "It is true that before he became the husband of Mary, St. Joseph was already a great saint, but by living with Mary, his holiness increased day by day."[91] He adds that she brought to him, as a sort of dowry, unlimited grace and virtue. Because of her great love for him, which was second only to her adoration for Christ, she procured for him the blessings of holiness and perfection from God.

The Rev. Joseph Mueller generally concurs with these ideas, writing in *The Fatherhood of St. Joseph*, "Joseph was ... most closely united with Mary, therefore ... on account of this, an abundance of grace must have come to him and his sanctity must have been increased more and more."[92] However, Mueller later emphasizes at great length that St. Joseph is inferior to the Virgin Mary and is not worthy of the same sort of veneration due her, known as hyperdulia. This is because the Virgin served as the physical mother in the incarnation of Jesus, while Joseph's role was only that of an adoptive or foster father. He was not genetically linked with Jesus, though he helped to raise Him. In addition, Mary cooperated much more directly in her Son's redemptive work. She witnessed and suffered with her Son during His passion and crucifixion, while St. Joseph was (presumably) dead. Mueller states, "From all this we can conclude with certainty that St. Joseph does not equal the Mother of God in rank and dignity."[93]

In another similarity to St. Anne, this close association with Jesus and Mary supposedly allows Joseph special intercessory powers. According to St. Theresa of Avila, because Jesus was subject to St. Joseph's authority on earth, He will continue to honor his requests in heaven. O'Rafferty writes:

> How ... powerful must be the prayer which St. Joseph directs for us to Jesus, whose foster father he was? For St. Joseph has only to show to the Son and the Mother the hands which have laboured so much for them, how much he has sweat to provide them with food, clothing and shelter, all the sacrifices that he has made for them. No, neither the Son nor the Mother can refuse St. Joseph anything when he reminds them of all that he did for them during thirty long years of his life on earth.[94]

In nearly all writings about St. Joseph, it is emphasized that, although he did not have sexual relations with Mary, their relationship should be considered "a true marriage." Mueller argues in favor of the validity of their marriage because they lived together and are referred to as spouses in the New Testament.[95] Filas discusses the matter at great length, stating that in the first centuries of Christianity, theologians "glossed over" the idea, since it seemed to imply sexual relations.[96] However, he emphasizes the idea that, despite its virginal nature, Joseph's and Mary's marriage was filled with great love. Love, he argues, exists in the heart, not in the exchange of sexual relations.[97] He concludes that because of the purely spiritual love inherent in their union, Joseph and Mary's relationship should be looked upon as the model for good marriage. He writes, "It is the sublime exemplar for all marriages and shows forth the basic goodness and opportunities for holiness in this state of life."[98]

Despite, or in many cases because of, its celibate nature, the union of Mary and Joseph would serve as the ideal model for both married women and nuns. If living entirely chastely was not possible, married women were encouraged by the Church to have sexual relations only with the aim of raising Christian children. While some rejected this paradigm as unrealistic, choosing to emulate Anne rather than Mary, many strove to live as free from lust as possible. Of course, the ultimate expression of this ideal was the choice to become a nun rather than marry. As lifelong virgins, nuns were thought to be truly imitating Mary more than even the most modest wife. Like her, they gave themselves over entirely to the love of God, becoming brides of Christ who preserved their virginity throughout their lives for Him.

7

The Virgin's Virgins

Nuns and Mary

At the dawn of the thirteenth century, St. Dominic, perhaps best known as the saint to whom the Virgin Mary entrusted the Rosary, founded his still-existing religious order. Notably, he started communities for nuns as well as monks, and it was to the first Dominican nun, Cecilia Cesarini, that he described his mystical visions to be recorded for posterity. In one of them, Dominic saw Jesus and Mary accompanied by the adherents of many religious orders other than his own. Convinced that no Dominican had been admitted to heaven, the saint began to weep. In response, Jesus assured him that He had entrusted Dominic's Order to Mary. At her Son's request, the Virgin Mary then opened her cloak, showing that many Dominican monks and nuns were concealed within its folds. Author Denis Wiseman, who relates this tale to contemporary readers, concludes it with the statement, "What is significant for our purposes is the conviction of Blessed Cecilia ... that the Order was personally protected by Mary."[1]

Although the Virgin has been held up as a model for all women throughout history, it has always been widely accepted that she maintains a special relationship with nuns. Female monasticism as we know it, however, scarcely existed before the twelfth century. It was not entirely unknown — the first "rule," or guide to daily life, specifically for nuns was created in the sixth century by Caesarius of Arles, a bishop in Gaul.[2] At the time of William the Conqueror's invasion of England in 1066, nine convents existed there.[3] Nonetheless, although there are no precise records of how many religious orders existed during the early years of the Catholic Church, it is certain that before 1200, monks vastly outnumbered nuns.[4]

Prior to the twelfth century, female monastics most commonly lived in "double monasteries," religious communities which included houses for both monks and nuns, often side by side. However, as the medieval era progressed, male religious leaders became increasingly concerned about this proximity and

St. Dominic, founder of the Dominican Order (courtesy Chant Art).

its possible consequences. Warning monks against the temptations of the double monastery, Bernard of Clairvaux stated, "To be always with a woman and not have sexual relations with her is more difficult than to raise the dead."[5]

As a result of this institutionally sanctioned paranoia, nuns were forced to separate from their brothers in religion and move to locations suitably distant from them. In the thirteenth century, St. Francis of Assisi forced Clare, his most avidly pious female disciple, to live in a cloistered community far away from him. She protested that she wanted to live her life like Jesus' apostles, preaching and working in the world. Francis, however, insisted and Clare reluctantly accepted her fate. Resigned to the fact that her mentor had forced his female followers to remain "imprisoned forever," she founded a religious order still in existence today — the Poor Clares. In 1253, she became the first female author in history of a rule for nuns.[6]

Clare, a woman ahead of her time, was not only forced to retire from public life permanently by her mentor, she was also misunderstood by subsequent generations. In her article, "Imitatio Christi or Imitatio Mariae? Clare of Assisi and Her Interpreters," Catherine M. Mooney argues that St. Clare actually saw herself as a follower of Jesus, not Mary. Many contemporary scholars have asserted that Clare was "uniquely feminine" and have even characterized her as a Madonna figure.[7] She was first explicitly compared to the Virgin after her death, at the ecclesiastical Process for her canonization. Fifteen nuns who served under her rule as abbess testified, in response to questions put to them by ecclesiastical interrogators, that no other woman, except the Virgin Mary, was as holy as Clare.[8]

Her anonymous hagiographer, who began his work shortly after her death, calls her "the footprint of the Mother of God." Clare herself also frequently used the idea of footprints in her own writing — however, in every case, the feet in question belonged to Jesus, not Mary. Encouraging her fellow nun Agnes of Prague in her adoption of holy poverty, she praised her in several letters for following in the footsteps of the poor and humble Jesus Christ. Her own request to the pope for her order to live without possessions was couched in similar terms, stating that she wished to "cling to the footprints of Him who for us was made poor."[9] Pointedly, in none of her letters or other writings did she mention imitation of Mary, female saints, or any other women.

Mooney theorizes that medieval authors, such as Clare's hagiographer, compared Clare to the Virgin rather than Jesus in a possibly unconscious desire to reserve Jesus as a model for men, leaving women to follow the subordinate Mary. Similarly, artists frequently created iconographic depictions of her standing near the Virgin Mary or in Marian poses. In the fresco adorning the basilica of St. Francis in Assisi, Clare is shown mourning over the dead body of Francis like a Mater Dolorosa. By contrast, art commissioned by the Poor Clares themselves frequently depicts her travels alongside Francis. In one notable piece from the thirteenth century, she is shown multiplying bread to feed those who listened to them, as Christ did in the miracle of the loaves and fishes.[10]

There was another reason for Clare's unintended association with specifically female piety, and perhaps it is the most significant one of all. The order of friars established by Francis wished to renounce responsibility for and relationship with their female branch. While Clare served as abbess of her order, the Franciscan minister General Haymo of Faversham convinced the pope that Franciscan clergymen had no responsibility to serve as the Poor Clare's spiritual directors. Furious, Clare responded by sending away the friars who obtained food for her order, stating that if the sisters had to live without spiritual "food," they could also forgo the more material kind. Faced with a convent filled with starving nuns, the pope gave in to Clare's demands.[11]

To keep nuns from resenting their separation from the world in general and men in particular, male religious leaders began to emphasize the role of the "Bride of Christ." Both Mary and nuns are referred to by this title, and these cloistered virgins have often been considered her earthly counterparts. In the twelfth century, theologian Aelred of Rievaulx explored the idea of the Virgin Mary as the Bride of Christ, conflating her with the woman in the Song of Solomon. Through the use of somewhat convoluted symbolism, he asserted that although she had married both God the Father and the Son, her virginity remained intact.[12]

The centrality of chastity to nuns' lives was certainly nothing new, even during the medieval era. As early as the fourth century, women who wished to imitate Mary were consecrated to Christ in a public "pact of virginity." Each one who took part in this sacred ceremony had a veil placed on her head by a bishop. She then took a vow of lifelong celibacy. By the late medieval era, nuns such as Saint Catherine of Siena were having mystical visions of their marriages to Christ, complete with jewel-encrusted rings and saints as wedding guests.[13] Ulrike Strasser describes the ceremony commonly used for German nuns in the seventeenth century:

> Novices began to send out invitations to kin, friends and guests of honor, whose presence they desired at their wedding day. Like secular brides, the women who were destined to marry God wore wreaths of varying sizes symbolizing chastity and social status and investing them with the identity of the virgin ready to receive her groom.[14]

This ceremony would be the first and last time the newly consecrated nun would publicly appear in the community. She would then effectively vanish from society behind her cloister's walls. Even when a fellow member of her convent died, a Renaissance-era German nun would not appear in public to mourn. Instead, societal expectations compelled her to turn the body over to secular men, so that they could carry it to its final resting place — usually located in an all-male monastery. Although contemporary nuns are generally much more visible in their communities, the wedding symbolism when they take vows is still quite strong. The ceremony used today for consecrating nuns includes veils, rings, feasts and three days of retreat like a honeymoon.[15]

A member of the Poor Clares. St. Clare was reluctant to found this order and only did so at St. Francis' insistence (courtesy Chant Art).

It was commonly believed during the medieval era that Brides of Christ were destined for special privileges in heaven after their deaths, where they would be crowned and united with Jesus, the mystical spouse for whom they had carefully preserved their virginity. Both Mechthild and St. Gertrude, thirteenth-century nuns and mystics, had detailed visions of the afterlife, in which they quite literally got to have the experience of being a holy Bride. Mechthild "finds the bed of love" in a beautiful palace, where Christ tells her to "put away the garments of fear and shame and all outward virtue" and "he gives himself to her and she herself to him," after which "their hearts can nevermore be separated."[16]

St. Gertrude experienced visions even more graphic than Mechthild's. In her writing, Jesus is referred to as "delicate caresser, gentlest passion, most ardent lover, sweetest spouse." She included a detailed description of him covering her eyes, ears, mouth, heart, hands and feet with kisses. In her book *Spiritual Exercises*, she encouraged nuns in prayer to say to Jesus, "In a kiss of your holy mouth take me as your possession into the bridal chamber of your beautiful love."[17] Gertrude claimed that, in heaven, she would be able to enjoy such personal attentions from Christ because she remained a lifelong virgin like Mary. Comparing her own future death to the Assumption of the Virgin, she even stated that she would also be invited to reign with Christ for eternity.

Two of the most important obligations of Brides of Christ have traditionally been celibacy, often thought of as keeping chaste for Jesus the bridegroom, and living sequestered. The two are actually interrelated, as enclosure was frequently deemed necessary for preserving the celibacy of those in religious orders. During the Middle Ages, nuns were supposed to stay at home with Christ, their mystical husband, serving his needs as good wives did their earthly spouses. Warning nuns that their husband Jesus was "jealous," male Church authorities exhorted them to remain in their cloisters, often solitary in individual "cells," refraining from going to public events or even food shopping.[18]

According to medieval theologians, Mary was the perfect model for both of these requirements for nuns. Not only had she retained her virginity throughout her life, she supposedly stayed home in quiet modesty, attending to the needs of her husband Joseph and her Son. In the twelfth century, theologian Peter Abelard wrote that nuns were earthly reflections of the Holy Mother. He stated that women who live full sexual lives are inferior beings, but nuns follow the honorable path of the Virgin Mary.

Admittedly, Abelard had personal reasons to present life in the cloister as particularly admirable. He was celibate until he was in his thirties, when he fell wildly in love with Heloise, his teenaged theology student. He secretly married and impregnated her, but they were soon separated by her irate uncle, who also had the unfortunate teacher castrated. At Abelard's request, Heloise became a nun, and he wrote her many letters praising female monasticism, perhaps as a means of consoling her about her life of chastity.[19] In Abelard's case, Bernard of Clairvaux's assertion that it was easier to raise the dead than remain celibate around women proved to be unfortunately true. Abelard's rueful advice to his son many years later was—if you can't be good, at least be careful.

Abelard, however, was not unique in encouraging nuns to identify with the Virgin Mary. Indeed, many other church leaders throughout the medieval era held her up as an example. One fifteenth-century sermon delivered to nuns at Carrow, England, asserted that the very habits they wore were symbols of "The Seven Dignities of the Virgin Mother." The smock was contrition and confession, the kirtle trust in God, the sleeves righteousness and mercy, while the boots were the will to amend sinful ways, as well as the desire to do good deeds and abstain from evil. The girdle, appropriately enough, was restraint from one's own will, the knives which hung from this girdle were perpetual joy which came from the love of God and hatred of sin, and the surplice was knowledge of God, revealing what each nun owed her sisters and the world. Perhaps most importantly, there was the mantle, which was faith, with seams of Christ's charity. The sermon ended with an admonition to the nuns to pray to the Blessed Virgin for edification and redemption.[20]

Popular literature of the time reflected Church teachings that nuns, at least ideally, had a special relationship with the Virgin Mary. It has been argued by scholars that Chaucer's Prioress in the *Canterbury Tales* represents the Virgin in the Mary-Eve dichotomy. This allegory of sin and redemption was made manifest among the pilgrims by the Prioress's contrast with the lascivious Wife of Bath. Scholar Elaine Filax, however, believes that Chaucer intended the nameless nun who tells the tale of St. Cecilie to be strongly identified with Mary as well. This theory is particularly interesting because it is likely that some medieval nuns, as the most educated women of their time, would have had access to Chaucerian literature. Many more of them would have identified with the humble "second nun," instead of the Prioress, with her privileged position as the head of a convent.

Filax states, "*The Second Nun's Tale* reflects the earlier idealization of Mary as a model to be followed: virginity as a source of strength, submission to the will of God, and the miraculous paradox of virginity engendering fertility."[21] Somewhat strangely, Chaucer's nun refers to herself as a "son of Eve." Such seeming gender confusion is, in fact, a means of placing emphasis on her own Mary-like virginity. She is making a subtle reference to the idea set forth by Sts. Jerome and Ambrose that female virgins cease to be women when they sacrifice their sexuality. The only other option for these "not-women" is to become, in some sense, men.[22] This idea is further brought home by the lack of visual description accorded the nun by Chaucer. Displaced by her spirit, her body is entirely absent or invisible due to her virginity.

Popular medieval literature abounds with "miracle legends," in which Mary directly intervenes to help nuns adhere to the behavioral ideals of celibacy and living cloistered. One of the most interesting of these tales is about a young

English nun who is "exceeding fair of face, a most sweet and comely maid." Because of her beauty, a local knight tempts her to escape from the convent and share his bed. After falling in love with him, she agrees, stealing the key to the locked convent door. However, when she attempts to open it, it is as if some unseen barrier has been placed between the keyhole and purloined key. Quite simply, try as she might, she cannot open the door. The frustrated nun tries in vain for three nights in a row.

At last, on the third unsuccessful night, she prays to the Virgin Mary, asking for her aid in opening the door. Once she has done this, however, it is revealed to her that Mary's invisible presence has been blocking the key all along. The Virgin's hand, which had been in front of the keyhole for the past three nights, is bruised and bleeding from the key. She tells the young nun that she will have to push it entirely through the injured hand if she is determined to get out. When the nun pleads with Mary to move her hand, she replies that she is protecting the nun's virginity and that the lock, if opened, would also be opening the gate of hell. At this, she repents of her sin and is carried back to her cell by Mary, who also kindly replaces the key in its proper place, so that the escape attempt is never discovered by the other nuns.

Amidst the canon of miracle tales, this story stands out as particularly instructive, with its undeniable call for nuns to recognize the virtues of a chaste and cloistered life. It begins with a sort of prologue which overtly states Mary's special relationship with nuns, their role as Brides of Christ, and the safety of life in a convent. At the very beginning of the story, it is stated:

> Saint Mary, Queen of Virgins, hath a very special love for those children of hers that serve her in the cloistered life, having given their troth to Jesu Christ her Son; and she watches over them right tenderly and shields them from danger if she can, that they may every one come safely to their heavenly nuptials, as did the blessed Saint Catherine.... Many are the snares that Sathan sets to tempt Our Lady's daughters from their home. For those that live in convents are, as it were, a company kept safe in a strong castle that is defended by the chivalry of God, where none may reach them from without to wound or slay.[23]

Quite a few medieval miracle legends of the Virgin Mary focus on the importance of celibacy for nuns. However, in some stories, Mary actually aids nuns who sin against her, failing to uphold the ideal of chastity. Such tales emphasize her forgiving, merciful nature, as well as her maternal protectiveness for nuns, her spiritual daughters. Mary, understanding from personal experience the difficulty of remaining a virgin, has particular sympathy for nuns who fall into this sort of temptation. In one such tale, a particularly pious abbess attracts the attention of the devil with her unusual goodness, who then leads her into the sin of fornication with her page. She becomes pregnant, and the nuns she supervises report her immorality to the bishop. Just before he arrives, Mary causes the child to be removed from her womb and given into the care of a local hermit. When the bishop arrives, the abbess is providentially free of all signs of pregnancy.

In *Spiritual Economies*, Nancy Bradley Warren argues that the miracle of the pregnant abbess symbolizes female empowerment through monasticism. Through the intercession of the most powerful woman of all, Mary, the abbess is able to control her own body and its productive capabilities. Warren writes, "The abbess and the Virgin Mary as maternal authority figures provide exemplars of female self-sufficiency upon which women can model subject positions of spiritual and temporal autonomy. Female monasticism is therefore suggestive of opportunities to women living in the world."[24]

There is a similar story about a devout nun named Beatrice, who is enticed by a cleric to secretly give up her place in the convent and lose her virginity to him. After he has his way with the unfortunate Beatrice, he abandons her. Having no other means to sustain herself, she becomes a whore. She unhappily continues on in this way for fifteen years, until she receives a mystical visit from the Virgin. It turns out that Mary has disguised herself as the nun and lived in the convent under her identity for the entire fifteen years. Beatrice is free to return home to her cloister with no one the wiser, which she joyously does.[25]

Many contemporary feminists rail against the sacrifices traditionally required of nuns, arguing that lifelong chastity and isolation are unnatural. Marina Warner bitterly inveighs against the idea of Brides of Christ, stating, "The icon of Mary and Christ side by side [as man and wife] is one of the Christian Church's most polished deceptions: it is the very image and hope of earthly consummated love used to give that kind of love the lie."[26] Yet, it was because of such isolation that many nuns found themselves thriving. Elizabeth Abbott writes:

> For the women summoned to their vocation by God ... the compulsory vow of celibacy was seldom a privation. For them, it was an instrument of faith, and of personal independence.... Best of all, the convent offered a nun that elusive commodity — solitude — in the form of a room or cell of her own.[27]

In her article "Everyday Life, Longevity and Nuns in Early Modern Florence," Judith C. Brown points out that on average, nuns who lived during the Renaissance era had significantly longer lifespans than their married contemporaries. This was partly because virginity protected them from maladies related to childbearing. Married women not only suffered from the immediate danger of dying in childbirth; their bodies, worn out from repeated pregnancies, were often more vulnerable to disease. In addition, the isolation of the convent provided protection from the spread of contagious diseases such as typhoid and bubonic plague. This was particularly effective in cloisters that provided for individual cells for nuns, rather than communal sleeping quarters. The few diseases that made it into the convent did not subsequently spread among the sisters.[28]

Chastity and isolation also made it possible for medieval nuns, undistracted by the demands of family life, to create art, literature, and music, much of which reflected their devotion to the Virgin. The cloister was almost the only place in medieval life where scholarship for women was encouraged. Nuns were instructed to follow the example of the Virgin Mary in this, who was frequently depicted in medieval art with a book in her hand. Imagery of the time showed Mary as a serious scholar during every stage of her life — learning to read as a child at St. Anne's knee, having her reading interrupted at the Annunciation, and even deep in a book on a donkey's back during the flight into Egypt. Jo Ann Kay McNamara writes, "Practical and religious concerns required [nuns] to have a good education. Reading was one of the prescribed activities in the rule of Aachen and most canonesses had other skills, particularly in music and the art of copying and illuminating manuscripts."[29]

This emphasis on education in nunneries naturally resulted in women who sometimes became excellent writers, artists, and musicians themselves. The brilliant tenth-century nun Hroswitha of Gandersheim produced a volume of plays, a book of poetry, and a history of the reign of Otto I.[30] A significant amount of her writing contained Marian themes. Notably, she composed the first narrative in Latin verse of the birth of the Virgin. In addition, she was the first to record a tremendously popular miracle legend, in which the archdeacon Theophilus sells his soul to the devil in exchange for worldly success. Repentant, he appeals to Virgin for help, who saves his soul by personally wresting the blood-signed contract from the devil's grasping fingers.[31]

During the twelfth century, however, an abbess gifted both in theological writing and musical composition would focus even more intensely on the Virgin in her work. Hildegard of Bingen's music is much better known in contemporary society than Hroswitha of Gandersheim's writing. Recordings of pieces she composed nearly nine hundred years ago are common all over the world, and they are frequently performed live. Effusive in her adoration of the Virgin Mary, Hildegard referred to her as a fruitful branch and the source of primeval light.[32] She also wrote music in which Mary is praised as a shining jewel by the citizens of heaven, calling attention to her roles as the "new Eve" and the archetype of the Mother Church. Her connection with Holy Communion was also emphasized by Hildegard, who wrote that Jesus became flesh through the agency of His mother's womb, as well as through the transmutation of the Eucharist.[33]

Many nuns throve in what is probably the most deliberately Marian and feminist religious order in history — the Brigittines. Still in existence today, it was established in the fourteenth century by the influential and highly charismatic Saint Birgitta of Sweden, who strongly identified with the Virgin Mary. In contrast to St. Clare, who reluctantly confined herself to the cloister at the behest of St. Francis, Birgitta installed her daughter as abbess of the Brigittines and continued on her travels. There were, after all, still kings in the world to advise and the Pope to criticize.

When Brigittine nuns take their vows, the postulants are preceded by a red banner depicting Christ on one side and the Virgin Mary on the other. The Holy Mother and her Son are meant to be perceived here as co-redeemers, as if they are two sides of the same coin. When a new nun is accepted into the community, she is proclaimed not only Christ's spouse, but also his "virgin mother."[34] Even the Brigittines' daily church services are highly Marian. Warren states:

> Unlike the divine service performed by nuns in other orders, the Brigittine nuns' offices, which vary with the days of the week, focus on the Virgin Mary, her work in the process of the Incarnation, and her role in salvation history. The female lineage through which humankind is saved, and especially Mary's maternal transmission of salvation, appear prominently in several services.[35]

Scholarship and the individual understanding of theological lessons are highly emphasized in the Brigittine Order, where Mary is considered both the model and embodiment of female wisdom. Like almost all religious orders, Brigittine monastics are prohibited from owning personal property — however, their very notable exception to this rule is that nuns may have as many books as they want. Since the inception of the Order, lessons have always been written and spoken in the nuns' mother tongue instead of Latin, long associated with masculine knowledge and the scholarship of men.[36] In one of St. Birgitta's many visions, an angel revealed to her that the vernacular words of the lessons shape a coat for the Queen of Heaven.

Given the highly feminist nature of the Brigittine order, it is somewhat surprising that it was not stamped out of existence by the Church patriarchy or a king who felt threatened by so much female empowerment. In England, however, the success of the Order, complete with its 700-year-old abbey at Syon, can be attributed to the early fifteenth-century king Henry V. Due to his spectacular victory at the Battle of Agincourt, he was proclaimed King of France as well as England. However, his claim to the French throne was based entirely on his matrilineal heritage. In order for Henry's assertion of his divine right to the French throne to be justified, people had to accept that royal blood could be passed on through women.

This made the king unusually progressive about women's issues for his time and particularly interested in Mariology. According to Nancy Bradley Warren's explanation of his logic, "Just as the Word becomes Flesh through Mary's female body, the divine right of kingship is transmitted through women to Henry, in whom it is made incarnate."[37] The king did many things to encourage his people in both England and France to make this connection. In his 1415 victory procession, a symbolic choir of young maidens welcomed Henry in song as the sovereign of England and France.

That same year, he also spent enormous amounts of money establishing a monastic house at Syon for the Brigittine nuns.[38] Henry's sister-in-law, Margaret, duchess of Clarence, subsequently became so attached to the Brigittine nuns here that she obtained special permission from the Pope to live near the abbey. The nuns, who were normally strictly cloistered, were allowed to visit Margaret, and she was given papal permission to go inside their sanctuary.[39]

It cannot be said, however, that joining a convent was always a positive experience for women. In strict contrast to the contented Brigittine scholar-nuns of the fifteenth century were the unwilling Italian nuns of the sixteenth. One very unfortunate side effect of the nunnery as an alternative to marriage was that girls were sometimes coerced to take the monastic veil. In sixteenth-century Italy, expectations for how much a bride's parents would spend on her dowry and wedding were astronomically high. Even a very wealthy family could be bankrupted by marrying off several sisters. As a result, half of the upper-class girls in Italian cities such as Florence and Venice were cloistered. Bastard daughters, spinsters, and widows, who could be a drain on family purses, were frequently dispensed with by sending them off to the convent. Girls were often cloistered before they were old enough to truly understand what was happening to them — those as young as five were sent to nunneries, while the average age was nine.

Marian imagery was never far from these unfortunate women. Patriotic Venetians frequently used her symbolism to represent the city itself, since it was entirely enclosed by water. Like Mary, Venice was also considered perfect, invincible, and eternally persevering.[40] According to Mary Laven's book *Virgins of Venice*, even prostitutes in Renaissance-era Italy felt adoration for their Holy Mother. Laven relates a true story in which two of them, Laura Todeschin and Signora Grana, went to the Venetian church of Santa Maria Maggiore in 1612 to make their devotions on Candlemas. Separated from the prostitutes only by a brick wall, the nuns of Santa Maria Maggiore were going about their Marian holiday prayers at exactly the same time.[41]

Some unwilling nuns used their monastic education to write, not praises of the Holy Virgin, but scathing indictments of what they considered their imprisonment. Florentine female monastic Beatrice del Sera wrote extensively of nuns' misery, while Venetian nun Arcangela Tarabotti penned an attack on fathers who forced their daughters into the convent.[42] Rebellion came in many forms, both large and small. Visiting bishops of Italian convents were often horrified to find the sisters keeping pets and hoarding personal supplies of food and wine. Reluctant nuns also wore low-cut dresses, grew their hair long and curled it, and even wore high-heeled shoes.[43] The most discontented among them sometimes took lovers, an event common enough that there was even a nickname for men who had a proclivity for nuns—"monachini."[44]

During this time period, Shakespeare introduced Isabella, one of the best-known fictional nuns ever to have been created. In *Measure for Measure*, she staunchly defends her chastity against the advances of Angelo, the corrupt nobleman who offers to spare her condemned brother's life in exchange for taking her virginity. Robert N. Watson argues that Shakespeare intended Isabella as a symbol of Marian piety. Lucio, the first male in the play who speaks to her, initially addresses her with the greeting, "Hail, virgin," referencing the Annunciation. Later, Angelo proposes to deflower her in an enclosed garden, a symbol of Mary's chastity.[45]

However, Isabella ultimately cannot keep her Marian-inspired virginity. At the end of *Measure for Measure*, her hand in marriage is claimed by the Duke, who, unlike Angelo, at least does not attempt to dishonor her. Unfortunately, he also refuses to respect her intention to become a nun. Shakespeare, though, had little choice but to marry off poor Isabella, a novice who had not yet taken her final monastic vows. The Bard lived in the Protestant-ruled country of England, where all monasteries, convents, and abbeys had only recently been dismantled by Henry VIII. In such a political climate, it would not have been appropriate to offer King James I a play in which the most virtuous female character becomes a nun.

In the Western world of today, there are few, if any, unwilling nuns. Women in the twentieth and twenty-first centuries have had career options open to them inconceivable to their female ancestors. No longer limited to marriage or the convent, some contemporary women still have chosen to become nuns. Unlike female monastics of earlier centuries, nuns who feel that they have lost their vocation are free to leave the cloister at any time. However, there is little evidence that most nuns today still feel a strong connection to the Virgin Mary. Writings both by and about female monastics contain few references to her, and those who look to her as a model seem few and far between.

Over the course of the past century, however, there have been a few times and places in which devotion to the Virgin among nuns has been strong. In the 1950s and early 1960s, just before Vatican II, there was a flowering of Marian piety among Catholics. Responding to the demand, a great deal of Mariological literature was produced, such as Sister M. Marguerite Andrew's *Journal for Mary*. This book, recorded as a series of journal entries for 1960, takes the reader through the Marian year, focusing, for example, on the Rosary during October, when the Feast of the Rosary occurs. Sister Andrew's journal begins with a tantalizing but never fully explained assertion of why she is devoted to Mary:

> Then came a time when I had a precarious toe-hold on the edge of an abyss; and desperately, to keep balance, to avoid the sight of the terrifying depth, I wrenched myself back and turned; and there — there you were [Mary], filling my whole horizon. I knew you then as the Refuge of sinners, the Comforter of the afflicted. Yes, you have filled my whole horizon ever since.[46]

Even in the twenty-first century, nuns of Hispanic origin often continue to feel connected to Mary, despite the Church's post–Vatican II de-emphasizing of her role. In Rebecca J. Lester's 2005 book, *Jesus in Our Wombs*, the lives of contemporary Mexican nuns are explored in fascinating detail. In Mexico, the Virgin of Guadalupe's image is on everything from bumper stickers to tattoos to the most sanctified of church windows. Even the title of Lester's book itself strongly suggests nuns' identification with the Holy Mother. Like her, after all, they carry Jesus in their wombs.

A modern nun prays to Mary. From a private scrapbook, 1940s (courtesy Chant Art).

A modern nun asks the Virgin for spiritual guidance. From a private scrapbook, 1940s (courtesy Chant Art).

For these nuns, identification with the Virgin Mary usually begins when they hear God's "call" to their vocation. The postulants, just starting on the path to lifelong monasticism, are taught that like Mary, they have been singled out by God for specific reasons. Although His true motivations are often unknown to these young women, they believe they have been chosen to serve God in a radical way. During the initial stages of their studies, one of the primary goals of the postulants is to become certain that they have, indeed, been called. Once they lose their doubts, they are supposed to completely assent to God's will, just as Mary did when she declared herself God's handmaid, agreeing to bear Jesus.[47]

Once they have taken the veil, these women continue to emulate Mary's virtues to the best of their abilities. Much like their counterparts in medieval Europe, they are taught that, just as the Virgin did, they should become servants, wives, and mothers to Christ. In order to accomplish this in the way that is most pleasing to God, they must truly follow the Virgin Mary's example. Lester states, "Like obedience, the dispositions of humility and purity take on a feminine cast for the sisters, and they are encouraged to look directly to Mary for guidance on how to manifest [these virtues] in their daily lives."[48] Just as she atoned for Eve's willfulness with complete submission to God, so they also must be obedient, especially to higher-ranking nuns. Obedience and humility are manifested in everything from completing their chores to showing up on time to their classes.[49]

The importance of sexual purity is emphasized, and the postulants are taught that it can be learned from Mary's example. According to the nuns, she achieved the most sublime state of marriage and motherhood through chastity. Despite, or more likely because of, her perpetual virginity, she was the perfect mother and wife. And the spiritual rewards for becoming like the Virgin are supposedly well worth the struggle. According to Lester, "They are encouraged to take Mary — inviolate and chaste, yet supremely receptive to God — as their model. If they are successful, they, like Mary, will come to experience — in their deepest interior — the kiss of God."[50]

If the proffered reward of experiencing "the kiss of God" seems oddly familiar, historically speaking, that is because it is. It certainly can be compared to the union with Jesus in heaven that nuns were promised during the medieval era. These Mexican nuns, at least to some degree, live in a convent untouched by time. It is certainly debatable, however, whether this is a negative thing. After all, female monastics during the Middle Ages often enjoyed an unusually high level of satisfaction with their lives. Although the life of a nun in a Hispanic country is certainly alien to most contemporary women's personal experience, there is no reason to devalue it. The *Dictionary of Mary*, published in 1985, states:

> It is not hard to see why and in what way Mary is the perfect example of what [nuns] strive to become.... The contemplation which they devote to Mary

reminds them, clearly and indelibly, of the vocation to which they have been called.... Relying on Mary and the motherly help she never fails to offer, they progress more easily and more rapidly in their "following of Christ" as nearly as humanly possible.[51]

Particularly during the medieval era, such contemplation sometimes became intense and personal. In every historical period, a few nuns have always gone beyond the bounds of simple piety to become visionaries and mystics. Women who had this sort of experience sometimes believed that they could communicate directly with saints, Jesus, and, of course, the Virgin Mary. Their challenge was figuring out how to convince Church authorities that their visions were genuine. In the context of women's religious history, it is important to examine who was accepted as a true mystic, as well as who was dismissed as a misguided madwoman. It is even more important, however, to discover why.

8

Mystics and Miracles

Touched by the Virgin's Hand

Since pre-Christian times, the term "mystic" has been used to refer to people who experience things which are, by their very nature, inexplicable. Somehow, mystics are supposedly able to move out of the realm of bodily life and into a purely spiritual world. This most often occurs while the visionary is in a trance which suddenly and uncontrollably takes over her body. During the Middle Ages, women who were acknowledged as genuine mystics by Church authorities enjoyed unequalled social privilege. They traveled with impunity to holy sites around the world, gave their advice to grateful bishops and kings, and were frequently canonized as saints after their deaths.[1]

Although the rewards for being a recognized visionary were quite high, few sought out this honor, since it was difficult to get the Church's official sanction. Those who claimed to have mystical experiences that were not subsequently accepted by Church authorities often suffered as a result. This was particularly common for women, who were vulnerable to the accusation of witchcraft. An unverifiable claim of preternatural experiences could even be life-threatening to the mystic. Fifteen cases have been documented of female visionaries being brought before the Spanish Inquisition on charges of "feigned sanctity."[2]

If she were lucky, a discredited female mystic was simply thought of as an unfortunate victim of clever demonic spirits. During the medieval era, the devil's excellence at duplicity was widely acknowledged, and women, who were considered weaker-willed than men, were supposed to be especially susceptible. In the seventeenth century, Jesuit theologian Martin Antoine Del Rio claimed this was because women's constitutions were "damper and more viscous" than men's. As a result, their passions were violent. They were likely to confuse dreams with visions, and more dangerously, to succumb to suggestions from the devil.[3]

At the trial of St. Joan of Arc, a fifteenth-century mystic and military hero, her interrogators alleged that her visions came not from God but from fairies, cleverly disguised as saints. Because fairies were frequently associated with demonic forces, this assertion made her claims of mystical experiences particularly suspect.[4] More apallingly, medieval hagiographer Francisco de Arcos wrote of a pregnant Flemish girl who was told in a vision that she was equal in merit to the Virgin Mary. She rejoiced, certain that she and her child had been chosen for special honors by God. Much to her horror, however, she discovered she had been misled by the devil when she subsequently gave birth to a monster.[5]

Sometimes, however, discredited visionaries were not benignly dismissed as demonic victims but instead denounced as frauds. Women from the lower classes of society were considered likely to make false claims, since becoming an accepted visionary was one of the very few paths to wealth and esteem available to them.[6] Federico Borromeo, archbishop of Milan from 1595 to 1631, asserted that women between the ages of thirty and forty were prone to vanity, which led them to fabricate visions.[7] Attempts were sometimes made to banish them from a church, a dioceses or even a city.

Margery Kempe, perhaps the most famous discredited mystic in history, was unwelcome just about everywhere she traveled. She made religious authorities uncomfortable by insisting upon wearing the virginal white clothes that she claimed Jesus and the Virgin Mary had instructed her to wear. This was considered particularly offensive because she had been married and borne many children. Her attire ultimately caused the frustrated Archbishop of York to have her objectionable presence removed from his diocese. Worse, she called attention to herself and distracted parishioners by weeping loudly during sermons, which she also believed Christ and the Blessed Mother wished her to do.[8] She once cried so persistently, supposedly at heavenly behest, that a well-known traveling preacher declared to his entire congregation that he wished she were out of his church.

Women who wanted to be accepted as true visionaries had to prove themselves to a special commission of exclusively male esteemed theologians. When one claimed to have received mystical communication from heaven, a panel of such men was convened to rigorously question her. Jean Gerson, a noted fifteenth-century expert on spiritual visions, was frequently called upon to evaluate such cases. Frequently, the main criterion he used for making judgments was the nature of the woman herself. A true mystic, he wrote, should possess the five virtues of the Virgin Mary at the Annunciation: humility, willingness to accept counsel, patience, accuracy and charity. He added that the visionary should conform to all Church approved ideas about faith and morality, show great caution in reacting to her visions, and not have any obvious ulterior motives, such as the desire for personal gain.[9]

Nearly all women who were accepted as mystics during the medieval era were nuns— in most cases, those who had been cloistered since childhood. Such experiences were almost always considered the exclusive domain of "Holy Women" who practiced lifelong celibacy. Thirteenth-century theologian Caesarius of Heisterbach believed that Mary revealed herself to virgins exclusively.[10] Although not a nun, St. Joan of Arc famously had to endure repeated gynecological examinations, in order to ascertain that she was pure enough to receive divine visions. Even the standard epithet which accompanies her name, "La Pucelle," means "the maiden." Numerous depositions from the soldiers she led on the battlefield attested to the fact that she was so spiritually pure that it was impossible to desire her. Indeed, in her presence, they ceased to feel sexual interest in any woman at all.[11] Secular women like Kempe who said they had direct interactions with the divine were generally considered presumptuous at best and dangerously heretical at worst.

Two women who whose claims of mystical visions were accepted by both the Church and society at large were St. Elizabeth of Schonau and St. Gertrude the Great. By medieval standards, both women led exemplary lives, taking the nun's veil at an early age. Elizabeth, child of a pious Rhineland family, was placed in a Benedictine nunnery at the age of twelve.[12] She was well known for fasting and other "mortifications of the flesh," so much so that Hildegard of Bingen wrote letters to her, urging her to eat more and keep up her strength. Gertrude entered the convent at the age of five (young even by medieval standards), having been taken under the wing of St. Mechtilde when she was orphaned. As a child postulant, she was an exceptionally brilliant student. In Gertrude's writings, she claimed that she had to repent for studying so much as a young girl that she neglected her prayers.[13]

During the Middle Ages, most nuns felt particular devotion toward Mary, whom they considered their model, the Virgin of Virgins. It is certainly not surprising that she figured prominently in both the visions of Elizabeth of Schonau and Gertrude the Great. However, each of these famous mystics interacted with her in a very different manner. A significant part of this variance had to do with the theological wisdom that was accepted in each woman's century. The fact that each of these nuns had visions that were in line with Church teachings of their day had everything to do with their official acceptance as visionaries. Often, the reasoning that the Church fathers used to determine the truth of a mystical experience was somewhat circular. Almost without exception, these were men with extremely conservative values who wished to see traditional religious doctrines upheld. The more a mystic's visions reinforced accepted theology, the more likely it was that she would be declared genuine.[14] Both Elizabeth and Gertrude, as educated nuns, would naturally have been very well versed in the predominant theology of the day. During the twelfth century, when Elizabeth was alive, Mary's role as the regal Queen of Heaven was particularly emphasized. In Gertrude's time, the thirteenth century, Mary was still perceived as regal—however, her role as the earthly mother of Jesus was coming more to the forefront of theological wisdom.

In Elizabeth's visions, Mary was powerful and somewhat frightening. She initially appeared to the mystic as a sort of combination of queen and priest, wearing white vestments, a purple mantle and a crown. The Virgin reassured the nun that she would not be harmed by these visions and blessed her with the sign of the cross, like a priest. Mary could also be a distant and surprisingly resentful figure in her interactions with Elizabeth. When the Virgin felt that the nun did not honor her enough, she refused to speak to her. Once, when displeased by such neglect, she refused to appear in the nun's visions until the convent's abbot performed Mary's divine office at Elizabeth's request. However, just as Elizabeth was beginning to question her relationship with her Divine Mother, she received a vision reminding her of the Virgin's simultaneous power and mercy. In it, Jesus threatened to destroy the world because of His anger at the sinfulness of mankind, and Mary intervened, protecting it from His wrath.[15]

Saint Gertrude the Great also experienced visions of Mary that were somewhat intimidating, but here the Virgin seemed more like an overbearing maternal figure. As a nun who was considered a "bride of Christ," Gertrude's overall sense of Mary's role in her life was that of her mother-in-law. Somewhat amusingly, this came complete with all the negative implications of that relationship. For several years on Christmas, Gertrude experienced very personal, emotionally charged visions of the Nativity, in which she was permitted to hold and care for the Christ child. However, on the day of Candlemas (February 2), the Virgin looked at her with a severe expression. Like a mother addressing an irresponsible babysitter, she demanded that Gertrude return the baby. This prompted great feelings of guilt in the mystic, who immediately began to beg for mercy. In a subsequent vision, hoping that Mary would behave more maternally toward her, Gertrude asked the Virgin to wrap her in Jesus' swaddling clothes. Peevishly, Mary refused.[16]

Throughout her life, Gertrude experienced conflicted feelings about the woman who was supposed to be her Holy Mother. Unlike many nuns, Gertrude did not identify herself with Mary, and she could not even view the Virgin as a true maternal figure in her life. Rather, this "bride of Christ" had to be protected by her "spouse" from her frequently disapproving mother-in-law. As with Elizabeth, Mary sometimes expressed that she felt neglected by Gertrude, who focused much of her devotion on Jesus.

Ultimately, however, Gertrude and the Virgin were capable of calling a truce. Like a good mother-in-law, Mary would then offer her gifts. These, however, were of a strongly metaphorical nature. The Queen of Heaven planted symbolic Marian flowers in Gertrude's heart, such as the rose of charity and the violet of humility. On another occasion, the Virgin gave her a magnificent necklace of precious gems symbolizing Marian virtues, such as purity and tranquility. Several times, Gertrude also had visions of the Blessed Mother's tenderly maternal presence at the deathbed of one of her fellow nuns, as she held

Acknowledged Marian visionary St. Gertrude the Great (courtesy Chant Art).

the suffering person's head in her hands. Even in these visions, Mary was still dressed in regal purple vestments, similar to the clothing Elizabeth of Schonau saw her wearing.[17]

A century after Gertrude had her visions, the brilliant, charismatic Saint Birgitta of Sweden became a mystic who seemed to be the exception to every established rule. She had a distinct advantage over many would-be female visionaries, in that she was born into a highly influential, aristocratic family. It was generally accepted that she had little to gain by claiming to have mystical experiences. Nonetheless, it is somewhat astonishing that her visions were almost universally accepted as true, despite the fact that Birgitta was neither a nun nor even a virgin. At the age of fourteen, she was obliged by her family to marry an aristocratic young man named Ulf, with whom she eventually had eight children. Her background would later place her in a unique position among saints. Her cult became tremendously popular among secular medieval women, who felt that they could identify with her far more easily than most other female saints, who were usually canonized nuns.

By this time in history, the Virgin Mary's role as a human woman and mother to Jesus was decidedly emphasized over her Queen of Heaven aspect. In Birgitta's visions, the maternal side of Mary was certainly predominant. When the mystic was twelve years old, she claimed that the solicitous Holy Mother had appeared at her side to help her with a particularly difficult piece of embroidery. Ultimately, though, it was Birgitta's subsequent experience as a mother which allowed her to identify so strongly with Mary. When the future saint was in her forties, after the death of her husband, she decided it was time to pursue her religious calling. To do this, she had to pay the terrible price of leaving her children behind, the youngest of whom was only nine years old. Finally, she received a vision in which a demon tried to inflame the love of her children within her. It hoped to increase her maternal feeling so much that it would interfere with her love of Christ. Reluctantly, she came to believe that it was the will of God that she should leave them. This would afterwards give her a personal perspective on the anguish of the Mater Dolorosa, separated from her Son at his death.

Birgitta had many other experiences over the course of her life which strongly fixed the association of Mary with motherhood in her mind. She firmly believed that assistance from the Virgin had saved her during the particularly difficult birth of one of her children. In addition, one of the strongest and clearest visions she ever had was that of Mary's painless and instantaneous delivery of Jesus. Even for a medieval woman, Birgitta was particularly attached to the idea of Mary as the Blessed Mother. She wrote that she would have chosen eternal suffering in hell if Mary had not been the Mother of God.[18]

Birgitta's important life's work as an acknowledged mystic, prophet, and the founder of a religious order was presaged by an experience that took place both in her physical body and the spiritual realm. While staying at a Cistercian

138   8. Mystics and Miracles

St. Birgitta of Sweden — a charismatic and scholarly Marian mystic (courtesy Chant Art).

monastery in Alvastra, she felt a living child turning around and around in her heart. Mary soon appeared to Birgitta, reassuring her that it was not the work of the devil but "a sign of the arrival of my Son into your heart."[19] This led the future saint to understand that she was meant to bring Christ's word into the world, just as the Virgin had incarnated Christ's body.

An incredibly strong identification with Mary gave Birgitta the confidence to take on extraordinary power in the world. When she wished to say something controversial, she claimed that she was merely conveying the words of the Queen of Heaven to her earthly subjects. Somewhat astoundingly, Birgitta claimed that Mary had revealed to her the truth of the Immaculate Conception — the idea that the Virgin herself had been conceived without sin.[20] This was not accepted as official church doctrine until 1854, when it was proclaimed by Pope Pius IX.[21] Taking on the voice (and to some extent, the role) of the Holy Mother, she criticized Magnus, the King of Sweden. She called him "boyish" and said that because of his childish behavior, he needed to listen to her motherly advice. She even used this same maternal tone to chastise Pope Urban for traveling to Avignon, rather than staying in Rome, where Birgitta plainly felt he belonged.

So powerful was this mystic's conflation with the Virgin, she was able to pass it on to others, as a kind of heritage. One of her lasting contributions to the world is the founding of the Brigittine religious order, in which both male and female members were instructed to glorify the Virgin. There were no gender restrictions on joining the Order, but it was always to be governed by an abbess, who was head of the organization, as the Virgin Mary was Queen of the Apostles.[22] Men were tolerated in the Order primarily because they were thought to be serving God in the way that the Virgin's husband Joseph had done so — through his service to Mary. Speaking as the Blessed Mother, Birgitta recorded in her Revelations, "[Joseph] espoused me with the intention of serving me, holding me in the light of a sovereign mistress, not a wife."[23] Ultimately, through a sort of deputization, Birgitta was able to convey her identification with the Virgin to all future abbesses of the Order.

In nearly all relevant scholarly literature today, the remarkable work of Saint Birgitta seems inevitably linked with that of Margery Kempe (1373–1440), the discredited mystic. Kempe was coincidentally born in the same year that Saint Birgitta died, and she also experienced visions in which the maternal role of Mary was emphasized. At first glance, she seems to have little else in common with the venerable saint. However, there are actually some resemblances which are striking. Both of these women spent the early parts of their lives as wives and mothers. Birgitta bore eight children, while Kempe had the remarkable number of fourteen. As mothers, they both had the same difficulty with one of their sons — both young men were guilty of the sin of lechery.[24] Birgitta's son Karl supposedly died unrepentant for his love affair with Queen Joanna of Naples, so the Virgin and the saint had to join forces to save his soul from hell.

In one of Birgitta's visions, Mary argued on his behalf that his mother's "prayers, tears, and almsdeeds alone have blotted out Karl's countless venial sins and unfulfilled penances."[25]

In their early forties, both Birgitta and Margery received mystical communications from heaven, calling them to leave their families behind and pursue spiritual lives. When Kempe set out on her pilgrimages, she was certainly very much aware of St. Birgitta's life and works. Although she had only recently died, her *Revelations* were well known in England. In Kempe's writings, sometimes it seems that she is modeling her life on the saint's. At other times, however, she seems to be almost in competition with her. In the visions recorded by Margery, Jesus and Mary repeatedly reassure her that she is being shown sacred things that were also revealed to Birgitta. However, Kempe is also told that some things she has been allowed to see were never disclosed to the saint.[26] One difference between the visions of St. Birgitta and those of Margery Kempe is particularly significant. Kempe received maternal care from Mary, but she never had anything like Birgitta's "spiritual pregnancy." It was through this particular mystical experience that the saint became identified and conflated with the Virgin. Throughout her life, Margery claimed to be Mary's daughter, but, unlike Birgitta, she never presumed to act or speak as the Virgin herself.

Intriguingly, Kempe's early visions shared some of the attributes of St. Gertrude's. Early in *The Book of Margery Kempe*, she mentions a vision in which she, like Gertrude, was entrusted with the care of the Christ child, wrapping him in his swaddling clothes.[27] Most of the time, however, Margery did not act as a divine babysitter. Her primary role was that of daughter, and Mary represented herself to the discredited mystic as her Heavenly Mother. Significantly, the Virgin usually addressed Kempe as "Daughter." Like any good mother, Mary was constantly reassuring her, especially when Margery felt persecuted by those who doubted her pious devotion. When she visited Mary's burial site on a pilgrimage, the Virgin told her (similarly to her Magnificat speech about herself), "My son Jesus will flood you with so much grace that the world will sing your praises."[28]

In a later vision, in which Kempe attended at Mary's deathbed, she received reassurance that she would be welcomed into heaven when she died. The Virgin then added, "Daughter, be sure that I will be your own true mother to you. I shall help you, strengthen you, just as a good mother should her own daughter."[29] Perhaps Mary's most accessibly maternal act was her repeated exhortation to her daughter Margery to eat. The Virgin explained to her that all the crying (sometimes during sermons) Kempe was doing sapped her strength and that she had to eat, "for love of her."[30]

Given their numerous similarities, the inevitable question arises—why were St. Birgitta's visions met with practically universal acceptance, while the unfortunate Margery Kempe's found ridicule? Or, more simply, how did Birgitta get away with it? Perhaps the most concrete explanation is that, unlike

Margery Kempe's, the advent of Birgitta's mysticism was accompanied by a sign which could be perceived by unbiased witnesses. William A. Christian Jr. defines a "sign" in this context as "something that could be seen, smelled, or touched by others beside the seer, some manifestation of divine presence or impingement upon the natural world that could be independently verified."[31]

When she experienced the aforementioned "spiritual pregnancy," in which the Christ child lay in her heart, she immediately asked the respected Church authorities present to verify it. Two of her confessors, Prior Peter Olofsson and Canon Mathias of Alvastra, attested that they had seen and touched the movement "with great amazement on top of the lady Birgitta's clothes, which she had over her heart."[32] The Swedish saint also had the distinct advantage that, as a result of her "pregnancy," she subsequently was conflated with the Virgin. Swedish art historian Aron Andersson asserts:

> Her mystical pregnancy can be understood as a physical sign of her identification with Mary's role as the mother of Christ, just as stigmata were seen as a physical sign of other mystics' imitation of Christ. Through this experience, she was imbued with 'prophetic authority,' allowing her to write, instruct and speak on behalf of God.[33]

Finally, Birgitta was considered credible because of her unique social position. At the time she began having visions, she was widowed, which signified the "authenticity" of her calling.[34] Freed from the contaminating influences of sexuality and childbearing, she was considered free to devote herself entirely to spiritual pursuits. Also, there was little possibility of her feeling the need to become a mystic in order to gain money or increase her social position. She was a wealthy, aristocratic widow, a cousin to the King of Sweden. As such, she already had access to all the financial and social advantages any woman of her time could have had. Most people assumed that her spiritual calling was likely to be genuine.

Mystical experience among women claiming to receive visions of Mary is certainly not limited to the medieval era. In contemporary society, many have asserted that they have been touched by the Virgin Mary's hand. Catholic Church authorities today are also no less cautious about visionaries than their medieval predecessors were. On the Catholic Culture website, the Archbishop of Tours lists the major criteria for determining whether a vision is genuine. First, he writes, it must conform to Gospel Revelation and the dogma of the Church. The seer's message, ultimately, must be "in complete agreement with the Word," as interpreted by Church teachings.[35] Another important criterion is the "truthfulness" of the seer. Church investigation into a claim of mystical experience always includes an inquiry about the visionary's psychic equilibrium, conditions of life, and level of maturity.

In her book *Apparitions, Healings, and Weeping Madonnas*, Lisa J. Schwebel includes much more detailed information on the criteria used to determine the reliability of a vision. She states that the seer must be both pious and honest, exhibiting positive advances in sanctity after receiving the divine communication. The mystic must also have a great deal of personal integrity, which encompasses her sincerity, straightforwardness, and simplicity. She has to be determined physically and mentally healthy by unbiased authorities. Finally, as with St. Birgitta, it is considered more decisive proof if signs are present to verify the miracle. Most frequently, subsequent healings and miracles take place as a result of or at the site of the vision(s).[36]

One of the most noteworthy Marian visionaries of relatively recent history was Catherine Laboure, an early nineteenth-century French nun. According to Catholic belief, she received direct orders from the Virgin Mary to have the Miraculous Medal created. Arguably the most significant piece of Marian jewelry since the Rosary, the Miraculous Medal has been credited with cures for ills ranging from insanity and leprosy to hernias. There are also reports that it has accomplished conversions of hardened sinners and provided for the protection of believers during wars, shipwrecks, and duels.[37]

Seen in the most pragmatic light, it cannot be denied that Laboure's visions came at a politically expedient time. The Miraculous Medal, created at the behest of the Virgin in 1832, features an image of Mary surrounded by the words, "O Mary, conceived without sin, pray for us who have recourse to thee." The inclusion of the phrase "conceived without sin" is meant to emphasize that Mary herself was created asexually by her parents, Anne and Joachim. This doctrine, known as the Immaculate Conception, was officially proclaimed Church dogma by Pope Pius IX in 1854.[38] It is still considered important enough by Church authorities to merit official commemoration each December 8 with the celebration its own liturgical feast. There is, admittedly, a time difference of 22 years between the creation of the Miraculous Medal and the proclamation of the Immaculate Conception dogma. However, it is certain that Church authorities were beginning to give the matter serious thought at the time of Laboure's initial vision.

In addition to having her vision at the right time, Catherine Laboure had all the qualifications for an officially sanctioned female mystic. Even before she became a nun, it was clear that she possessed all the traditional womanly virtues. According to her official biography, *Venerable Catherine Laboure*, she was a model housekeeper as a young girl, attending to the cooking, cleaning, and care of younger children with "unremitting assiduity." She was also an unusually pious child, fasting on Fridays and Saturdays. She knelt to pray on hard pavement for such long intervals that she eventually contracted arthritis of the knees.[39]

Somewhat unsurprisingly, Laboure decided that her calling in life lay within a religious community as a nun. Her older sister, M. Louise, a Superioress in the order of the Daughters of Charity, encouraged her vocation, despite the protestations of their father. When Catherine was considering whether it was all right to leave her family and join a convent, M. Louise wrote, "A religious

Catherine Laboure — mystic whose Marian visions led to the creation of the Miraculous Medal (courtesy Chant Art).

may be compared to a soldier who in time of peace guards the city; a Daughter of Charity to one who faces the enemy."[40] In 1830, when Catherine Laboure was still a postulant, she deliberately swallowed a piece of St. Vincent de Paul's linen surplice, in the hopes that it would help her to have a Marian vision. Apparently, her effort was successful, since that very night she was led by an angel in the shape of a small child to an empty chapel, where she saw Mary for the first time.

Notably, the Virgin of Catherine's vision was far more inaccessible, powerful queen than maternal figure. She appeared in a blaze of white light, and on her hands were three rings which radiated beams of light "the color of jewels." Mary explained that these rays represented graces she gave to those who asked for them. Emphasizing her purity — this was, after all, a vision reinforcing the Immaculate Conception — was an abundance of the color white. In addition to radiating white light, Mary wore a veil of that same color which fell to her feet, and her hair was bound in a "fillet ornamented with lace."[41] Despite the somewhat intimidating nature of these visions, Catherine was willing to rest her hands in the Virgin's lap while they spoke together.

Reinforcing Catherine Laboure's credibility as a visionary, she never sought any public recognition for herself. Even when Mary shared prophecies about upcoming political upheaval, the pious nun never sought to involve herself in any affairs of state. Indeed, Laboure did not ever inform secular authorities about what she had been told. Until after her death, only her confessor knew that she had any connection whatsoever with the Miraculous Medal. For forty-six years after Catherine had her mystical experiences, she took care of the elderly and tended her convent's chicken coop. She died in 1876 and was canonized as a saint in 1947.

In 1953, the Virgin supposedly interceded to help a young woman named Antonina Iannuso. She lived in Sicily, at a time when all of Italy was still ravaged and depopulated by the horrors of World War II. Iannuso was a somewhat unlikely visionary — a woman who chose to pursue the secular path of marriage and motherhood. Her encounter with the Virgin occurred when she was pregnant with her first child, a son who would be born on Christmas Day.

Suffering from a difficult pregnancy which included convulsions and temporary blindness, she looked up at an image of the Madonna hung over her bed and found that it was weeping. Suddenly, she was healed of all the pregnancy's complications. In the presence of numerous witnesses, this plaster-of-Paris image continued to cry for four days. Samples of the tears were collected in sterilized tubes and sent to a laboratory to be analyzed. Ten days later, it was announced that the liquid was "analogous to human tears."[42] Due to the fairly decisive evidence of this sign, after only a few days, Iannuso was accepted as a true visionary by Catholic authorities.

Miraculous healings of "incurable" illnesses and injuries were subsequently attributed to this Weeping Madonna image, which was enshrined underground.

The delighted Archbishop of Syracuse proclaimed, "Weeping is fecund ... As the rain that falls from on high irrigates the countryside ... so it happens in the realm of the spirit. A woman who weeps always becomes, in the very act, a mother."[43] In a time when Italy desperately needed to be rebuilt and repopulated, Church authorities were eager to accept the encouraging sign of a weeping Madonna, who cared deeply and personally for a pregnant woman.

The officially encouraged interest in Mary as Mater Dolorosa (The Mother of Sorrows) which occurred in postwar Italy had a strong historical precedent. In the fourteenth century, during the time of the Black Plague, Europeans' focus on the Lady of Sorrows bordered on obsession. Art and literature frequently depicted her crying as Jesus was crucified, and a confraternity specifically dedicated to contemplating her Sorrows was founded in Flanders.[44] The mystic Miguel Noguer experienced a vision in which Mary appeared to him as a sobbing child of seven, warning that if people did not cease their blasphemous ways, Christ would send a great epidemic of bubonic plague.[45]

Since that time, the Weeping Madonna has seemed to resurface regularly at times of great crisis. Her presence in this incarnation is an effective means of reinforcing the idea of divine compassion for human suffering. Catholics even claimed that a statue of the Virgin wept outside of a cathedral in Saigon when the Viet Cong took the city. Due to the socio-political realities of her day, Iannuso found easy acceptance as a true mystic, despite her usually discrediting status as a pregnant, married woman. The birth of her son on Christmas also came to be considered a sign by many believers, conflating her with the Madonna.

In contrast to Laboure and Iannuso, there are many self-proclaimed mystics of modern times who never receive the sanction of the Catholic Church. If there is a contemporary equivalent of Margery Kempe, it is certainly Veronica Leuken. This mother of five claimed her first vision of Mary in 1970, when she was 47 years old. The Virgin appeared to her at St. Robert Bellarmine Church in Queens, New York, instructing her to hold prayer vigils and establish a shrine to Our Lady of the Roses there.[46] She soon had a small group of followers gathering at the site, praying and chanting. A Catholic newspaper in Quebec picked up Leuken's story, and by 1973, busloads of Canadians wearing distinctive white berets were arriving each week to take part in her vigils.

Parishioners of St. Robert Bellarmine, as well as those who lived in the church's vicinity, soon began to complain of the vigilites, who were regarded as something of a public nuisance. The monsignor of St. Robert Bellarmine Church asked the indignant Veronica to move her gatherings to another location. Worse still for Leuken and her followers, Catholic authorities issued an official report denying that anything of a supernatural nature was occurring there. Officials of St. Robert Bellarmine Church removed the statue of the Virgin Mary, put up a fence, and secured a court order barring vigils on the property. Somewhat defeated, Veronica Leuken moved her followers to a nearby grassy mall.

In 1974, civic leaders asked police to force the vigilites to leave this location as well. The conflict between Leuken's followers and their opponents became increasingly heated. A neighborhood resident was clubbed in the head by police while protesting near the vigil site. Soon afterwards, residents planned to pre-empt the vigil by holding an early bicentennial celebration on the mall. A virtual riot ensued, and police had to be called in to separate the two sides. The confrontations finally reached a climax when 2,500 worshippers faced off against 900 area residents.

As the violence increased, Mary's communications with Veronica Leuken took on a more dire tone. The Virgin began imparting a message of impending doom, warning that unless more people lived a life of prayer, penance and sacrifice, a giant comet called the Ball of Redemption would hit the earth, killing billions. Ultimately, Leuken ended the face-off when she told her followers that Mary had instructed her to move the vigils to Flushing Meadows–Corona Park, where they are still held to this day.[47]

It is interesting that Catholic Church authorities, who accepted Iannuso as a mystic and visionary in the space of only ten days, were so quick to dismiss Leuken's claims. In his work, *The Apparitions of the Blessed Virgin Mary Today*, Father Rene Laurentin classifies her experiences in an appendix with the heading "Apparitions without Credibility." In a paragraph in which he seems to be scolding Veronica Leuken and others who have attested to similar experiences, the priest states,

> Lack of spiritual guidance in an area that abounds in temptations and psychophysiological traps allowed them to deviate, to confuse their own drives with the movements of the Spirit.... Not that one wants to throw the first stone, but rather one prays that these so-called visionaries will find their way back from these ambivalent experiences to a humble faith.... In many cases, they were left to their own devices because their very failure had caused them to be abandoned and left without advice of any sort.[48]

He goes on to discuss at some length why Leuken's visions, in particular, were found unbelievable by the Catholic Church. Laurentin states that they contain "evident errors," including heavenly denunciation of two high-ranking Cardinals as "men given to Satan." According to Veronica Leuken, these men substituted an impostor, altered by plastic surgery, for the Pope. They then supposedly confined the true Pope to his rooms as a prisoner. As a result of this, Leuken claimed that Mary was weeping with her hands over her eyes because the Church was being transformed into a satanic synagogue.

It can certainly be said that Father Laurentin is following the centuries-old Church practice of only giving credit to mystical experiences which reinforce accepted dogma. Veronica Leuken's visions are treated like Margery Kempe's decision to wear virginal white on her spiritual quest. In both cases, Church authorities did not take kindly to personal piety's conflict with officially approved theology. However, it must be acknowledged that Leuken's assertions are, at best, highly improbable. Most contemporary Christians value verifiable claims over inherently personal mystical experiences. In order to be believed, it is necessary for modern day visionaries to substantiate their contentions with observable evidence.

Throughout history, the issue of determining true visions and miracles has always been complicated. Mystical experiences related to Marian statues, for example, could be particularly confusing. A well known one which occurred during the Renaissance era is the case of the Jesus Oak. In the 1630s, a Dutch grocer named Peter van Kerckhoven was disturbed by a "gigantic, gnarly, lightning-riddled old tree called the Devil's Oak, used for centuries as a meeting place by hunters and thieves."[49] He frequently had to pass it in the course of his business, and it never failed to unsettle him. Finally, he bought a wooden statue of the Madonna and Child, vowing to hang it there and sacralize (meaning to make holy with a sacred object) the frightening tree. He unfortunately forgot this promise to God until he was on his deathbed, when he requested, as a dying wish, that his children carry out his vow. His son Philip did so, and within five years, beginning with the healing of a child's hernia, the Jesus Oak became a site of divine miracles.[50]

As a place of miraculous events, the Jesus Oak is particularly problematic for several reasons. Neither Peter nor Philip van Kerckhoven claimed that they had received a visitation from the Virgin or any other divine entity requesting that they make the Devil's Oak a holy site. It was the grocer himself who decided to do so. Also, the fact that it was a tree which was so transformed calls up associations with centuries of pagan nature magic. Was it through the agency of the tree or the Madonna statue placed in it that these miracles were taking place? Were the Kerckhovens some sort of magicians, unbeknownst even to themselves?

Similarly, in 1636, a violent storm struck the port of Genoa, Italy causing many ships to be wrecked. Among the items salvaged from the storm by local sailors was the figurehead of a ship called the Madonna della Pieta, which depicted the Virgin and Child. After they repaired and repainted it, the sailors brought it to the nearby church of San Vittore. Curiously, the statue, which had originally been intended for the pragmatic and largely secular purpose of being a ship's figurehead, became the focus of a tremendously popular cult.

A famous blind songwriter was commissioned to compose something in honor of the image, and thousands of people began arriving daily to leave the statue offerings of candles, silver crowns, necklaces, and crosses. Despite disapproval from local Church leaders, the sailors themselves directed devotions to this Madonna image and even conducted exorcisms there. In the face of such tremendous popular belief, Church authorities eventually decided it was better to get behind belief in the image than to oppose it. In 1637, Church authorities named the statue Nostra Signora della Fortuna and gave it official sanction as a holy object capable of performing miracles. Despite the initial reluctance of the Genovese clergy, the sailors had gotten their way.[51]

8. Mystics and Miracles

If it has traditionally been somewhat problematic for the Catholic Church to determine which mystical visions of the Virgin were genuine, the same can be said for miracles. Such questions gained new importance during the Renaissance, when criticism of Catholic acceptance of miracles rang from the pulpit of every Protestant church. The Reformers were particularly opposed to those accomplished through the idolatrous agency of holy relics and statues. Martin Luther, arguably the leader of the Protestant movement, insisted that Catholic miracles were in truth, "lying wonders of the Antichrist."[52] Renaissance-era Catholic theologian Thomas More, however, dismissed such accusations. He wrote:

> The simplest fool knows that Our Lady is in heaven and that her image here with us is merely an image ... and if Catholics speak among themselves that a statue of the Virgin healed this one or that, they understand well that the statue is not doing this itself but rather God through it.[53]

However, even among Catholics, there has traditionally been a great deal of confusion and disagreement about Madonna statues and supernatural power. In 1786, the Grand Duke of Tuscany, Peter Leopold, issued a decree in which he commanded that no church in the area he ruled was to contain more than one Marian image. Leopold stated, "These different images have led to thousands of strange ideas among the people, such as the idea that there are several different Virgin Marys."[54] Ordinary Catholics, it seems, were regarding various depictions of the Madonna as separate and distinct supernatural beings.

Michael P. Carroll emphasizes that this idea is common even among Italian Catholics of the twentieth century. According to Carroll, much like the saints, each Madonna has a separate and distinct identity. Unlike the saints, however, who generally specialize in helping with one particular aspect of human life (safe childbirth, finding lost objects, traveling) all Madonnas possess a more generalized power to heal and protect. He sites a 1958 study of religious belief in Basilicata, in which an older Italian woman chided a young man who had been in seminary for his belief in only one Virgin Mary. "You studied with the priests for eight years, and you haven't learned the differences between the Madonnas?" she asked, incredulously.[55]

Partly because of popular credence in a multitude of Madonnas, Italian lay Catholics came to believe that individual Madonna statues desired veneration. In order to bring themselves more attention from humans, images of the Virgin would accomplish miracles. As a result, the statues themselves would encourage their own cults. One example of such belief is included in the seventeenth-century account of the Madonna della Pieta, located near Naples. The author states, "Not wanting to be held in ... low regard, the image began to dispense a great number of miracles and favors."[56]

Similarly, in Italy, there is the traditional practice of keeping certain statues of the Virgin covered with veils. This naturally leads to a chicken-and-egg sort of inquiry—are the images kept veiled because people believe they are powerful, or is popular belief in their efficacy a direct result of covering them? Added to this is the idea that, on the rare occasions when these statues are unveiled, they possess extraordinary power. Each year in Sicily, those who believed they were possessed by evil spirits would gather on the eve of the Assumption of the Virgin (August 14) for the unveiling of the Madonna di Trapani. The uncovered Virgin Mary, it was believed, forced the spirits out of the bodies they inhabited. Bystanders were careful to cover their mouths with rosaries in order to prevent the expelled spirits from entering them instead.[57]

There is even a story about an early seventeenth-century archbishop of Pisa, who got too curious about a veiled statue. He ordered a workman to uncover the image of St. Maria sotto gli organi, in the presence of two canons of the cathedral. Before the workman could entirely remove the veil, the archbishop was seized with a violent shivering fit, and he urgently shouted to cover it again. However, it was too late. The archbishop died soon afterwards, one of the canons committed suicide, and the other died a bit later in dire poverty. The unfortunate workman, who was guilty only of following the bishop's orders, went blind.[58]

As early as the fourteenth century, members of the Lollards, a sect considered heretical by mainstream Catholics, began to argue against the use of images. John Wycliffe, one of the earliest theologians to assert that the spiritual use of images had become excessive, was suspicious of Marian statues partly because women found them so attractive. He stated that the lavishly painted statues of the Virgin, frequently dressed up in clothes and jewels by adoring women, were comparable to the pagan idol of Diana described in the Bible. Certainly, women of late medieval times could be extreme in their admiration for sculpted Marian images. In the fifteenth century, a woman named Joan Tule wrote in her will that her wedding ring was to be left to the Mary statue at Salisbury Cathedral. Even Thomas More had to admit that women's veneration of images could become excessive. He wrote that London wives would sometimes gape up at the statue of the Virgin by the Tower until they imagined it smiled at them.[59]

One particularly tragic consequence of Reformation-era suspicion of Marian statues is that they were frequently defaced or destroyed. Acts of vandalism could sometimes be relatively harmless, such as in the case of Hugh Knight. In 1441, he was excommunicated for putting a temporary false beard on a Madonna statue at Newport chapel with candle smoke.[60] However, the vandals could also be unsettlingly violent, like the parish clerk of Byfield in Northamptonshire. In 1416, he cut off the head of a Mary statue in his own parish and burned it.[61]

In response to such acts, Catholics placed increased emphasis on traditional stories of Mary's revenge on those who desecrated her image. Supposedly, the Virgin repaid iconoclasts in kind—inflicting upon them the same mutilations they visited upon her statues. Seventeenth-century English author Sir Edward

Hoby, a Protestant, made light of such claims. One character, a minister, in Hoby's work, *A Curry Combe for a Coxe–Combe*, remarks, "I never heard before that a mild Lady [Mary] did cut off so many Gentlemen's noses."[62]

The veneration of images experienced a great resurgence in England during the sixteenth-century reign of the Catholic queen Mary Tudor. After the deaths of Henry VIII and Edward VI, her Protestant father and brother, English Catholics were delighted to bring their images and relics out of hiding, where they had been, disgraced, during the Protestant regime. When Queen Mary first entered London in 1553, depictions of the Virgin and other saints were proudly displayed in windows for the first time in many years. In 1559, Protestant John Jewel, writing with disgust of this Catholic restoration, stated, "What a wilderness of superstition has sprung up in the darkness of Marian times."[63]

Prior to the sixteenth century, conflation of Marian Christianity with what is now deemed superstition was simply taken for granted. Lay people and clergy alike believed in all forms of magic, as well as supernatural beings such as fairies and ghosts, just as they had unquestioning faith in the existence of God. It was not uncommon for folk magic spells to combine some aspects of pagan nature worship with Marianism. This Renaissance-era folk charm to dispel rats is an excellent example — the vermin were commanded to depart by sun, moon, air, stars and firmament, "as sure as Mary gave birth to the Son of God."[64]

Marija Zavjalova points out in her online article that in Lithuania, traditional spells "preserve[d] certain characteristics of pagan outlook," due to the late introduction of Christianity into the region.[65] Michael P. Carroll makes a similar claim about the Southern region of Italy. He argues that the area was geographically protected from the anti-magic stance decreed by the 1563 Council of Trent. As a result, Catholicism in Southern Italy retained more elements of the supernatural.[66]

According to Zavjalova, traditional Lithuanian spells may interchangeably request the aid of personifications of nature (fire, sun, or oak), pagan deities (Baltic gods such as Perkunas the Thunderer and Svasistkas), and Christian forces (God, Mary, Jesus, saints and angels), while still being considered "white" or holy magic. On the other hand, love spells are always regarded as black magic, regardless of whether Christian or pagan forces are involved. Spells invoking the Virgin usually have to do with protecting against illness or curing the sick, though Marian magic related to agriculture is not unknown.[67]

During the Renaissance, belief in the efficacy of amulets was also common, particularly among women. A seventeenth-century prostitute named Aldegonde Walre admitted at a trial that she wore magic amulets around her neck. She claimed that they were effective in warding off anyone who intended to stab her — until a priest, fearing their magical properties, burned them.[68] Catherine de Medici, a sixteenth-century Queen of France who was desperate to produce an heir, wore "an amulet containing the ashes of a large frog to encourage the birth of a male child."[69]

However, this was not a great leap of logic from the Church-approved actions of England's sixteenth-century queen, Catherine of Aragon. On numerous occasions, she offered jewelry to the statue of Our Lady of Walsingham, in the hopes of conceiving an heir. Faith in such amulets also seems less naïve when it is taken into account that Pope Pius V was actively encouraging belief in another sort of magic necklace. In 1573, he declared that the Turks had been defeated in battle because faithful Christians had prayed for the Virgin's aid with their Rosaries.[70]

Despite their vaunted freedom from both superstition and the Virgin Mary, even Protestants believed in magic. Queen Elizabeth I sanctioned the killing of witches, though she herself employed John Dee — her official court magician. It is worth noting, however, that Dee was summarily dismissed by her successor, James I, who decidedly did not approve of magicians of any kind. In the book *Enforcing Morality in Early Modern Europe*, E. William Monter raises the possibility that Marian devotion, in conjunction with the idea of courtly love, actually brought about European fervor for persecuting witches. Because these movements increased the status of women in society, the idea of the witch, conversely, took hold. After all, if some women were pure and good, like the Virgin Mary and the idealized courtly Lady, it stood to reason that others were evil, like the witch.

Monter unfortunately goes on to dismiss this idea, claiming that sinful Eve, not the witch, was perceived as the mythological counterpart of the Virgin. He adds that courtly love and Marian devotion, movements of the twelfth century, were too far separated in time from witch hysteria, a fifteenth-century phenomenon.[71] Still, the idea of a connection remains intriguing. It could even be argued that if Eve is the Virgin's counterpart, the witch is the natural antithesis to the lady of courtly love. The presence of both the Lady Guinevere and the witch Morgan le Fay in the King Arthur cycle, possibly the ultimate literary expression of the ideals of courtly love, seems to substantiate this.

During the Middle Ages, it was believed that Mary could, and often did, save the souls of those who had been seduced by black magic, such as witches. One of the most famous of all miracle tales is that of Theophilus, a previously virtuous man who is tempted into obtaining the aid of a Jewish necromancer. This evil sorcerer helps him to sell his soul to the devil, in exchange for riches and success. Theophilus ultimately repents of his sin, so the Virgin personally wrests his soul contract from the devil's grasp, sparing him condemnation to hell.[72] Similarly, in "The Dove that Returned," a young man desperate with unrequited love goes to a heathen sorcerer, who helps him enter the service of the devil. His beloved agrees to marry him as a result of the dark magic, but Mary ultimately intervenes to save them both.[73]

In her article "The Virgin and the Devil," Iona McCleery points out that, in the Theophilus legend, Mary's role as a mother is particularly emphasized in many of its retellings and is considered the main source of her power. The medieval author Berceo, who composed a Theophilus poem, refers to her as "mother" in it twenty-six times. McCleery asserts, "It was through her Divine Motherhood, her power to give birth, that Theophilus was redeemed."[74] Also, in the Theophilus legend, his relationship with the Virgin Mary is a particularly medieval one — that of vassal to the lord he serves. When Mary saves him from his pact with the Devil, she is, in some sense, acting as a lord reasserting her rightful authority. Although similar Devil-pact tales, such as Faust, emerged in later centuries, Mary was given no role in them. This was largely because the ideas of Divine Motherhood and vassalship gradually faded with the advent of Reformation theology and the new social order of the Renaissance.[75]

In the fourteenth century, ritual magic and Marian mysticism were directly combined by the self-proclaimed visionary John the Monk. He asserted that she was the inspiration and guide for his magical text, *The Book of Visions of the Blessed and Undefiled Virgin Mary, Mother of God*. The Queen of Heaven supposedly appeared to him in a series of dreams, persuading him to abandon the study of the *Ars Notoria of Solomon*, which was condemned by church authorities. In place of this sinister book, Mary promised to personally reveal to him an alternative, benevolent system of magic. Such claims of divine intervention, however, did not stop John's book from also being condemned by the Catholic Church. In 1323, all the copies that Church officials could find were burned, largely because the author refused to keep the practice of his new magic secret.[76]

Though scientific advances in subsequent centuries dispelled much superstition, both Catholic and Protestant Christianity have continued to be intertwined with magic. In a series of interviews conducted over the course of a few years, from 1907–1909, several Scottish Protestant ministers admitted to a belief in fairies. One such man, the Rev. Donald MacDonald, seemed to feel that they were beings not quite angels or devils. Instead, they were "those who left heaven after the fallen angels."[77] Another Protestant minister, identified only as "a native of Ross-shire," referred to groups of fairies as "spiritual orders" and stated that they could be invisible "just as Our Saviour became invisible though in the body."[78] His interview concluded with a fascinating story he claimed as truth about a woman who used to offer milk libations to fairies. "The woman was later converted to Christ and gave up the practice, and as a result one of her cows was taken by the fairies."[79]

Somewhat unsurprisingly, given their much stronger tradition of supernatural belief, Catholic clergymen in Ireland asserted that magic was inseparable from religion. A Catholic theologian from Galway stated that magic used to call up evil spirits is unholy and forbidden by the Church, but "holy magic is practiced by carrying the Cross in Christ."[80] He added that in certain places where pagan sacrifices had been practiced, evil spirits gained control and had to be driven out by exorcism. Certainly, this priest's beliefs were consistent with the centuries-old Catholic idea that all magic is either demonic or divine.

It could be "secret knowledge of the wise, just as Christ revealed secrets to his disciples ... [or] dallying with the devil."[81]

It is likely that the main reason for the long continuation of such beliefs is that Catholicism was a sort of bridge between the rural practice of paganism and contemporary Christianity, with its many sects and variations. As Catholicism took hold, pagan festivals and rituals were subsumed into the new religion, in order for converts not to lose all that was comforting and familiar to them. The returning sun of the winter solstice became God's Son at Christmas, the Light of the World. More controversially, important functions and qualities of agrarian goddesses such as Demeter and Brigid were attributed to the Virgin Mary. As goddesses before her had been perceived for thousands of years, she became the Great Mother, the Star of the Sea, and the Lady of the Harvest.

9

Transformations

From Pagan to Christian to the Uncertain Future of Mary

Whatever their faults, no one could accuse the citizens of the middle-Eastern city of Ephesus (the Ephesians of the Bible) of lacking enthusiasm for their religious beliefs. At the dawn of Christianity, St. Paul visited the city to preach and try to gain converts for his new religion. In response, enraged crowds nearly incited a riot, vociferously shouting the praises of the city's patron goddess, Diana. The unfortunate preacher had to leave town.[1] Several centuries later, when Christianity had a significant following, a council of bishops was convened in Ephesus to debate a very important point of dogma. Should the Virgin Mary be considered mother of only the human aspect of Jesus, or did she actually give birth to God, as well? In 431, the Council of Ephesus met in a Marian church adjacent to the temple of Diana, whose worship had been suppressed by the Emperor Theodosius only fifty years before. One column with the goddess's image had been incorporated into the new church, symbolizing the common ground shared between the two Divine Mothers.[2]

Unsurprisingly, in this city so devoted to the Great Mother, Mary was declared the Theotokos, or God-Bearer, a title previously held by Diana.[3] This announcement was met with an explosion of joy by the Ephesians. They led the bishops back to their lodgings with torchlit processions and shouts of praise for the Theotokos. In later centuries, it was popularly believed that Ephesus was the place where the Virgin lived between the time of Jesus' ascension and her death.

Particularly for feminist historians, it is intriguing that the decision reached at the Council of Ephesus may have been greatly, though indirectly, influenced by a woman. According to Kate Cooper's article "Contesting the Nativity," Pulcheria, sister of the fifth-century Byzantine emperor Theodosius II, claimed that the Virgin Mary was her divine counterpart. Significantly, previous emperors had presented themselves as the earthly representatives of other gods—Diocletian had conflated himself with Jupiter, while Julian the Apostate had chosen the sun god Helios. Pulcheria's goddess, then, was Mary. To make the association stronger, she claimed lifelong virginity for herself, an assertion which was loudly contested by her detractors.

It is possible that Pulcheria came by her affinity for Mary because of the sermons given by a former Bishop of Constantinople named Atticus. He asserted that all women were blessed through Mary's virgin birth of Jesus. Because of her, they could not be considered accursed, despite the sinfulness of other women in the Bible, such as Eve, Delilah, and Jezebel. In the fifth century, the Constantine church even declared the 26th of December an annual holiday called the Virginity Festival, to commemorate Mary's erasing the sin of Eve.[4] Naturally, Pulcheria would have valued an association with a divine being whose actions had granted women such spiritual redemption.

In 431, she planned a ritual reenactment of the Nativity, in which she would take the role of Mary. However, her ceremony was prevented by Nestorius, who held the office of Bishop of Constantinople at the time. He claimed that such a rite would be sacrilegious. In retribution, shortly before the Council of Ephesus, she persuaded Emperor Theodosius to relieve Nestorius of his position. As a result, he was unable to voice his objections to bestowing the title of Theotokos on the Virgin.[5]

If people in Ephesus came to equate the Virgin Mary with their traditional goddess, they were hardly alone. Benko states, "The rapid spread of the cult of Mary is due in no small measure to the fact that people could so easily transfer to it the worship they had offered to their pagan goddess."[6] In the fourth century, women in Thrace and Upper Scythia, lands near the Black Sea, created rituals for the Virgin Mary rooted in the ancient goddess faith of their region. They baked sacred loaves of bread, which were ritually offered up to Mary in a ceremony lasting several days that involved singing and praying. There is a long tradition of such practices—the ancient Roman writer Ovid composed a poem encouraging women to offer millet cakes to the Theban goddess Mater Matuta at her annual summer festival.[7]

However, Epiphanius, the Bishop of Salamis, found this practice alarmingly inappropriate for good Christian women. He declared them heretics and gave them the derogatory name "Collyridians," meaning "followers of a small loaf of bread,"[8] the title by which they are unfortunately still known today. Stephen Benko writes that scholars have since more accurately described them as "Philomarianites" (those who love Mary). It is unlikely, though, that these women would have used any name for themselves other than Christians.[9] Not content with merely calling them nasty names, the bishop proceeded to write at length against them. Prefiguring the arguments of Protestant Reformers centuries later, he stated, "With adulterous intent they have rebelled against the one and only God, like a common whore who has been excited to the wickedness of many relations and rejected the temperate course of lawful marriage to one husband."[10]

Possibly, the main reason Epiphanius compared these women to whores and generally found them so offensive had to do with the nature of the bread they made. In ancient societies, there was a tradition of offering the Goddess baked goods shaped like female genitals. In Syracuse, sesame and honey cakes in vagina shapes called "Mylloi" were baked for Demeter as part of the festival of Thesmophoria. The triangle-shaped poppy seed cakes still eaten by Jews at Purim probably originated in pagan times as representations of the goddess Ishtar's genitals.[11]

It was almost certainly the concern with fertility in a largely agrarian society which motivated women to offer such pastries to their goddesses. Such traditions never entirely died out, even centuries later. For hundreds of years in Scotland, the first ears of corn harvested were made into a bannock called "Mary's fatling." A piece was ritually eaten by each member of the family, then hymns to the Virgin were sung while they walked "sun-wise" around a bonfire.[12] Similarly, in the city of Bagnara, participants in an annual procession wore wreaths of corn ears on their heads and necklaces of macaroni, which they laid as gifts at a Madonna statue's feet. Images of the Virgin were traditionally showered with wheat and corn in the city of Lucera on feast days, and in Sicily, such statues were offered large sheaves of grain.[13]

This same primal need for fertility also caused the legend of the Virgin's Grain Miracle to become overwhelmingly popular during the medieval era. It appears thematically in every art form of the time, from troubadours' songs to the stained glass of churches to the pages of medieval manuscripts. In *The Goddess Obscured*, Pamela Berger explains, "The assimilation of pagan imagery to later Christian concepts is to be expected when we realize that both grew out of the human experience of the agricultural cycle."[14]

At least on the surface, the tale of the grain miracle is quite simple. The Holy Family, pursued by Herod's soldiers on the Flight into Egypt, passed by a farmer who was plowing and sowing his field. Mary told the farmer that, if he was questioned by soldiers about whether he had seen them, he should reply, "Yes, when I was plowing and sowing my field." He agreed, and the Holy Family resumed their journey. Instantaneously, the newly planted grain sprouted, grew tall, and was ready for harvest. When soldiers came by shortly afterwards and questioned him, he answered just as the Virgin had instructed him. His response was technically true, though in the normal course of things it would have meant that the Holy Family had passed by several months before. The soldiers made the natural assumption that the grain had grown as usual, and they were thrown off the trail.[15]

This story, which cemented Mary's association with the successful growth of crops, was a means for farmers to reclaim their traditional grain goddesses. According to Lewis Dayton Burdick's work, *Magic and Husbandry*, there is an

Mary as Our Lady of the Harvest (courtesy Chant Art).

early Russian version of this legend in which Mary carries an image of the sun god, "showing that the story is of pagan origin and springs from belief in magic."[16] Pamela Berger states, "Farmers would sometimes attempt to re-create, in a more acceptable Christianized form, their earth mother and her ceremonial. This same adaptation process was likewise applied to the Virgin Mary."[17] During the medieval era, plays and pantomimes in which the Grain Miracle was acted out were frequently performed. They were met with much popular enthusiasm but the condemnation of Church authorities, who disapproved of their pagan origins.

Medieval plays about this tale frequently featured a scene in which the Virgin was led entirely around the field by Joseph. It seems to be a particularly strange inclusion, given the Holy Family's need for haste. This aspect of the drama could almost certainly only be a Christianized version of pagan spring rites. In this simple traditional ceremony, farmers would stage a procession in which an image of the grain goddess was carried around the edges of their fields. This was supposed to encourage the crops to grow, as well as magically protect the fields, farmers, and their families from harm.[18] In some versions of the Grain Miracle, other plants and trees were incorporated, further emphasizing Mary's role as a controller of the earth's fertility. In one version, a tree bends down to offer her its fruit.[19] In another, basil plants helpfully hide the Holy Family from their pursuers. The mint plant, however, acts against the Virgin, calling out her hiding place to the soldiers. In punishment, it is cursed forever afterward to have flowers but no seeds.[20]

As Christianity, with its predominantly masculine concept of God, spread across Europe, the worship of countless local goddesses was merged with veneration of the Virgin. In her article "In Woman's Image: An Iconography for God," Wioleta Polinska states:

> It is striking that historically not only "God the Father" and the Son but also the Holy Spirit were shown embodied as males.... It is within these restrictive conceptualities for God that the historical emergence of feminine names for God needs to be seen.[21]

Worship of agrarian goddesses seems to have been particularly strong in pre–Christian Russia and the Ukraine. A popular goddess of this region, Mary-Rusalka, was a tree deity associated with birds and animals who became intertwined with the Virgin Mary. For centuries, Russians and Ukrainians continued their ancient folk custom of dressing birch trees in women's clothes and decorating them with ribbons. Originally intended to honor their beloved tree goddess, over time, this became a means of venerating Mary.[22] A popular Christmas song from Russia still refers to the Virgin "carrying the seedcorn."[23]

Northern European pagan folk customs were also transformed into Christian celebrations. In regions of England, Scotland, Wales and Ireland, the pagan May Queen had traditionally been crowned with flowers and married to the Green Man in a fertility rite that took place annually on May 1.[24] This festival

From Pagan to Christian to the Uncertain Future of Mary 159

The Virgin Mary surrounded by symbols of the wheat and grape harvests (courtesy Chant Art).

was largely replaced by May Day celebrations, in which statues of the Virgin covered with flowers were carried in processions down flower-strewn streets. The custom of parading with Madonna statues spread throughout medieval Europe. In Spanish rural villages, images of the Virgin were carried through the streets every year to ensure sufficient rain for the crops. There is even a thirteenth-century tale from Liege in which a drought occurred because villagers neglected to appeal to Mary. Her name and image were accidentally omitted in a procession with statues of saints, intended to procure divine assistance with obtaining the right amount of rain.[25]

It was commonly believed that statues of Mary could miraculously bring rain in times of drought, as well as provide protection against extreme storms. The Madonna of Impruneta (a town near Florence) was perhaps the most celebrated rainmaker in history. This statue was rewarded with garlands of flowers if spring rains were normal, but it was covered in rubbish if there was too much, flooding the crops.[26] In fourteenth-century Italy, it was believed that honoring the Virgin Mary on Saturdays protected the grapevines from "tempests." And a black Madonna statue was supposedly responsible for keeping the town of Murat (Cantal) safe from lightning.[27]

At least one traditional agrarian custom which was Christianized specifically applied to women. Annually, on February 2, women who had given birth over the course of the previous year would come to church for a purification ceremony in which they received a specially blessed candle. This was meant to mirror the Purification of the Virgin Mary, which supposedly took place on that date after Jesus was born. In pre–Christian times, women would carry torches through the fields each year in February, to purify the ground for new seeds. They did this as a way of ritually re-enacting the earth goddess Demeter's search for her daughter Persephone, the maiden goddess of spring. It was believed that doing so would help to obtain the goddess's goodwill and a successful harvest.[28]

Alistair MacGregor's article "Candlemas: A Festival of Roman Origin" focuses on the transition process of this celebration from pagan to Christian. In the twelfth century, Pope Innocent III wrote that the "holy fathers" had been unable to do away with the beloved custom in honor of Demeter and Persephone, so it was turned into a Marian festival.[29] Candles were almost certainly made the focus of this ceremony in order to conflate it with Demeter's torch festival. Furthermore, the Latin for wax candle is "cereus," a word remarkably similar to the goddess's Roman name "Ceres." Additional proof linking the two holidays together comes from the fact that clergy always wore black vestments for Candlemas, the color traditionally used to symbolize Ceres' mourning for her daughter.[30] The ritual was thus carried over into the post–Christian world, purifying women with candles (torches) before a new "seed" could be planted in their wombs.

One goddess that was more or less directly transmuted into the Virgin

Mary was the Egyptian deity Isis. Like Mary, this maternal goddess was known for protecting young children and women in labor. Such areas of specialization reflected many women's concerns, so she became tremendously popular in Rome after Egypt became a province of the Empire. Benko writes:

> The Greek and Roman goddesses were in charge of all female functions, presiding over marriage, childbirth, and similar issues.... In popular piety simple believers still turn to [Mary] with the same problems our pagan ancestors brought to their goddesses.[31]

Art featuring Isis was transformed into Marian imagery. Like the Virgin, Isis was frequently depicted seated on a throne, suckling her divine infant son (the god Horus). Pagan statues of Isis and Horus were "baptized" and rededicated as Marian objects.[32] This Christian effort was so successful that, well into the medieval era, images originally intended to portray Isis still appeared on Christian altars as representations of Mary. Perhaps the most famous example of this is the black statue of Isis in Paris that was venerated as the Virgin Mary until the sixteenth century.[33]

A transformed pagan goddess ritual took place as recently as 1979, when Pope John Paul II visited the much-venerated statue of the Black Virgin of Czestochowa, in his home country of Poland. For the occasion, this Madonna was dressed, not in the flowers of fertility, but in a robe and crown covered in magnificent jewels to symbolize her role as the Queen of Heaven. This heavily adorned statue was then carried through the streets in a procession. Benko points out:

> Such crownings are strongly reminiscent of ancient processions honoring statues of goddesses, such as Athene, with a new peplos [Greek women's robe].... This seems to be the way that devoted followers of the goddess, from pagan to modern times can best express their love for the one they sense to be alive behind her material likeness. A queen, after all, must have wealth.[34]

In his work *The Virgin Goddess*, Stephen Benko's most controversial assertion is that more than just the maternal qualities of ancient goddesses were transferred over to Mary. Her very status as the Virgin Mother, he claims, was a result of early Christians' efforts to conflate Mary with the much-loved goddess Cybele. Benko believes that for the central Christian idea of salvation, it is Jesus' death and resurrection that matter, not Mary's lack of a sexual nature. He writes:

> For minds accustomed to thinking in the categories of the prevalent pagan culture, the mother of the Son of God could have no lesser dignity than the Great Mother of the gods, the favorite subject of popular piety in the East.[35]

It was, in other words, Mary's status as both a virgin and mother that allowed her to be equated with Cybele, notably the first deity in recorded history to bear the title of Virgin Mother. This somewhat radical claim is substantiated by similarities between Christ's crucifixion and resurrection and the legend of the death of Cybele's consort, Attis. In penance for his unfaithfulness to her, he castrates himself at the foot of a pine tree (cross) and dies. Pieta-like, Cybele ministers to his dead body, giving it the proper funerary rites and mourning. Attis, however, is resurrected, and the Great Mother Cybele rejoices in her renewed hope and joy.[36] It is also worth noting that the still existing Marian church of Monte Vergine (the Virgin's Mountain) near Naples, Italy, was originally a shrine for the goddess Cybele. Many stones from the original pagan structure were used to build the site's current church.[37]

Places long associated with goddess worship in many European countries were frequently transformed into sacred Marian sites. Edgar and Canute, Christian kings of England in the tenth and eleventh centuries, respectively, found pagan worship at holy rivers, wells, and fountains particularly difficult to discourage. Indeed, it persisted so strongly, despite Church disapproval, that the kings had to enact laws against it.[38] In other countries, however, the less contentious solution of turning the sites into Christian holy places was often utilized. In France, Chartres Cathedral, a church particularly rich with Marian artistic imagery, was built over a spring sacred to the Gallic Goddess in pre–Christian times.

It was the Irish, however, who seemed to take to this idea with the greatest enthusiasm. In Ireland, 86 percent of all Christian shrines, including Our Lady of Knock, are based on wells once dedicated to the Celtic goddess Brigid. This deity was also transformed herself — into the still popular St. Brigid. St. Patrick, in a rite amusingly reminiscent of a Celtic fertility ritual, supposedly "Christianized" Brigid's sites by thrusting his staff into each of her holy wells.[39] As late as 1850, Irish scholars such as William Wilde, father of the famous writer Oscar Wilde, were asserting that Christian rites held at holy wells were (perhaps overly) influenced by pagan practices. He stated, "Unchristian rites and ceremonies ... still attend the practices observed there by the uneducated."[40]

As the Roman Empire became medieval Europe, increasing numbers of pagan goddesses were transformed into the Virgin Mary. However, Marianists of the time were not content to stop there. Even the Jewish faith was not immune from Marian piety. In the ninth century, prolific Christian author and monk Rhabanus Maurus proposed a solution to the centuries-old theological problem of Queen Esther. This Jewish heroine of the Old Testament interceded with her husband, King Ahasuerus, to save her people from genocide. However, the inclusion of Esther's story in the Bible troubled medieval theologians, since she did not seem to be particularly pious. In fact, God's name does not even appear throughout the entire first ten chapters. Rhabanus' answer to this quandary was simple; he proposed that she prefigured the Virgin Mary. According to this medieval theologian, Esther, the Queen of Persia, showed concern for her people, the Jews, just as Mary, the Queen of Heaven, feels for her people, the Christians. As Esther interceded with Ahasuerus to save the Jews from destruction, the Virgin will intercede with Christ on Judgment Day to save sinners from hell.[41]

With few exceptions, people saw little cause to take issue with the blending of Christian and pagan ideology that comprised religion in the Middle Ages. All of this changed, however, with the advent of Protestant Reformers during the sixteenth century. Martin Luther, the founder of Lutheranism and one of the first successful reformers of the Church, began to radically downplay the importance of Mary. Stating that it was better to take too much away from her than from the Grace of God, Luther began to see faith "like a zero-sum game in which the more Mary loses, the more Christ wins."[42]

Luther strongly denied that God had chosen her to bear Jesus as a result of any special merit of her own. Mary, he said, had no trace of divinity. He claimed that she was sinful, like the rest of humanity, and utterly dependent on divine Grace. Insisting that she had no part in Christ's decisions on Judgment Day, he instructed his followers to appeal to Jesus alone for salvation.[43] Strengthening the Father by casting out the Mother, Luther denied the feminine dimension of the sacred, declaring himself firmly against "the still unimpeachable vision of the old Earth-cults."[44]

As a result of the Protestant Reformation begun by Luther, women were given fewer career options. Female monasticism, largely the product of a society that venerated the Virgin, was non-existent in the Protestant faith. The possibility of becoming a nun or powerful abbess in a convent was suddenly gone. After all, if Mary was a simple housewife, surely all women were meant to be the same. Ruether asserts, "Luther went on to insist that women's sphere was limited to the household by divine decree."[45] Perhaps nothing indicates this more clearly than the fact that in the sixteenth century, Reformers added the word "obey" to marriage vows for women.

Despite this anti-feminist climate, Elizabeth I, the Protestant Queen of England, was quick to use the dissolution of all things Marian to her advantage. Our Lady of Walsingham, the most beloved shrine to the Virgin in England, had been destroyed by her father, King Henry VIII, complete with its Madonna statue known as the Virgin Queen. There is some possibility that the act had personal overtones, since he had unsuccessfully appealed to Our Lady of Walsingham for a male heir. Shrewdly taking Mary's title of Virgin Queen for herself, Elizabeth set about filling the void left by the dismantled Cult of the Virgin. She began the Cult of Gloriana, with herself as the secular replacement for Mary.[46] Over the course of her reign, this Marian association was increasingly important. It became the justification for remaining permanently single and not producing an heir to the throne. Elizabeth's assumption of the role of Virgin Queen gave her status as a single woman divine associations, imbuing her unprecedented decision with God's tacit approval.

The idea of associating Tudor-era Queens with the Virgin Mary did not begin with Elizabeth. Surprisingly, Anne Boleyn, Elizabeth's mother, was associated with Mary, despite her status as the patroness of English Protestantism. In one of her official coronation pageants, a song was presented which praised

Mary surrounded by her symbols, many of which were appropriated by Queen Elizabeth I (courtesy Chant Art).

Anne's heraldic white falcon in Marian terms—for its virginal chastity and its fruitfulness. Another included a tableau featuring a lady with a sign saying "Come my love, you shall be crowned," simultaneously evoking the language of both the Song of Songs and the Coronation of the Virgin.[47] In a somewhat ironic turn, Boleyn was also associated in these pageants with her namesake, St. Anne, the Virgin Mary's mother, who famously bore only female children. Trouble with her children's gender ultimately brought about Boleyn's demise at the command of her husband.

Elizabeth's sister and immediate predecessor, Mary I, was particularly strongly associated with the Virgin Mary. In part, this was necessary to establish her right to rule. As the first queen regnant since Matilda in the twelfth century, conflating Queen Mary with her divine counterpart in heaven helped to overcome English reluctance to female rule. The Marian identification, however, was somewhat inevitable, since the Queen restored Catholicism to her nation and even shared the Virgin's name.[48] William Wizeman emphasizes this association in his article "The Virgin Mary in the Reign of Mary Tudor":

> The accentuation of the cult of the Virgin in Marian England also found expression in the praise of Mary Tudor.... Authors associated their Queen with the Queen of Heaven in language used otherwise exclusively for the latter, to underscore Queen Mary's essential role in England's re–Catholicization. As one Mary possessed an essential role in salvation, so the other possessed an essential role in England's participation in salvation. Both Marys were intercessors, acting for others' redemption.[49]

Unlike Queens before her, however, Elizabeth intended to eclipse the Virgin Mary, rather than simply become conflated with her. This desire was made obvious by her startling action at Euston Hall, the home of Edward Rookwood, a secret Catholic. Euston Hall was a planned stop for Elizabeth on a "royal progress," a journey commonly undertaken by a monarch who wished to survey his or her domain. In the midst of a country dance presented for the Queen's entertainment, a statue of the Virgin Mary was discovered, hidden under some bales in Rookwood's hay house. Apparently disgusted, Elizabeth commanded that the image should be placed in the fire. Hackett comments, "The Virgin Mary is set up against the Virgin Queen Elizabeth; the 'false' virgin is destroyed, thereby reinforcing the authority of the 'true' virgin."[50] Rookwood had his estate confiscated as punishment for his recusancy.

Elizabeth incorporated into her official portraits a multitude of symbols that had traditionally been used to denote Mary, including roses, pearls, stars, and the moon. Just as Catholics had traditionally demanded veneration for depictions of the Virgin, images of Queen Elizabeth came to be, at least in some sense, revered. According to Frances E. Dolan, in 1591, a man known only by the name of Hacket was brought up on charges of treason. Among his offenses was an assault on a portrait of the Queen, which he "maliciously" attacked by thrusting an "iron instrument" into the heart of her painted image. He paid the ultimate price for his violent political commentary — the conviction led to his execution.[51]

In order to compensate for the lack of Marian feasts, new patriotic holidays were added to the calendar. November 17 became Accession Day, an annual commemoration of Elizabeth's taking the throne of England. Far more offensive to Catholics, however, was the celebration of the Queen's birthday each September 7, which coincided with their liturgical feast for the birth of Mary. Protestants took Queen Elizabeth's birthday to be something of a divine omen, signifying that God himself wished her to be conflated with the Virgin. Eventually, this was further substantiated by the fact that Elizabeth's death occurred on March 24 — the eve of the Annunciation.[52]

The Queen's campaign to eradicate the Virgin Mary in favor of herself was largely successful. Protestant English subjects began to substitute the phrase, "Long Live Eliza" for "Hail Mary." There was even a strange case in which a man called Miles Fry renamed himself "Emanuel Plantagenet," claiming that he was the miraculous son of Elizabeth and God. According to Fry's 1587 letter to court official Lord Burghley, he believed that he was taken from Elizabeth at birth by the Angel Gabriel and brought to his adoptive mother, Joan Fry. Levin comments:

> Fry's delusion is an interesting subtext on Elizabeth's presentation to her people as their "mother," a Virgin Queen who substituted for the worship of the Virgin Mary. For poor Miles Fry, Elizabeth's self-presentation was all too successful.[53]

Anti-Marianist feeling became so strong during Queen Elizabeth's reign that less than fifty years after her death, the English House of Commons ordered that all pictures representing the Virgin Mary should be burned.[54] This, however, was after the disastrous reign of Charles I, the only English king in history to be deposed and beheaded. His marriage to an openly Catholic princess, who became conflated with the Virgin Mary, did nothing to endear him to his Protestant subjects. Admittedly, some of their objections to him were of an entirely secular nature, having to do with the merits of divine right (vs. constitutional monarchy). Others, however, objected to his rule largely on religious grounds.

James I arranged a marriage for his heir, Charles, to a Catholic French princess named Henrietta Maria. As part of the marriage contract, she was permitted free exercise of her religion, as well as her own chapel. Even more dangerously, she was allowed to control her children's education and religious allegiance until they were thirteen. For the first time since the reign of the infamous "Bloody Mary," England had a Catholic Queen who was likely to raise heirs to the throne in the "popish" faith.[55]

Henrietta Maria did nothing to dispel Protestant consternation about her Catholicism. She declined to attend, let alone participate in, her husband's coronation, since it was a ceremony of the Church of England. Refusing to receive her crown from a "heretic," she became the first uncrowned consort in English history.[56] Openly devoting herself to the Virgin, she dedicated her elaborate new chapel at Somerset House to Mary. It became the location for meetings of the Arch-Confraternity of the Holy Rosary, which Henrietta Maria led herself. The chapel itself contained many images of the Virgin Mary, and its Capuchin staff adopted her as their official patron. Like Elizabeth before her, Henrietta Maria became conflated with the Virgin, but in this case, the association for most of her subjects was a negative one.

She was frequently referred to as a "mediatrix" for Catholicism — just as Mary intervened on behalf of her devotees with Jesus in heaven, it was believed that Henrietta Maria interceded for English Catholics with King Charles. So great was her supposed influence over her husband, political writers of the time began referring to the idea of "The Great Eclipse," in which Henrietta Maria, symbolized by the Marian-identified moon, was eclipsing the authority of King Charles, who was associated with the sun.[57]

Her conflation with the Virgin was further reinforced by her abundant fertility. Much to the chagrin of English Protestants, God seemed to bless this foreign Catholic queen with nearly constant pregnancy. Ultimately, she bore nine children, ensuring the succession of her bloodline to the throne. Echoing the nature symbolism of Mary, Henrietta Maria was referred to by Catholic supporters as a "fruitful vine."[58] Calling upon the Virgin Mary in her traditional role of protector of women in childbirth, Henrietta Maria prayed for her assistance at each labor. Once, during a particularly "bad lying-in," the Queen asserted she was the recipient of Mary's direct intervention.[59]

When the victory of Protestant forces compelled Henrietta Maria to flee the country, her Somerset House chapel was broken open and defaced by order of Parliament. The Capuchins who staffed it were imprisoned.[60] However, the Marian Queen had the proverbial last laugh. Just as the English Protestants had feared, her son Charles II, who was brought back to the throne in the Restoration, was secretly Catholic and asked for Catholic last rites just before his death.

Despite the long history of Marian devotion, there are no guarantees for its survival in the future. However, there are plenty of signs indicating that humanity's need for a female face of God has never abated. For some women today, the desire for the divine feminine is so intense, they feel compelled to entirely break away from Judeo-Christian modes of thought and practice. Rosemary Radford Ruether documents the recent rise of Wicca, a still existing goddess-centered religious movement in her book *Goddesses and the Divine Feminine*. She states:

> Circles of women and some men gathered around worship of the "Goddess," presumed to be the original deity of human history. Goddess worship was linked to "female" values that promoted peace, harmony with nature, and love

for all.... The reclaiming of Goddess worship took on the vision of a redemption of humanity.[61]

Despite the attractions of a true goddess-oriented religion, the majority of contemporary Western women still find it unacceptable to live without any form of Christian faith. Claire E. Wolfteich's 2002 book *Navigating New Terrain: Work and Women's Spiritual Lives*, shows that some still manage to think of the Virgin Mary in a positive light, despite the anti–Marian rhetoric common in society today. Like the work of previous feminist scholars, her book points out that, during the 1960s and 1970s, many women became deeply dissatisfied with the idea of Mary as a behavioral model. Wolfteich mentions Mary Gordon, a writer of this era who referred to the Virgin as "a stick to beat smart girls with."[62]

However, she counters this example with the 1964 letters to *Commonweal* magazine of a woman who referred to herself as "Mrs. James Arnold." Defending the choices of working Catholic women, she wrote that modern women could say "yes" to God, like Mary did, "over the cradle, the lecture podium, the automatic washer, the wheel of a car, the kitchen range or the desk — or over all of them."[63] In a more contemporary example, Wolfteich mentions a woman named Eileen Farrell, who stated in an interview given in 2000 that "The Blessed Mother is my friend."[64] Finally, there is Wolfteich's own assessment of the Virgin Mary as an example for women:

> Most [women] can respond to God by walking along one of a number of different paths. What is most important is that — no matter the particular path, no matter the confusing or painful steps along the way — we find it in us to whisper a yes to God. Mary stands before us as a model for this task.[65]

In contrast to Wolfteich's confident Marian spirituality, many women have found it necessary to form a sort of uneasy truce with Christianity. Somehow, they reconcile the religious beliefs they have held since earliest childhood with their yearning to recognize themselves in God's image. Perhaps nothing in our society is a clearer indication of this than the overwhelming popularity of Dan Brown's 2003 novel *The Da Vinci Code*. Some churches, especially more traditional Protestant ones, have chosen to simply ignore its influence on contemporary women's spirituality. However, despite the fact that it is a work of fiction, it has permanently altered how many people think of Mary Magdalene and even Jesus. It has also provided the basis for a dialogue among millions of people about gender roles within the Church.

10

Two Marys

The Virgin and the (Repentant) Whore

The Da Vinci Code is a novel which has sold over forty million copies since its publication in 2003. In it, author Dan Brown suggests that, for almost 2000 years, the Catholic Church covered up Jesus' marriage to Mary Magdalene, as well as the subsequent birth of their child. He also proposes that there is a parallel Christian community which venerates Mary Magdalene as Christ's wife and protects their descendants. Despite the book's status as a work of fiction, the ideas it contains have taken root in the minds of millions of contemporary people. Many have even come to believe that there has indeed been a Catholic conspiracy that has carefully covered up Jesus' marital status for thousands of years. Others, while rejecting the literal truth of the book, began thinking of Mary Magdalene as the manifestation of the Divine Feminine. Naturally, this groundswell of devotion to Magdalene has caused much consternation among more mainstream Christians, including clergy members.

In an article for the internet publication *Catholic Online*, Maurice Timothy Reidy, obviously somewhat exasperated by the persistence of Brown's ideas, attempts an eight-point explanation of why this novel has remained extremely popular. Reidy's reason number four, "Women and the Church," cites women's interest in what has been termed "the lost sacred feminine" in *The Da Vinci Code*. He states, "I suspect the notion that the church 'subjugated women' resonates with many women today ... they might find something attractive about a Christian community that reveres 'the feminine.'"[1] Such assertions would probably be considered extreme understatements by many feminist scholars, such as those quoted in Kara Alaimo's *Da Vinci Code* article for *Women's E-News*. Rosalind Miles, founder of the Center for Women's Studies at Coventry Polytechnic, simply dismisses the book's popularity. She claims it has only been so well received because the author is a man and the work is fiction. However, Judith Plaskow, professor of religious studies at Manhattan College, believes that current interest in Brown's novel is based on — and has resulted in — "questions about women's place in religious history for a lot of people who never thought about it before."[2]

Before the publication of the *Da Vinci Code*, however, the idea that Mary Magdalene was a viable, and even preferable, model for women had been proposed. In 1993, Susan Haskins issued a challenge to Christian women in her book *Mary Magdalen, Myth and Metaphor*. In this work, she claims that women's interest in Magdalene was strong even in the 1950s and early 1960s, when the Church was actively encouraging girls to look to the Virgin Mary as their model. A few girls had the "ingenuity and imagination" to pattern their lives instead on that of Mary Magdalene, who had sinned and been forgiven. She further asserts that certain societal ills, such as the Catholic Church's refusal to ordain women, are the direct result of idealization of the Virgin. Haskins states:

> It is perhaps time to recognize the true feminine model [Mary Magdalene], one which, according to the gospels, embodies strength, courage and independence, all feminine qualities which the Church has attempted to suppress by subordinating women to the model it has created, the passive virgin and mother.[3]

Girls who chose Magdalene as a role model in the mid-twentieth century were, at least to some degree, setting themselves in opposition to Church teachings. However, even some respected theologians of the time wished to cleanse Magdalene's image of its traditional taint. An article called "Mary Magdalene in Scripture and Tradition" by Episcopalian minister Francis C. Lightborn appeared in the spring, 1959 issue of *Religion in Life*. Boldly defending Magdalene's honor, Lightborn begins his work with the statement, "Mary Magdalene is a much maligned woman."[4] He goes on to argue that, despite popular belief, there is no real scriptural evidence that she had a career as a prostitute before meeting Jesus. Rather, her true role in the New Testament was something much different. She was a member of a group of women who accompanied Jesus on His travels, providing Him with financial support. He writes, "If this be true, we may see in Mary Magdalene and her fellow workers a prototype of ... ladies' aid societies, women's guilds, and the like."[5]

In 1969, the Catholic Church renamed the day dedicated to her in the liturgical calendar (July 22), calling it the Feast of Mary Magdalene, Witness to the Resurrection, instead of its previous appellation, the Feast of Mary Magdalene the Repentant Sinner.[6] Galen C. Knutson, a Lutheran minister, praised the decision to change the focus of her feast day, calling it "an act of courage" of the Catholic Church. As early as the seventh century, there was a sharp divergence between Eastern and Western official teachings about her, and the post–Vatican II Church was starting to heal this rift. Knutson explains, "In the West, Mary Magdalene was being portrayed as a penitent prostitute, while in the East she was believed to have lived with Mary, the mother of Jesus, and with John, was a teacher of holiness and was herself a virgin."[7]

The sixth-century theologian Gregory the Great was probably originally responsible for casting her in the role of penitent whore. In the eleventh through thirteenth centuries, this idea was popularized by Dominican clergy at Vezelay, France, where her bones were thought to be.[8] Even in medieval Europe, however, there were those who questioned Gregory's version of Mary Magdalene. In the sermons of Dominican priest St. Vincent Ferrer, she is characterized not as a whore but a *cortezia*, "a girl of easy manners whose behavior may be considered more as frivolous, unconsciously encouraging gossip, than as sinful."[9]

In the fifteenth century, Valencian abbess Isabel de Villena presented a similar version of Magdalene in her touching work, *Vita Christi*. The daughter of writer Enrique de Villena, Isabel shows her inherited talent in a particularly poetic passage. In it, she describes Mary Magdalene crying behind her fan at her discovery of true love for Jesus. De Villena's Magdalene, though certainly guilty of being frivolous girl, is unquestionably a virgin. Her bad reputation is derived from malicious gossip, not actual sexual acts.[10]

In France, interest in Mary Magdalene was renewed in 1516, when the court of Francis I undertook a pilgrimage to two of her shrines. In commemoration of this event, the Queen Mother, Louise de Savoy, commissioned a lavishly illustrated biography of the saint.[11] Perhaps influenced by these events, the following year, theological scholar Jacques Lefevre d'Etaples published a critique of Magdalene's traditional characterization as a repentant whore. In the furor that ensued, d'Etaples was censured by the theological faculty of the Sorbonne, and his work was banned by the pope himself. Fifteen major treatises were written on the topic during the subsequent three years, and the controversy ultimately raged for the next 350.[12]

Although generally considered a whore, Mary Magdalene also served as an accessible, realistic role model for women during the Middle Ages. Medieval theologian Hildebert of Le Mans pointed out that there were far more people who sinned and repented than lived a blameless life, like the Virgin Mary. Therefore, more people "profit from the example of Mary Magdalene."[13] Some medieval preachers, such as the Franciscan friar Ludovicus and Dominican preacher Tommaso Agni da Lentini, proposed that the Virgin Mary and Mary Magdalene represented two complementary paths to salvation. The Virgin's was the way of innocence, while Magdalene's road was that of penance.

Le Mans asserted that their sharing the name of Mary, which meant Star of the Sea, was no coincidence. Both, he claimed, are metaphorical lights to follow — one the great light of virtue and immaculate life, the other the lesser light of penitence and life made white after sin.[14] In the twelfth century, wandering preacher Robert of Arbrissel (who apparently attracted quite a large female following) emphasized this idea when he founded a double monastery for women at Fontevrault. Virgins and widows were to live in a house "under the patronage of the Virgin Mary," while the residence for "penitents" was dedicated to Mary Magdalene. Eleanor of Acquitaine, the famously feminist medieval queen of France and, subsequently, England, retired to Magdalene's house at the end of her life.[15]

Like Queen Eleanor, who was considered far from saintly in her day, many aristocratic women during the Renaissance found Mary Magdalene appealing. They commissioned art which portrayed her fashionably dressed in the opulent gowns and jewels most popular among their contemporaries. This was probably because she represented the promise of their own salvation, despite the worldliness of their daily lives. Feminist scholar Grieco writes:

> Many women of the elite found in the Magdalene a model of sanctity that promised them an eventual pardon for the ostentatious consumption and parade of worldly wealth they were obliged to adopt in order to maintain their husbands' rank and social prestige as well as their own. Fully cognizant of contradiction between their worldly ways the otherworldly ideals of the Church, these women doubtless saw in the Magdalene a promise of future redemption.[16]

Magdalenist theologians of the time claimed that her sincere repentance, combined with vigilance in guarding her chastity after conversion, transformed Mary the Sinner into a virginal enclosed garden, like the Virgin Mary. Because of this, Magdalene was rewarded in heaven with a floral crown, otherwise reserved for virgins, and a position at the head of the heavenly choir. This idea was received enthusiastically by married women, who had previously been taught that their sexuality made them eligible for only thirty percent of the blessings available to virgins.[17] Mary Magdalene was looked upon as the woman who redeemed Eve's sin of sexuality in a more realistic and accessible manner than the Virgin Mary. Haskins writes:

> With the intensified emphasis on her role as repentant sinner in the Middle Ages, she represented the sexuate feminine redeemed, and therefore rendered sexless. In this way, she stood for Eve redeemed, not, like the Virgin, as Eve's antithesis, but rather as her more fully developed counterpart.[18]

It was also commonly believed during the Middle Ages that Mary Magdalene had a good and longstanding relationship with the Virgin Mary. Paintings created during the late medieval and early modern period depict her being present at several important events in the Virgin's life. She is frequently there when Jesus is not present, attending even the Holy Mother's assumption into heaven.[19] Magdalene was sometimes conflated with the bride at the Biblical wedding at Cana, where Jesus performed his first miracle at his mother's behest. So prevalent was this idea in medieval society that Jacobus de Voragine, who seemed to find it rather offensive, took great pains to deny it in *The Golden Legend*.[20]

In medieval art and literature, Mary Magdalene was often portrayed as the Virgin Mary's sole female support during Christ's crucifixion. It was sometimes said that Jesus' mother repaired to Magdalene's house during His flagellation.[21] In other medieval legends, she supported the Virgin Mary when she fainted at the foot of the cross, though this was a controversial idea. Theologians such as St. Ambrose believed that the Virgin reacted calmly to the crucifixion because she had foreknowledge of her Son's resurrection.[22]

Some medieval theologians bristled at the idea that the Holy Mother could have had such a close relationship with a sinful woman like Magdalene. However, according to the narrative of medieval miracle legends, the Virgin Mary generally took an attitude of kindness and forgiveness toward "fallen women." In one such tale, a nun is tempted by a man into leaving the safety of her convent for him. Once he has deflowered her, he abandons her, and she is forced to become a prostitute to support herself. Returning to her cloister years later in despair, the erstwhile nun finds that the Virgin Mary had taken on her face and form in the convent for all the years she was absent. This unforeseen circumstance allows her to return joyously with no one the wiser. In another legend, the Virgin Mary intercedes with Jesus to obtain forgiveness for an unrepentant whore, whose only act of piety is to pray on behalf of a holy hermit.[23]

Many people during the medieval era believed that the two Marys sometimes worked together to help people. When a peasant in northern France labored in his field on Mary Magdalene's feast day, lightning supposedly struck him in retribution, severely burning his legs and killing his oxen. The Marys subsequently took pity on him, however. Magdalene cured his burns, then the Virgin restored his ability to walk on the feast day of her Assumption.[24] In the thirteenth century, Italian nun Gherardesca da Pisa had a vision in which both the Virgin and Magdalene helped her recover from combat with a demon. Mary Magdalene stripped Gherardesca of her tattered and bloody garments and wrapped her in a cloak, while the Virgin found fresh clothing for her and gave her the kiss of peace.[25]

Medieval theologian Raymond of Capua wrote that God intended for the Virgin Mary and Mary Magdalene to have a mother-daughter relationship.[26] In the medieval bestseller, *Meditations on the Life of Christ*, however, they seem more like mother and daughter-in-law. In this book, the apocryphal story is told of Jesus visiting the Virgin before His Scriptural appearance to Magdalene. After He has spoken with His mother, He asks her permission to seek out Mary Magdalene. Haskins states, "Much in the way of a mother whose son has put her before his wife, and therefore her daughter-in-law, the Virgin approves 'very much.'"[27]

Arising simultaneously with the belief that Magdalene interacted with the Virgin—both during their earthly lives and in heaven—was ideology that conflated the two Marys. Magdalene also began to take on the roles of both virgin and mother. She was considered by many theologians to be sexually sinless, either because her post-conversion purity had restored virginity to her or because she was a "virgin of the mind." By the thirteenth century, she was also seen as a mother figure, with "generative, nutritive and protective qualities."[28]

Miracle legends about Magdalene frequently involved her intercession on behalf of childless women, those who had difficult births, or those whose infant children died. Her association with motherhood was so strong in Italy that "nuptial dolls" were frequently made in her image for brides' trousseaux. They were particularly beautiful, since their magical function was to help women produce attractive children. Supposedly, a baby would resemble the saint's image that a mother used for contemplation while pregnant.[29]

In the fourteenth century, Giovanna I was heir to the Angevin kingdoms of Provence and Naples, as well as the faith of a strongly Magdalenist family. She appealed to the saint for aid during her difficult first pregnancy and, apparently, succeeded in obtaining it. In return for Mary Magdalene's divine intervention, Giovanna promised that she would provide an annual endowment to the saint's Neapolitan shrine of one hundred measures of salt. Records exist of the "debt" being paid. When she was in a ship caught in a terrible storm at sea, the queen appealed to Magdalene for help again. Echoing the Virgin's roles of "Star of the Sea" and "Help of Sailors," Mary Magdalene came through for Giovanna. The saint was rewarded with a gift of nine hundred gold florins for her basilica at Saint-Maximin.[30]

Many of the Virgin's traditional spiritual functions were assumed by Magdalene. In the fourteenth century, pilgrims' badges featuring Mary Magdalene's image were sold by the Dominican custodians of the Saint-Maximin shrine. They were meant to inspire the faithful to repent of their sins, as Mary Magdalene had.[31] Wealthy women provided funding for new churches in her honor, as well as elaborate devotional books about Magdalene. In the fifteenth century, English countess Isabel Bourchier commissioned the friar Osbern Bokenham to write a life of Mary Magdalene to aid in her meditations. She asserted in a letter to him that she had "special devotion of pure affection" for the saint.[32] Like the Virgin's resting place, Magdalene's burial site became an important location for her post-mortem miracles. The faithful who visited her tomb had all manner of troubles cured there. The sick were healed, the blind had their sight restored, and those possessed by demons were relieved of their spiritual interlopers.[33]

Magdalene also began appearing in the visions of holy women, such as the fifteenth-century saint, Francesca Romana. The mystic claimed that Mary repeatedly emphasized the need for humility and self-abasement in order to attain God's love.[34] Julian of Norwich, the remarkable female fourteenth-century visionary and theological author, expressed in her writings a desire to be with Magdalene at Christ's passion. Elisabeth Koenig explains, "[Julian] wants to 'be like' Mary Magdalene; she wants to participate in Christ's passion and to learn of God's love from that experience as she imagines the Magdalene to have done."[35] Fortunately for Julian, this opportunity later comes, by means of a vision, although she is very ill and in a great deal of pain at the time. During her suffering, almost as if she is taking part in a passion play, she assumes the role of Mary Magdalene at the foot of the cross. She is permitted to see Jesus' suffering through the saint's eyes, as well as experience her subsequent joy at the Resurrection.[36]

One role Magdalene came to share with the Virgin, which initially seems particularly strange, is that of patroness of orders of nuns. However, as one who had sat at the feet of Jesus to learn his teachings, she was considered an ideal model and guide for the contemplative life. One Dominican preacher, Guillaume Peyraut, wrote that while Mary Magdalene's liturgical feast day (July 22) was celebrated by everyone, it was of particular importance to enclosed nuns. This was primarily because they lead the contemplative life, of which Mary was the example and mirror. By the mid-twelfth century, convents of Benedictine, Premonstratensian, and Cistercian nuns dedicated to Mary Magdalene had been founded throughout Europe. By the early fourteenth, however, Italy had far outstripped any other country in its quantities of Magdalenist enclosed nuns.[37]

During this time, many Italian monastic women, even in convents not directly associated with the saint, assumed the name Sister Magdalena or Madalena when they took their vows to become nuns. However, this is hardly surprising, since the name was popular overall. In Tuscany, Maddelena was one of the most popular names for baby girls.[38] A religious order was established in fourteenth-century Naples called the Order of Magdalene, which consisted of nuns who were reformed prostitutes. The members of this order were sometimes called Magdalenettes.[39] Sancia, wife of the Angevin king Robert the Wise, who was very devoted to Mary Magdalene, founded a Magdalenist convent for reformed prostitutes in 1342. It was so successful that she founded another one later that year, though the second was dedicated to Mary of Egypt, another prostitute-turned-saint.[40]

A similar institution called the Magdalen house was set up in mid-eighteenth century London, though the women it housed did not become nuns. It was established by a philanthropic merchant named Jonas Hanway, in order to give prostitutes an alternative to leading sinful lives. Hanway was also somewhat well known, during his lifetime, for being the first man in London to carry an umbrella. The institution attracted the attention of famous men such as Horace Walpole, whose account of his visit there is still in print, as well as Dryden, who composed hymns for the residents.[41]

Perhaps most important for medieval women, however, was that both the Virgin Mary and Mary Magdalene provided them with examples to counter misogynistic Church teachings. When women were accused of being uncontrollably sexual, they could point to the Virgin Mary in response. Mary Magdalene was the counter-argument against the Church-sanctioned idea that women should be seen and not heard. Hadn't her words, after all, first brought the news of Jesus' Resurrection to the Apostles? In addition, there was the widely believed apocryphal story about Magdalene's travels in France, where she preached among the pagans. Beatrice, the thirteenth-century Angevin queen, claimed that her family line stemmed from the first monarch of Provence converted to Christianity by Mary Magdalene.[42]

During the second half of the fourteenth century, the idea of Magdalene as the messenger of good, Christian ideas increased in popularity, especially among women. Christine de Pisan, bestselling author of the *Book of the City of Ladies*, argued in her work that if women's speech was "blameworthy and of ... small authority, as some men argue," Jesus would not have chosen "the blessed Magdalene" to announce the Resurrection to the apostles.[43] During this same period, St. Catherine of Siena used the example of Mary Magdalene's ministry to justify her own decision to preach. Despite widespread censure, Catherine took to the pulpit, claiming that God had commanded her to do so. According to this medieval saint, the Lord wanted women, such as Magdalene and herself, to preach in order to confound arrogant men's pride. This was accomplished by the example of females who, weak and ignorant as they were, could nonetheless save souls.[44]

Also in the late fourteenth century, the heretical sect known as the Lollards made its mark on history. Members believed that both men and women had the authority to preach, an idea which Church authorities considered incredibly dangerous. When a Lollard named Walter Brut was tried for heresy in 1381, he held up Magdalene's example as a part of his defense. He claimed that "blessed Mary Magdalen" had converted pagans to Christianity with her public preaching and, as a result, she was given the title "Apostle of Apostles."[45] In subsequent centuries, many women who dared to preach, such as Maria de Santa Domingo and Alijit of Windesheim, similarly looked to Mary Magdalene as their model.

Throughout the medieval era, many parallels were perceived between the Virgin Mary and Mary Magdalene. However, there were some key differences, as well. Despite Magdalene's honorable status as a reformed sinner and revered saint, it was never forgotten that the Virgin Mary's virtues were far greater. After all, she had never led a sinful life in the first place. Some medieval saints, such as Francesca Romana and Birgitta of Sweden, adamantly maintained that Jesus appeared to his mother first after His Resurrection, despite Biblical evidence that he initially visited Mary Magdalene.[46] This idea, which has been under debate for centuries, has led to disagreement about which Mary the Gnostic Gospels (famously referenced in the *Da Vinci Code*) actually referred to. In these writings, she is identified as the Mary who was first witness to Christ's Resurrection.

In addition, many believed that Mary Magdalene had to do extensive penance for her sins before she attained her heavenly reward. According to popular legend, she became a hermit after the ascension of Jesus, retreating to a cave at La Sainte–Baume. There, she miraculously lived without food for thirty-three years. Her strict regimen of fasting and prayer inspired many subsequent saints to take as little sustenance as possible, particularly Catherine of Siena, who conflated herself with Magdalene. It was said that Mary Magdalene learned to levitate in mystical ecstasy, a power St. Catherine of Siena also supposedly possessed.[47]

According to medieval hagiographers, Magdalene was from a wealthy, aristocratic family. Biographers of saints frequently attributed such backgrounds to them because "high birth implied noble character and the requisite spiritual qualities for saintliness."[48] This was also supposed to have made her a more appropriate friend and companion for Christ. However, the very assumption of noble birth for Mary precluded her from being a true prostitute. According to the mystery plays of medieval France and Germany, Magdalene refused any money offered for her sexual services, primarily because she was wealthy enough not to need it. In this version of the life of Mary Magdalene, her choice to live promiscuously was motivated by lust, not poverty.

According to popular medieval belief, both Magdalene and the Virgin were very beautiful. Unlike the mother of Jesus, however, Mary Magdalene was regarded as a symbol of vanity and lust. Amusingly, because of this strong association, she became the patron saint of perfumers, glovers, hairdressers and cosmetic makers.[49] She also became connected in the medieval mind with the frivolity of music and dancing.

In 1249, the priest Eudes Rigaud visited the priory of Villarceaux and was horrified to find that the nuns there sometimes put on farcical performances, which included dressing up in "worldly costumes" and dancing. He chastised them, comparing them to Mary Magdalene before her conversion.[50] H. Colin Slim writes, "Many literary and visual sources from the fourteenth through the sixteenth centuries testify that Mary Magdalen was ... a dancer."[51] In 1300, a play from St. Gall portrays her doing a round dance with another woman and two men. During the sixteenth century, several pieces of choreography were named after her, such as Pierre Attaingnant's basse dance, "La Magdalena" and Antonio del Pifaro's pavane "La Madalena."[52]

One of the most well known artistic representations of Magdalene ever created is the 1519 engraving by Lucas van Leyden, *Dance of the Magdalene*. In it, she appears simultaneously in three different artistic scenes. In the foreground, she dances with a man, while in two background scenes, she participates in a stag hunt and is lifted into the sky by angels. The most commonly accepted interpretation of these images is that van Leyden juxtaposed the worldly (hunting and dancing) and saintly (communion with angels) aspects of her life. However, some recent scholarship has called this into question.

In her article, "Is She Dancing?," Liesel Nolan points out that the stag, particularly when hunted, is a common iconographic symbol for Christ. The hunting scene in the painting, therefore, could have been intended to signify Magdalene's encounter with Jesus. The foreground could also have a different meaning—Mary Magdalene, resplendent with her glowing halo, is not participating in the worldly enjoyment going on around her. Instead of dancing, she is bringing Christ's message to the revelers through her preaching.[53] If this interpretation is correct, it is likely that van Leyden was trying to rehabilitate Magdalene's image. His famous artistic work was illustrating the idea that her supposed worldliness was, in reality, a part of her mission to convert pagans.

Mary Magdalene became associated with the renunciation of vain and worldly things, and her feast day on July 22 was meant to inspire Christians to do the same. The Bolognese noblewoman Diana d'Andalo gave up her silks and jewels to become a Dominican nun on one such feast day in the thirteenth century. During the same time period, Magdalene's feast day was used for the passage of a Neapolitan sumptuary law regulating luxury goods. Finally (and horrifyingly), in 1529, Thomas Manny was brought to trial for the murder of his lascivious wife. Although he admitted his guilt, he defended his actions with the explanation that July 22, the day of the murder, was the appropriate time to kill a whore.[54]

Efforts to rehabilitate Magdalene's image were continued over the course of several centuries, since her role as the Biblical Whore carried on irrevocably in popular consciousness. During the Victorian era, this was partially responsible for a strong revival of interest in her. Kruppa states, "The Victorian fascination with the Magdalen took many forms: fiction, the visual arts, religious prescription, and, inevitably, in analogies of 'fallen women.'"[55] During the nineteenth century, fears about female immorality were particularly strong, and unmarried girls were constantly supervised. Many good Christians of the time were engaged in "rescuing" prostitutes, a form of charity work popular with both men and women. Even Charles Dickens took on the cause, providing funding for a house where those who wished to give up their "sinful" occupations could live for free. Such charitable Victorians frequently pointed to Magdalene as an example, both for the prostitutes themselves and those who were dubious about their potential for reform.[56]

As peculiarly Victorian as the preoccupation with saving prostitutes might seem, this movement had its precedent in the medieval era. As early as the twelfth century, they were considered an important social problem, partly because they were so numerous in urban areas. During this time, Cardinal Jacques de Vitry wrote that, because of their great numbers, whores in Paris had become bold enough to openly solicit passing holy men. Even more shocking to the Cardinal was that they frequently shouted, "Sodomite!" at those who piously refused them. Debate rose up about whether it was immoral for the Church to accept alms from women who had earned the money by selling themselves. The eventual resolution was that it was all right, provided the women had prostituted themselves solely from economic necessity and did not enjoy their shameful work. At the end of the twelfth century, Pope Innocent

III urged all Christians to try to "reclaim" whores for respectable society, offering an official remission of sins for men who married them.[57]

Even during the prudish Victorian era, however, not everyone was willing to accept the "guilty until proven innocent" mode of thought concerning Mary Magdalene. One peripatetic American preacher, Moncure Conway, argued that the concept of her immorality was inconsistent with her portrayal in the New Testament. When the Bishop of London referred to her as "the penitent," Conway wrote to the *Westminster Gazette*, challenging him to provide scriptural evidence for this characterization. Unfortunately for Moncure Conway, defending Magdalene's honor was an uphill battle in the nineteenth century. At this time, there was much social currency to be gained by characterizing her as a harlot.

The subject of the Magdalene as the ultimate fallen woman allowed Victorian artists a means of "treat[ing] human sexuality in a socially acceptable form."[58] Among pre–Raphaelites particularly, much artistic emphasis was given to the beauty of her hair, which was invariably worn loose. In both the medieval and Victorian eras, only young girls wore their hair loose, as a symbol of innocence. Respectable women were expected to put it up when they "came of age," and any who didn't were suspected of moral laxity.[59] In a medieval French legend, Mary cuts her hair off when she recognizes her own sinfulness. Little wonder, then, that the Magdalene images of artists such as Rossetti and Sandys portray her with hair lush enough to grace any shampoo advertisement.

It would likely have amused Rossetti, who rejected the Victorian idea that art should serve a moral purpose, that after he died, his Magdalene work was deemed unsuitable for a church. His family's vicar rejected their proposal to install a memorial stained glass window in the chapel where Rossetti was buried, based on his painting *Mary Magdalene at the Door of Simon the Pharisee*. Distressed at the idea, the minister argued that an image of Magdalene tearing at her hair and garments was "unlikely to inspire devotional thoughts ... and in some cases, it might rather do the reverse."[60] Oscar Wilde, who kept a version of Burne-Jones's *Christ and the Magdalen* in his rooms at Magdalen College, Oxford, would surely also have found this quite humorous. Being neither religious nor heterosexual, Wilde's interest in Burne-Jones's painting was based entirely on its aesthetic appeal.

Images of Magdalene the Whore continue to shock pious people even in contemporary times, when societal standards of morality are less absolute. As recently as the early 1980s, director Martin Scorsese stirred up controversy with his movie *The Last Temptation of Christ*. Conservative Christians all over the world took offense at its representation of Magdalene as a tattooed prostitute capable of leading Jesus into carnal thoughts. They stood outside movie theaters, protesting the screening of the film, and one Paris cinema was even bombed by religious extremists.[61]

Fifteen years later, Dan Brown's idea of the "lost sacred feminine" in *The*

Da Vinci Code was the next Magdalene-related controversy to enter public consciousness. Though not entirely lacking precedent, Brown's characterization is far less substantiated by Western theology than Scorsese's. The idea of Magdalene as the divine feminine has appeared in the writings of small Christian sects, long deemed heretical by Church authorities. However, this body of work is dwarfed by the numerous tomes that have been produced throughout history, quite often by respected theologians, about the Virgin Mary as the Co-Redeemer, the Salvatrix, the Female Face of God. Perhaps the answer to the problem of the missing divine feminine has been there all along, but has simply never been offered to contemporary Christian women. Sensationalism, after all, has always been more accessible than scholarship.

Despite this, new and challenging academic work continues to be produced on the Virgin Mary as the face of the divine feminine. In 1993, Stephen Benko's book *The Virgin Goddess, Studies in the Pagan and Christian Roots of Mariology* was published. In it, he argues convincingly that devotion to Mary stems from and is the result of pagan goddess worship. He states:

> The Mariological principle, i.e., veneration of the motherhood of Mary, is much more indebted to pagan belief and practice than many scholars are willing to admit ... the conclusion seems inevitable that Mary eventually fulfilled the same role and filled the same need in Christian theology and piety.[62]

Later, he quotes Pope John Paul II's assertion that women look to Mary to find the secret of living their femininity with dignity and achieving their own true advancement. Benko comments that a pagan who wanted to explain the need for goddesses could have "written this statement with very little change."[63] Finally, in the conclusion to his book, he asserts, "Mary is the direct continuation of the pagan goddesses."[64]

In their work *The Myth of the Goddess: Evolution of an Image*, Anne Baring and Jules Cashford devote an entire chapter to the Virgin entitled "Mary: the Return of the Goddess." They state unequivocally, "Mary is the unrecognized Mother Goddess of the Christian tradition."[65] They also refer to well-known mythology scholar Robert Campbell's assertion that she inherited all the names and forms of the Western goddess. Explaining her importance in Western culture, they state, "The pervasive influence and significance of Mary can be understood by seeing her in the context of the millennial tradition of the mother goddess, as its latest embodiment."[66] The primary aim of Baring and Cashford's work seems to be showing all of the traditional goddess-roles she has assumed over time. According to these scholars, she is the Great Mother Goddess, the Goddess of the Heavens, the Nature Goddess, the Goddess of the Underworld-Death, and even the War Goddess.[67]

Rosemary Radford Ruether implicitly concurs with the assertions of Baring and Cashford, as well as Benko, in *Goddesses and the Divine Feminine: A Western Religious History*. She argues, "Never touched by sin, incorruptible, ascending to the celestial realm immediately after death to be crowned as queen of heaven, appearing in endless visions, and celebrated in tens of thousands of pieces of art, she is functionally the Christian Goddess."[68] Anthropologists Victor and Edith Turner's theories also include the idea that the Virgin Mary is "the ultimate symbol of the symbolic feminine."[69] However, the Turners disagree somewhat with contemporary Mary-as-Goddess ideology. The feel that she is cannot be considered a true Christian goddess, since her place in society over time is changeable. Her status is ultimately culturally determined, dependent on views about women in Western culture as a whole.

Assertions of Mary's divine nature by academic theologians also frequently find challengers from within the Catholic Church, such as priest and popular writer Andrew Greeley. He argues that Mary, like many pagan goddesses, does indeed fill the roles of eternal feminine and ultimate other. However, he states, her essential humanity ultimately distinguishes her from them. She "goes far beyond them precisely because of her humanity... Mary is better than a goddess because she reveals the true God and inclusive, androgynous deity."[70]

Recent scholarship has further begun to challenge the strictly Western goddess concept of Mary. Maria Reis-Habito conflates the Virgin with Guanyin, the primary female bodhisattva in the Buddhist faith. Scholars of Chinese religion have recently referred to Guanyin as "the Buddhist Madonna." Accounts have also been related of Japanese Christians who lived during the Edo period, when Christians were persecuted, keeping iconic statues that resembled Mary and Guanyin simultaneously.[71] There are also many examples of traits that the two divine women have in common. These include numerous apparitions, healing powers, and intercessions on behalf of the dead. Both also have a special association with sailors, whom they protect from the sea's dangers. Women who wish to conceive children or are suffering in childbirth frequently appeal to them, as well.[72]

For new converts to Christianity in China, there was historically a somewhat interchangeable relationship between Guanyin, who was known as "the sender of sons," and Mary. This is plainly illustrated in Xiaoping Lin's article "Seeing the Place: The Virgin Mary in a Chinese Lady's Inner Chamber." She relates the story of a recently converted pagan in late Ming-dynasty China who was destroying all the statues of gods in his house. This man went to his priest, complaining that his pregnant wife had saved the idol of Guanyin from the fires in order to insure the safe delivery of their child. The priest told him to simply replace her statue with a picture of the Mother of God. Then, he was to ask his wife to say seven Hail Marys and Our Fathers in front of the Virgin's image each day. In accordance with her husband's wishes, she did so, and the couple's son was brought forth with exceptional ease.[73]

Thomas Cleary and Sartaz Aziz discuss Mary in the context of the Sufi faith, in which she is looked upon with great reverence. They point out that an entire chapter of the primary Muslim holy book, the Qu'ran, is named after her. In this version of her story, she is dedicated to the service of God by her mother while still in the womb. Given over to the care of the priest Zacharias at a very young age, Mary is noticeably detached from worldly things, and she is visited by angels.

Her Arabic name Maryam can be translated as "concentration," a usage substantiated by the fact that Eastern wisdom sometimes considers pregnancy a metaphor for meditation. Another possible translation of her name signifies a woman who enjoys the company of men but is not "flirtatious, immodest or unchaste with them."[74] Cleary and Aziz believe that, seen through the eyes of someone who follows the Sufi faith, the story of Maryam is "a kind of outline map of the mystic path."[75] They also draw parallels between Maryam and Rabi'a, "the most famous of the female Sufis of the classical era," who was also a pure and holy virgin, devoted to God.[76]

The central issue, then, is not whether scholars will continue to study the Virgin Mary in the context of the divine feminine. Rather, it centers on whether the mainstream public will ever read their work. Such cerebral findings are nearly always published in obscure academic journals and books that will certainly never make the bestseller lists, unlike *The Da Vinci Code*. Even more problematically, they are inaccessible to the majority of the public due to their complex language and challenging ideology. Just as the majority of medieval lay women were cut off from theological wisdom due to a lack of education, most women today will never be exposed to the idea of the Virgin Mary as the divine feminine.

Alternately, however, there is the possibility that just as pagan goddesses were transformed into the Virgin Mary, she will in turn become Mary Magdalene. This new version of the divine feminine certainly seems to resonate with the dominant ideologies of the postmodern world. Supposedly a woman who renounced prostitution to marry Jesus and bear his child, Magdalene is inherently sexual and almost excessively self-aware. Her roles as career woman, wife, single mother, and reformed sinner-become-disciple make sense to most contemporary women. Unlike the unobtainable ideal of Virgin Mother, perhaps women today can look to Mary Magdalene as a more realistic spiritual role model.

We must be careful, however, to understand exactly what is being exchanged. Something was certainly lost when the pre–Christian goddesses became the Virgin. In order to truly gain Mary Magdalene as the new divine feminine, we will probably have to relinquish the Virgin Mary. If this is a conscious choice, rather than something that happens to our society unwittingly, we will be more likely to benefit from the change.

Yet, the precedent of the past does not seem to indicate that society as a whole will, in fact, be actively involved in such choices. Suddenly, where once there was a statue of Isis or Guanyin on the altar, the Virgin Mary was in its place. No one appeared to mind or even to notice. (Perhaps if some women did, they were too uneducated or marginalized to record their protestations

A girl prays to the Virgin Mary for happiness. From a 1920s holy card (courtesy Chant Art).

for posterity.) Are we heading toward a world in which images of Mary Magdalene adorn our houses of worship, instead of the Virgin? What will women's roles be in such a society? These are the questions that seem to be facing spiritual women in the twenty-first century. Hopefully this time, we will take a more active role in answering them than we did in the medieval era.

Chapter Notes

Chapter 1

1. Schoemperlen, Diane (2001). *Our Lady of the Lost and Found: A Novel.* New York: Viking (pp. 42–45).
2. Cunneen, S. (1996). *In Search of Mary: The Woman and the Symbol.* New York: Ballantine Books (pp. 9–10).
3. Ibid. p. XVI.
4. Johnson, E.A. (1985) "The Marian Tradition and the Reality of Women." *Horizons* 12 (1), 116–135 (pp. 121–126).
5. Warner, M. (1983). *Alone of All Her Sex: The Myth and Cult of the Virgin Mary.* New York: Vintage Books (p. 337)
6. Ibid. p. XXI.
7. Harrington, P.A. (1984). "Mary and Femininity: A Psychological Critique." *Journal of Religion and Health,* 23 (3), 204–217 (p. 204).
8. Ibid. pp. 215–216.
9. Donofrio, B. (2000). *Looking for Mary: Or the Blessed Mother and Me.* New York: Viking Compass (p. 70).
10. Ibid. p. 27.
11. Johnson, E.A. (2003). *Truly Our Sister: A Theology of Mary in the Communion of Saints.* New York: Continuum (p. 26).
12. Ibid. p. 30.
13. Ibid. p. 32.
14. Ibid. pp. 26–34.
15. Westerfield, N.G. (1999). "Mary of the Mirrors." *Theology Today,* 56 (3), 399.
16. Donofrio, B. (2000). *Looking for Mary: Or the Blessed Mother and Me.* New York: Viking Compass (pp. 206–207).
17. Bridgett, T.E. (1875). *Our Lady's Dowry: Or How England Gained and Lost That Title.* London: Burns and Oates (pp. 341–344)
18. Warner, M. (1983). *Alone of All Her Sex: The Myth and Cult of the Virgin Mary.* New York: Vintage Books (p. 325).
19. Buck, P.F., S.J. (1980). "The Marian Interpretation of the 'Song of Songs' in the Middle Ages (A.D. 1100–1500)." *Acta Congressus Mariologici-Mariani Internationalis Romae Anno 1975 Celebrati: Vol. IV. De culto mariano apud scriptores ecclesiasticos saec,* XII-XIII, 69–96 (pp. 94–95).
20. Graef, H. (1963). *Mary: A History of Doctrine and Devotion* (Vol. 1). New York: Sheed and Ward (p. 213)
21. Ibid. p. 214.
22. Van Scott, M. (1998). *Encyclopedia of Hell.* New York, NY: Thomas Dunne Books (pp. 290–291).
23. Peters, C. (2003). *Patterns of Piety: Women, Gender and Religion in Late Medieval and Reformation England.* New York, NY: Cambridge University (p. 67).
24. Warner, M. (1983). *Alone of All Her Sex: The Myth and Cult of the Virgin Mary.* New York: Vintage Books (pp. 321–322).
25. Harrington, P.A. (1984). "Mary and Femininity: A Psychological Critique." *Journal of Religion and Health,* 23 (3), 204–217 (p. 211).
26. Condren, M. (1999). *The Serpent and the Goddess: Women, Religion, and Power in Celtic Ireland.* San Francisco, CA: HarperCollins Publishers (p. 162).
27. Warner, M. (1983). *Alone of All Her Sex: The Myth and Cult of the Virgin Mary.* New York: Vintage Books (p. 316).
28. Van Scott, M. (1998). *Encyclopedia of Hell.* New York, NY: Thomas Dunne Books (p. 291).
29. Warner, M. (1983). *Alone of All Her Sex: The Myth and Cult of the Virgin Mary.* New York: Vintage Books (pp. 322–325).
30. Graef, H. (1963). *Mary: A History of Doctrine and Devotion* (Vol. 1). New York: Sheed and Ward (p. 40).
31. Cunningham, L. (1982). *Mother of God.* San Francisco, CA: Harper and Row (p. 67).
32. Warner, M. (1983). *Alone of All Her Sex: The Myth and Cult of the Virgin Mary.* New York: Vintage Books (p. 202).
33. Ibid. pp. 214–216.
34. Ibid. p. 215.
35. Cunningham, L. (1982). *Mother of God.* San Francisco, CA: Harper and Row (p. 126).
36. Warner, M. (1983). *Alone of All Her Sex: The Myth and Cult of the Virgin Mary.* New York: Vintage Books (p. 216).

37. Ibid. p. 231.
38. Voragine, J. de (1941). *The Golden Legend of Jacobus de Voragine* (G. Ryan and H, Ripperger, Trans.). New York: Longmans, Green. (Original work published 1298.) (p. 221).
39. Warner, M. (1983). *Alone of All Her Sex: The Myth and Cult of the Virgin Mary.* New York: Vintage Books (p. 18).
40. Voragine, J. de (1941). *The Golden Legend of Jacobus de Voragine* (G. Ryan and H, Ripperger, Trans.). New York: Longmans, Green. (Original work published 1298.) (p. 450).
41. Harrington, P.A. (1984). "Mary and Femininity: A Psychological Critique." *Journal of Religion and Health, 23* (3), 204–217 (p. 20).
42. Graef, H. (1963). *Mary: A History of Doctrine and Devotion* (Vol. 1). New York: Sheed and Ward (p. 223).
43. Voragine, J. de (1941). *The Golden Legend of Jacobus de Voragine* (G. Ryan and H, Ripperger, Trans.). New York: Longmans, Green. (Original work published 1298.) (p. 454).
44. Ibid. p. 454.
45. Graef, H. (1963). *Mary: A History of Doctrine and Devotion* (Vol. 1). New York: Sheed and Ward (p. 248).
46. Buck, P.F., S.J. (1980). "The Marian Interpretation of the 'Song of Songs' in the Middle Ages (A.D. 1100–1500)." *Acta Congressus Mariologici-Mariani Internationalis Romae Anno 1975 Celebrati: Vol. IV.* De culto mariano apud scriptores ecclesiasticos saec, XII-XIII, 69–96 (p. 91).
47. Graef, H. (1963). *Mary: A History of Doctrine and Devotion* (Vol. 1). New York: Sheed and Ward (p. 278).
48. Ibid. p. 217.
49. Warner, M. (1983). *Alone of All Her Sex: The Myth and Cult of the Virgin Mary.* New York: Vintage Books (p. 27).
50. Voragine, J. de (1941). *The Golden Legend of Jacobus de Voragine* (G. Ryan and H, Ripperger, Trans.). New York: Longmans, Green. (Original work published 1298.) (p. 524).
51. Ibid. p. 23.
52. Buck, P.F., S.J. (1980). "The Marian Interpretation of the 'Song of Songs' in the Middle Ages (A.D. 1100–1500)." *Acta Congressus Mariologici-Mariani Internationalis Romae Anno 1975 Celebrati: Vol. IV.* De culto mariano apud scriptores ecclesiasticos saec, XII-XIII, 69–96 (pp. 76–77).
53. Ibid. pp. 76–77.
54. Warner, M. (1983). *Alone of All Her Sex: The Myth and Cult of the Virgin Mary.* New York: Vintage Books (p. 59).
55. Graef, H. (1963). *Mary: A History of Doctrine and Devotion* (Vol. 1). New York: Sheed and Ward (p. 204)
56. Ibid. p. 309.
57. Abbott, E. (1999). *A History of Celibacy.* New York: Scribner (pp. 60–61).
58. Cunneen, S. (1996). *In Search of Mary: The Woman and the Symbol.* New York: Ballantine Books (p. 163).
59. Ibid. pp. 167–168.
60. Yalom, M. (1997). *A History of the Breast.* New York: Alfred A. Knopf (p. 48).
61. Johnson, E.A. (2003). *Truly Our Sister: A Theology of Mary in the Communion of Saints.* New York: Continuum (p. 76).
62. Gibson, G.M. (1989). *The Theater of Devotion: East Anglian Drama and Society in the Late Middle Ages.* Chicago: University of Chicago Press (p. 51).

Chapter 2

1. Pelikan, J. (1996). *Mary Through the Centuries: Her Place in the History of Culture.* New Haven, CT: Yale University Press (p. 8).
2. Warner, M. (1983). *Alone of All Her Sex: The Myth and Cult of the Virgin Mary.* New York: Vintage Books (p. 7).
3. Cunneen, S. (1996). *In Search of Mary: The Woman and the Symbol.* New York: Ballantine Books (p. 31).
4. Warner, M. (1983). *Alone of All Her Sex: The Myth and Cult of the Virgin Mary.* New York: Vintage Books (p. 3).
5. Ibid. p. 7.
6. Gaventa, B.R. (1995). *Mary: Glimpses of the Mother of Jesus.* Columbia, SC: University of South Carolina Press (pp. 51–52).
7. Galot, J., S.J. (1965). *Mary in the Gospel.* (S.M. Constance, Trans.) Westminster, MD: Newman Press (p. 3).
8. McHugh, J. (1975). *The Mother of Jesus in the New Testament.* Garden City, NY: Doubleday. (p. 55).
9. Brown, R.E., Donfried, K.P., Fitzmyer, J.A., Reumann, J. (Eds.) (1978). *Mary in the New Testament.* Philadelphia, PA: Fortress Press (p. 114).
10. Galot, J., S.J. (1965). *Mary in the Gospel.* (S.M. Constance, Trans.) Westminster, MD: Newman Press (p. 32).
11. Warner, M. (1983). *Alone of All Her Sex: The Myth and Cult of the Virgin Mary.* New York: Vintage Books (p. 177).
12. Gaventa, B.R. (1995). *Mary: Glimpses of the Mother of Jesus.* Columbia, SC: University of South Carolina Press (pp. 54–55).
13. Brown, R.E., Donfried, K.P., Fitzmyer, J.A., Reumann, J. (Eds.) (1978). *Mary in the New Testament.* Philadelphia, PA: Fortress Press (p. 139).
14. Galot, J., S.J. (1965). *Mary in the Gospel.* (S.M. Constance, Trans.) Westminster, MD: Newman Press (p. 72).
15. McHugh, J. (1975). *The Mother of Jesus in the New Testament.* Garden City, NY: Doubleday. (p. 73).
16. Cunneen, S. (1996). *In Search of Mary: The Woman and the Symbol.* New York: Ballantine Books (pp. 40–41).
17. Ibid. pp. 198–201.
18. Ibid. p. 41.
19. Ibid. p. 53.
20. Galot, J., S.J. (1965). *Mary in the Gospel.*

(S.M. Constance, Trans.) Westminster, MD: Newman Press. (p. 74).
21. McHugh, J. (1975). *The Mother of Jesus in the New Testament.* Garden City, NY: Doubleday. (p. 78).
22. Ibid. p. 94.
23. Ibid. p. 89.
24. Galot, J., S.J. (1965). *Mary in the Gospel.* (S.M. Constance, Trans.) Westminster, MD: Newman Press (pp. 79–80).
25. Gaventa, B.R. (1995). *Mary: Glimpses of the Mother of Jesus.* Columbia, SC: University of South Carolina Press (p. 61).
26. Cunneen, S. (1996). *In Search of Mary: The Woman and the Symbol.* New York: Ballantine Books (p. 43).
27. Gaventa, B.R. (1995). *Mary: Glimpses of the Mother of Jesus.* Columbia, SC: University of South Carolina Press (p. 42).
28. Ibid. p. 46.
29. Warner, M. (1983). *Alone of All Her Sex: The Myth and Cult of the Virgin Mary.* New York: Vintage Books (pp. 104–105).
30. Galot, J., S.J. (1965). *Mary in the Gospel.* (S.M. Constance, Trans.) Westminster, MD: Newman Press (p. 82).
31. Ibid. p. 97.
32. McHugh, J. (1975). *The Mother of Jesus in the New Testament.* Garden City, NY: Doubleday. (pp. 107–109).
33. Ibid. p. 112.
34. Brown, R.E., Donfried, K.P., Fitzmyer, J.A., Reumann, J. (Eds.) (1978). *Mary in the New Testament.* Philadelphia, PA: Fortress Press (p. 161).
35. Gaventa, B.R. (1995). *Mary: Glimpses of the Mother of Jesus.* Columbia, SC: University of South Carolina Press (p. 68).
36. Galot, J., S.J. (1965). *Mary in the Gospel.* (S.M. Constance, Trans.) Westminster, MD: Newman Press (p. 100).
37. Warner, M. (1983). *Alone of All Her Sex: The Myth and Cult of the Virgin Mary.* New York: Vintage Books (p. 21).
38. Gaventa, B.R. (1995). *Mary: Glimpses of the Mother of Jesus.* Columbia, SC: University of South Carolina Press (p. 80).
39. McHugh, J. (1975). *The Mother of Jesus in the New Testament.* Garden City, NY: Doubleday. (p. 362).
40. Galot, J., S.J. (1965). *Mary in the Gospel.* (S.M. Constance, Trans.) Westminster, MD: Newman Press (p. 107).
41. Cunneen, S. (1996). *In Search of Mary: The Woman and the Symbol.* New York: Ballantine Books (p. 55).
42. Warner, M. (1983). *Alone of All Her Sex: The Myth and Cult of the Virgin Mary.* New York: Vintage Books (p. 277).
43. Galot, J., S.J. (1965). *Mary in the Gospel.* (S.M. Constance, Trans.) Westminster, MD: Newman Press (p. 119).
44. Warner, M. (1983). *Alone of All Her Sex: The Myth and Cult of the Virgin Mary.* New York: Vintage Books (p. 287).
45. Ibid. p. 16.
46. Galot, J., S.J. (1965). *Mary in the Gospel.* (S.M. Constance, Trans.) Westminster, MD: Newman Press (pp. 151–152).
47. Cunneen, S. (1996). *In Search of Mary: The Woman and the Symbol.* New York: Ballantine Books (p. 46).
48. McHugh, J. (1975). *The Mother of Jesus in the New Testament.* Garden City, NY: Doubleday. (p. 367).
49. Ibid. pp. 392–393.
50. Gaventa, B.R. (1995). *Mary: Glimpses of the Mother of Jesus.* Columbia, SC: University of South Carolina Press (p. 3).
51. Ibid. p. 71.
52. Cunneen, S. (1996). *In Search of Mary: The Woman and the Symbol.* New York: Ballantine Books (p. 47).
53. Warner, M. (1983). *Alone of All Her Sex: The Myth and Cult of the Virgin Mary.* New York: Vintage Books (p. 15).
54. Ibid. p. 211.
55. Ibid. p. 218.
56. McHugh, J. (1975). *The Mother of Jesus in the New Testament.* Garden City, NY: Doubleday. (p. 377).
57. Galot, J., S.J. (1965). *Mary in the Gospel.* (S.M. Constance, Trans.) Westminster, MD: Newman Press (pp. 195, 199).
58. Gaventa, B.R. (1995). *Mary: Glimpses of the Mother of Jesus.* Columbia, SC: University of South Carolina Press (p. 90).
59. McHugh, J. (1975). *The Mother of Jesus in the New Testament.* Garden City, NY: Doubleday. (p. 403).
60. Cunneen, S. (1996). *In Search of Mary: The Woman and the Symbol.* New York: Ballantine Books (p. 56).
61. Gaventa, B.R. (1995). *Mary: Glimpses of the Mother of Jesus.* Columbia, SC: University of South Carolina Press (p. 95).
62. Galot, J., S.J. (1965). *Mary in the Gospel.* (S.M. Constance, Trans.) Westminster, MD: Newman Press (pp. 215–217).
63. Warner, M. (1983). *Alone of All Her Sex: The Myth and Cult of the Virgin Mary.* New York: Vintage Books (p. 18).
64. Brown, R.E., Donfried, K.P., Fitzmyer, J.A., Reumann, J. (Eds.) (1978). *Mary in the New Testament.* Philadelphia, PA: Fortress Press (p. 177).
65. Gaventa, B.R. (1995). *Mary: Glimpses of the Mother of Jesus.* Columbia, SC: University of South Carolina Press (pp. 74–75).
66. McHugh, J. (1975). *The Mother of Jesus in the New Testament.* Garden City, NY: Doubleday. (p. 405).
67. Galot, J., S.J. (1965). *Mary in the Gospel.* (S.M. Constance, Trans.) Westminster, MD: Newman Press (p. 203).
68. Riani, P.R. (1955). *Mary in the Twelfth Chapter of the Apocalypse.* Baltimore, MD: St. Mary's Seminary and University (p. 35).
69. McHugh, J. (1975). *The Mother of Jesus in

the New Testament. Garden City, NY: Doubleday. (p. 431).
   70. Spretnak, C. (2004). *Missing Mary: The Queen of Heaven and Her Re-Emergence in the Modern Church.* New York, NY: Palgrave MacMillan (pp. 210–211).
   71. Cunneen, S. (1996). *In Search of Mary: The Woman and the Symbol.* New York: Ballantine Books (p. 176).
   72. Matter, E.A. (1990). *The Voice of My Beloved: The Song of Songs in Western Medieval Christianity.* Philadelphia, PA: University of Pennsylvania Press (pp. 152–153).
   73. Ibid. pp. 154–155.
   74. Warner, M. (1983). *Alone of All Her Sex: The Myth and Cult of the Virgin Mary.* New York: Vintage Books (pp. 99–100).
   75. Astell, A.W. (1990). *The Song of Songs in the Middle Ages.* Ithaca, NY: Cornell University Press (p. 61).
   76. Ibid. pp. 62–64.
   77. Ibid. pp. 43–44

Chapter 3

   1. Underhill, E. (1905). *The Miracles of Our Lady Saint Mary: Brought Out of Divers Tongues and Newly Set Forth in English.* London: William Heinemann (pp. 167–177).
   2. Harthan, J. (1977). *Books of Hours and Their Owners.* London: Thames and Hudon (p. 13).
   3. Wieck, R.S. (1988). *The Book of Hours in Medieval Art and Life.* London: George Braziller. (p. 27).
   4. Poos, L.R. (1988). "Social History and the Book of Hours." In R.S. Wieck (Ed.), *The Book of Hours in Medieval Art and Life* (pp. 33–38). London: George Braziller. (p. 33).
   5. Harthan, J. (1977). *Books of Hours and Their Owners.* London: Thames and Hudon (p. 39).
   6. Ibid. p. 37.
   7. Penkneth, S. (1997). "Women and Books of Hours." In L. Smith & J.H.M. Taylor (Eds.), *Women and the Book: Assessing the Visual Evidence* (pp. 266–281). London: The British Library (p. 269).
   8. Harthan, J. (1977). *Books of Hours and Their Owners.* London: Thames and Hudon (p. 33).
   9. Penkneth, S. (1997). "Women and Books of Hours." In L. Smith & J.H.M. Taylor (Eds.), *Women and the Book: Assessing the Visual Evidence* (pp. 266–281). London: The British Library (p. 271).
   10. Ibid. p. 270.
   11. Bell, S.G. (1988). Medieval Woman Book Owners: Arbiters of Lay Piety and Ambassadors of Culture. In M. Erler & M. Kowaleski (Eds.), *Women and Power in the Middle Ages* (pp. 149–187). Athens, GA: University of Georgia Press. (p. 161).
   12. Penkneth, S. (1997). "Women and Books of Hours." In L. Smith & J.H.M. Taylor (Eds.), *Women and the Book: Assessing the Visual Evidence* (pp. 266–281). London: The British Library. (p. 269).
   13. Harthan, J. (1977). *Books of Hours and Their Owners* London: Thames and Hudon. (p. 32).
   14. Bell, S.G. (1988). "Medieval Woman Book Owners: Arbiters of Lay Piety and Ambassadors of Culture." In M. Erler & M. Kowaleski (Eds.), *Women and Power in the Middle Ages* (pp. 149–187). Athens, GA: University of Georgia Press (p. 162).
   15. Os, H. van (1994). *The Art of Devotion in the Late Middle Ages in Europe 1300–1500.* Princeton, NJ: Princeton University Press (p. 80).
   16. Harthan, J. (1977). *Books of Hours and Their Owners.* London: Thames and Hudon (p. 35).
   17. Saenger, P. (1985). "Books of Hours and the Reading Habits of the Later Middle Ages." *Scrittura e Civilta, 9,* 239–269 (p. 76).
   18. Harthan, J. (1977). *Books of Hours and Their Owners.* London: Thames and Hudon (pp. 35–36).
   19. Bell, S.G. (1988). "Medieval Woman Book Owners: Arbiters of Lay Piety and Ambassadors of Culture." In M. Erler & M. Kowaleski (Eds.), *Women and Power in the Middle Ages* (pp. 149–187). Athens, GA: University of Georgia Press (p. 160).
   20. Penkneth, S. (1997). "Women and Books of Hours." In L. Smith & J.H.M. Taylor (Eds.), *Women and the Book: Assessing the Visual Evidence* (pp. 266–281). London: The British Library (p. 270).
   21. Bell, S.G. (1988). "Medieval Woman Book Owners: Arbiters of Lay Piety and Ambassadors of Culture." In M. Erler & M. Kowaleski (Eds.), *Women and Power in the Middle Ages* (pp. 149–187). Athens, GA: University of Georgia Press (p. 162).
   22. Pizan, C. de (1989) *A Medieval Woman's Mirror of Honor: The Treasury of the City of Ladies* (C.C. Willard, Trans.). Tenafly, NJ: Bard Hall Press (Original work published 1405.) (p. 128).
   23. Ibid. p. 104.
   24. Bell, S.G. (1988). "Medieval Woman Book Owners: Arbiters of Lay Piety and Ambassadors of Culture." In M. Erler & M. Kowaleski (Eds.), *Women and Power in the Middle Ages* (pp. 149–187). Athens, GA: University of Georgia Press (p. 165).
   25. Wieck, R.S. (1988). *The Book of Hours in Medieval Art and Life.* London: George Braziller. (p. 27).
   26. Harthan, J. (1977). *Books of Hours and Their Owners.* London: Thames and Hudon (pp. 13–14).
   27. Os, H. van (1994). *The Art of Devotion in the Late Middle Ages in Europe 1300–1500.* Princeton, NJ: Princeton University Press (p. 170).
   28. Ibid. p. 172.
   29. Penkneth, S. (1997). "Women and Books of Hours." In L. Smith & J.H.M. Taylor (Eds.), *Women and the Book: Assessing the Visual Evidence* (pp. 266–281). London: The British Library (p. 266).
   30. Ibid. pp. 171–172.
   31. Penkneth, S. (1997). "Women and Books of Hours." In L. Smith & J.H.M. Taylor (Eds.), *Women and the Book: Assessing the Visual Evidence*

(pp. 266–281). London: The British Library (p. 272).
32. Cunneen, S. (1996). *In Search of Mary: The Woman and the Symbol.* New York: Ballantine Books (p. 187).
33. Os, H. van (1994). *The Art of Devotion in the Late Middle Ages in Europe 1300–1500.* Princeton, NJ: Princeton University Press (p. 20).
34. Ibid. p. 98.
35. Bell, S.G. (1988). "Medieval Woman Book Owners: Arbiters of Lay Piety and Ambassadors of Culture." In M. Erler & M. Kowaleski (Eds.), *Women and Power in the Middle Ages* (pp. 149–187). Athens, GA: University of Georgia Press (p. 173).
36. Harthan, J. (1977). *Books of Hours and Their Owners.* London: Thames and Hudon (pp. 80–81).
37. Ibid. p. 85.
38. MacGibbon, D. (1933). *Jean Bourdichon: A Court Painter in the Fifteenth Century.* Glasgow: Robert Maclehose. (p. 50).
39. Warner, M. (1983). *Alone of All Her Sex: The Myth and Cult of the Virgin Mary.* New York: Vintage Books (pp. 188–189).
40. Porcher, J. (1959). *The Rohan Book of Hours.* New York: Thomas Yoseloff (p. 6).
41. Butler, M.A. (1967). *Twice Queen of France: Anne of Brittany.* New York: Funk & Wagnalls (p. 152).
42. Ibid. pp. 168–170.
43. *Dictionary of Mary* (1985). New York: Catholic Book Publishing. (p. 251).
44. Kraus, H. (1982). "Eve and Mary: Conflicting Images of Medieval Woman." In N. Broude & M.D. Garrard (Eds.), *Feminism and Art History: Questioning the Litany* (pp. 79–99). New York: Harper & Row (p. 81).
45. Butler, M.A. (1967). *Twice Queen of France: Anne of Brittany.* New York: Funk & Wagnalls (p. 152).
46. Winston-Allen, A. (1997). *Stories of the Rose: The Making of the Rosary in the Middle Ages.* University Park, PA: Pennsylvania State University Press (pp. 155–157).
47. Miller, J.D. (2002). *Beads and Prayers: The Rosary in History and Devotion.* London: Burns and Oates (pp. 8–9).
48. Winston-Allen, A. (1997). *Stories of the Rose: The Making of the Rosary in the Middle Ages.* University Park, PA: Pennsylvania State University Press (p. 72).
49. Miller, J.D. (2002). *Beads and Prayers: The Rosary in History and Devotion.* London: Burns and Oates (p. 7).
50. Ibid. p. 87.
51. Winston-Allen, A. (1997). *Stories of the Rose: The Making of the Rosary in the Middle Ages.* University Park, PA: Pennsylvania State University Press (p. 14).
52. Miller, J.D. (2002). *Beads and Prayers: The Rosary in History and Devotion* London: Burns and Oates (pp. 89, 95).
53. Ibid. p. 88.
54. Winston-Allen, A. (1997). *Stories of the Rose: The Making of the Rosary in the Middle Ages.* University Park, PA: Pennsylvania State University Press (p. 116).
55. Ibid. p.112.
56. Ibid. p. 116.
57. Bridgett, T.E. (1875). *Our Lady's Dowry: Or How England Gained and Lost That Title.* London: Burns and Oates (p. 210).
58. Ibid. p. 204.
59. Winston-Allen, A. (1997). *Stories of the Rose: The Making of the Rosary in the Middle Ages.* University Park, PA: Pennsylvania State University Press (pp. 117–118).
60. Bridgett, T.E. (1875). *Our Lady's Dowry: Or How England Gained and Lost That Title.* London: Burns and Oates (pp. 206–207).
61. Ibid. p. 211.
62. Miller, J.D. (2002). *Beads and Prayers: The Rosary in History and Devotion.* London: Burns and Oates (p. 20).
63. Cunneen, S. (1996). *In Search of Mary: The Woman and the Symbol.* New York: Ballantine Books (p. 190).
64. Winston-Allen, A. (1997). *Stories of the Rose: The Making of the Rosary in the Middle Ages.* University Park, PA: Pennsylvania State University Press (pp. 100–101).
65. Warner, M. (1983). *Alone of All Her Sex: The Myth and Cult of the Virgin Mary.* New York: Vintage Books (p. 308).
66. Miller, J.D. (2002). *Beads and Prayers: The Rosary in History and Devotion.* London: Burns and Oates (p. 118).
67. Ibid. p. 119.
68. McClain, L. (2004). *Lest We Be Damned: Practical Innovation and Lived Experience Among Catholics in Protestant England, 1559–1642.* New York, NY: Routledge. (pp. 86–87).
69. Warner, M. (1983). *Alone of All Her Sex: The Myth and Cult of the Virgin Mary.* New York: Vintage Books (p. 307).
70. McClain, L. (2004). *Lest We Be Damned: Practical Innovation and Lived Experience Among Catholics in Protestant England, 1559–1642.* New York, NY: Routledge (p. 105).
71. Ibid. p. 97.
72. Ibid. p. 98.
73. Ibid. p. 103.
74. Miller, J.D. (2002). *Beads and Prayers: The Rosary in History and Devotion.* London: Burns and Oates (pp. 120–121).
75. Durham, M.S. (1995). *Miracles of Mary: Apparitions, Legends and Miraculous Works of the Blessed Virgin Mary.* San Francisco, CA: HarperCollins Publishers (pp. 164–165).
76. Heimann, M. (1995). *Catholic Devotion in Victorian England.* New York, NY: Oxford University Press (p. 59).
77. Ibid. p. 68.
78. Ibid. p. 66.
79. Ibid. p. 62.
80. Ibid. p. 63.
81. Miller, J.D. (2002). *Beads and Prayers: The Rosary in History and Devotion.* London: Burns and Oates (pp. 159–160).

82. Donofrio, B. (2000). *Looking for Mary: Or the Blessed Mother and Me*. New York: Viking Compass (pp. 206–207).
83. Ibid. p. 228.
84. Haughton, R. (1976). *Feminine Spirituality: Reflections on the Mysteries of the Rosary*. New York: The Missionary Society of St. Paul the Apostle (p. viii).

Chapter 4

1. Florendo, A.O. (2004). *The Liturgy of Flowers in a Mary Garden: A Contemplation*. New York, NY: Rosetti della Virgine Books (p. 54).
2. Krymow, V. (2002). *Mary's Flowers: Gardens, Legends and Meditations*. Cincinnati, OH: St. Anthony Messenger Press (pp. 21–22).
3. Ibid. p. 22.
4. Stokes, J.S. "Mary Gardens' Historical Perspective." 1995. 29 March 2006, <http://www.mgardens.org/JS-HP-MG.html>.
5. Moldenke, H. N. "Flowers of the Madonna." Dec., 1953. *Horticulture*. 29 March 2006, <http://www.mgardens.org/HM-FOTM-HO.html>.
6. Gambero, L. (2000). *Mary in the Middle Ages: The Blessed Virgin Mary in the Thought of Medieval Latin Theologians* (T. Buffer, Trans.). San Francisco, CA: Ignatius Press (p. 288).
7. Spretnak, C. (2004). *Missing Mary: The Queen of Heaven and Her Re-Emergence in the Modern Church*. New York, NY: Palgrave MacMillan (p. 211).
8. Krymow, V. (2002). *Mary's Flowers: Gardens, Legends and Meditations*. Cincinnati, OH: St. Anthony Messenger Press (p. 19).
9. Reimer, S. "Women in the Mary Garden Feed a Flowering of Spirit." *The Baltimore Sun*. Sunday, May 14, 1995. 29 March 2006, <http://www.mgardens.org/SR-SOD-BS.html>.
10. Donofrio, B. (2000). *Looking for Mary: Or the Blessed Mother and Me*. New York, NY: Viking Compass (pp. 13–15).
11. Krymow, V. (2002). *Mary's Flowers: Gardens, Legends and Meditations*. Cincinnati, OH: St. Anthony Messenger Press (p. 124).
12. Florendo, A.O. (2004). *The Liturgy of Flowers in a Mary Garden: A Contemplation*. New York, NY: Rosetti della Virgine Books (p. 24).
13. Saint-Jacques, D. P. "Women on Pilgrimage." Mar. 2004. *Terre Entiere* (C. Buuck, Trans.). 29 Mar. 2006, <http://www.saint-jacques.info/women>.
14. Webb, D. (2002). *Medieval European Pilgrimage*. New York, NY: Palgrave (p. 91).
15. Rawcliffe, C. (2002). Curing Bodies and Healing Souls: Pilgrimage and the Sick in Medieval East Anglia." In C. Morris and P. Roberts (Eds.), *Pilgrimage: The English Experience from Becket to Bunyan* (pp. 108–140). Cambridge, UK: Cambridge University Press (pp. 125–126).
16. Ibid. pp.125–126.
17. Dickinson, J.C. (1956). *The Shrine of Our Lady of Walsingham*. Cambridge, England: Cambridge University Press (pp. 36–37).
18. Hopper, S. (2002). *To Be a Pilgrim: The Medieval Pilgrimage Experience*. Gloucestershire, England: Sutton Publishing (pp. 67–68).
19. Ibid. pp. 69–70.
20. Rawcliffe, C. (2002). "Curing Bodies and Healing Souls: Pilgrimage and the Sick in Medieval East Anglia." In C. Morris and P. Roberts (Eds.), *Pilgrimage: The English Experience from Becket to Bunyan* (pp. 108–140). Cambridge, UK: Cambridge University Press (p. 121).
21. Hopper, S. (2002). *To Be a Pilgrim: The Medieval Pilgrimage Experience*. Gloucestershire, England: Sutton Publishing (pp. 67–68).
22. Rawcliffe, C. (2002). "Curing Bodies and Healing Souls: Pilgrimage and the Sick in Medieval East Anglia." In C. Morris and P. Roberts (Eds.), *Pilgrimage: The English Experience from Becket to Bunyan* (pp. 108–140). Cambridge, UK: Cambridge University Press (pp. 136–138).
23. Creasman, A.F. (2002). The Virgin Mary Against the Jews: Anti-Jewish Polemic in the Pilgrimage to the Schone Maria of Regensburg, 1519–25. *The Sixteenth Century Journal 33*, (4), 963–980 (pp. 971–972).
24. Hopper, S. (2002). *To Be a Pilgrim: The Medieval Pilgrimage Experience*. Gloucestershire, England: Sutton Publishing (p. 3).
25. Gambero, L. (2000). *Mary in the Middle Ages: The Blessed Virgin Mary in the Thought of Medieval Latin Theologians* (T. Buffer, Trans.). San Francisco, CA: Ignatius Press (p. 306).
26. Saint-Jacques, D.P. "Women on Pilgrimage." Mar. 2004, *Terre Entiere* (C. Buck, Trans.). 29 Mar. 2006, <http://www.saint-jacques.info/women>.
27. Hopper, S. (2002). *To Be a Pilgrim: The Medieval Pilgrimage Experience*. Gloucestershire, England: Sutton Publishing (pp. 162–163).
28. Hallissy, M. (1993). *Clean Maids, True Wives, Steadfast Widows: Chaucer's Women and Medieval Codes of Conduct*. Westport, CN: Greenwood Press (pp. 128–129).
29. Ibid. pp. 167–168.
30. Hopper, S. (2002). *To Be a Pilgrim: The Medieval Pilgrimage Experience*. Gloucestershire, England: Sutton Publishing (p. 7).
31. Ibid. p. 11.
32. Webb, D. (2001). *Pilgrimage in Medieval England*. New York, NY: Hambledon and London (p. 101).
33. Ibid. p. 82.
34. Webb, D. (2002). *Medieval European Pilgrimage*. New York, NY: Palgrave (p. 94).
35. Ibid. p. 102.
36. Aradi, Z. (1954). *Shrines to Our Lady Around the World*. New York, NY: Farrar, Straus and Giroux (p. 66).
37. Gill, S. (2004). "Marian Revivalism in Modern English Christianity: The Example of Walsingham." In R.N. Swanson (Ed.), *The Church and Mary*. Rochester, NY: Boydell Press (p. 349).
38. Ibid. pp. 351–352
39. Warner, M. (1976). *Alone of All Her Sex: The Myth and Cult of the Virgin Mary*. New York, NY: Vintage Books (pp. 236, 249–250).

40. Petitot, F.H., OP. (1950). *The True Story of Saint Bernadette*. Westminster, MD: Newman Press (p. 4).
41. Ibid. pp. 13–14.
42. Kaufman, S.K. (2005). *Consuming Visions: Mass Culture and the Lourdes Shrine*. Ithaca, NY: Cornell University Press (p. 73).
43. Ibid. p. 74.
44. Ibid. p. 75.
45. Cadegan, U. (1995). ""Images of Mary in Popular Periodicals."" *Marian Studies, XLVI*, 87–107 (p. 100).
46. Ibid. p. 311.
47. Boissarie, D. (1933). *Healing at Lourdes*. Baltimore, MD: John Murphy (pp. 29–39).
48. Harris, R. (1999). *Lourdes: Body and Spirit in the Secular Age*. New York, NY: Penguin Compass (p. 309).
49. Kaufman, S.K. (2005). *Consuming Visions: Mass Culture and the Lourdes Shrine*. Ithaca, NY: Cornell University Press (pp. 137–139).
50. Cadegan, U. (1995). "Images of Mary in Popular Periodicals." *Marian Studies, XLVI*, 87–107 (p. 97).
51. Ibid. pp. 100–101.
52. Apolito, P. (2005). *The Internet and the Madonna: Religious Visionary Experience on the Web* (A. Shugar, Trans.). Chicago, Ill: University of Chicago Press (p. 152).
53. Harris, R. (1999). *Lourdes: Body and Spirit in the Secular Age*. New York, NY: Penguin Compass (pp. 271–273).
54. Sered, S.S. (1986). "Rachel's Tomb and the Milk Grotto of the Virgin Mary: Two Women's Shrines in Bethlehem." *Journal of Feminist Studies in Religion, 2*(2), pp. 7–22 (p. 7).
55. Harris, R. (1999). *Lourdes: Body and Spirit in the Secular Age*. New York, NY: Penguin Compass (p. 361).

Chapter 5

1. *Dictionary of Mary*. (1985). New York, NY: Catholic Book Publishing (pp. 306–307).
2. Boyer, M.G. (1993). *Mary's day — Saturday: Meditations for Marian Celebrations*. Collegeville, MN: Liturgical Press (pp. 1–2).
3. *Dictionary of Mary*. (1985). New York, NY: Catholic Book Publishing (pp. 236–237).
4. Warner, M. (1976). *Alone of All Her Sex: The Myth and Cult of the Virgin Mary*. New York, NY: Vintage Books (p.281).
5. Andrew, S.M.M., RSM (1960). *Journal for Mary*. Boston, MA: Christopher Publishing House (p. 28).
6. Warner, M. (1976). *Alone of All Her Sex: The Myth and Cult of the Virgin Mary*. New York, NY: Vintage Books (p. 66).
7. MacGregor, A. (2002). "Candlemas: A Festival of Roman Origin." *Maria: A Journal of Marian Studies, 2*(1), pp. 26–45 (p. 33).
8. Wilson, S. (2004). *The Magical Universe: Everyday Ritual and Magic in Pre-Modern Europe*. New York, NY: Hambledon and London (p. 30).
9. Weiser, F.X. (1952). *Handbook of Christian Feasts and Customs*. New York, NY: Harcourt, Brace (pp. 299–300).
10. Wilson, S. (2004). *The Magical Universe: Everyday Ritual and Magic in Pre-Modern Europe*. New York, NY: Hambledon and London (pp. 30–31).
11. Warner, M. (1976). *Alone of All Her Sex: The Myth and Cult of the Virgin Mary*. New York, NY: Vintage Books (p. 299).
12. Ibid. p. 87.
13. Weiser, F.X. (1952). *Handbook of Christian Feasts and Customs*. New York, NY: Harcourt, Brace (pp. 286–287).
14. Wilson, S. (2004). *The Magical Universe: Everyday Ritual and Magic in Pre-Modern Europe*. New York, NY: Hambledon and London (p. 42).
15. Weiser, F.X. (1952). *Handbook of Christian Feasts and Customs*. New York, NY: Harcourt, Brace (pp. 23–24).
16. Elliott, D. (1993). *Spiritual Marriage: Sexual Abstinence in Medieval Wedlock*. Princeton, NJ: Princeton University Press (p. 225).
17. Weiser, F.X. (1952). *Handbook of Christian Feasts and Customs*. New York, NY: Harcourt, Brace (pp. 31–37).
18. Cooper, K. (1998). "Contesting the Nativity: Wives, Virgins and Pulcheria's Imitatio Mariae." *The Scottish Journal of Religious Studies, 19*(1), pp. 31–43 (pp. 38–40).
19. Abbott, E. (2000). *A History of Celibacy*. New York, NY: Scribner (p. 146).
20. Leyser, H. (1995). *Medieval Women: A Social History of Women in England 450–1500*. New York, NY: St. Martin's Press (p. 93).
21. Reed, T. (2003). *Shadows of Mary: Reading the Virgin Mary in Medieval Texts*. Cardiff, Wales: University of Wales Press (p. 56).
22. Amt, E. (ed.) (1993). *Women's Lives in Medieval Europe: A Sourcebook*. New York, NY: Routledge (pp. 23–24).
23. Underhill, E. (1905). *The Miracles of Our Lady Saint Mary*. London, England: William Heinemann (p. 263).
24. Atkinson, C. (1991). *The Oldest Vocation: Christian Motherhood in the Middle Ages*. Ithaca, NY: Cornell University Press (p. 123).
25. Wilson, S. (2004). *The Magical Universe: Everyday Ritual and Magic in Pre-Modern Europe*. New York, NY: Hambledon and London (p. 124).
26. Elliott, D. (1993). *Spiritual Marriage: Sexual Abstinence in Medieval Wedlock*. Princeton, NJ: Princeton University Press (pp. 176–179).
27. Shahar, S. (1983). *The Fourth Estate: A History of Women in the Middle Ages*. New York, NY: Methuen (p. 70).
28. Elliott, D. (1993). *Spiritual Marriage: Sexual Abstinence in Medieval Wedlock*. Princeton, NJ: Princeton University Press (pp. 284–286).
29. Leyser, H. (1995). *Medieval Women: A Social History of Women in England 450–1500*. New York, NY: St. Martin's Press (p. 106).

30. Gambero, L. (2000). *Mary in the Middle Ages: The Blessed Virgin Mary in the Thought of Medieval Latin Theologians* (T. Buffer, Trans.). San Francisco, CA: Ignatius Press (pp. 240–241).
31. Leyser, H. (1995). *Medieval Women: A Social History of Women in England 450–1500*. New York, NY: St. Martin's Press (pp. 109–111).
32. Elliott, D. (1993). *Spiritual Marriage: Sexual Abstinence in Medieval Wedlock*. Princeton, NJ: Princeton University Press (p. 169).
33. Leyser, H. (1995). *Medieval Women: A Social History of Women in England 450–1500*. New York, NY: St. Martin's Press (pp. 96–98).
34. Ibid. pp. 124–125.
35. Gambero, L. (2000). *Mary in the Middle Ages: The Blessed Virgin Mary in the Thought of Medieval Latin Theologians* (T. Buffer, Trans.). San Francisco, CA: Ignatius Press (p. 242).
36. Atkinson, C. (1991). *The Oldest Vocation: Christian Motherhood in the Middle Ages*. Ithaca, NY: Cornell University Press (p. 136).
37. Crawford, A. (Ed.), (1994). *Letters of the Queens of England*. Gloucestershire, England: Sutton Publishing (p. 87).
38. Wilson, S. (2004). *The Magical Universe: Everyday Ritual and Magic in Pre-Modern Europe*. New York, NY: Hambledon and London (p. 131).
39. Crawford, A. (Ed.), (1994). *Letters of the Queens of England*. Gloucestershire, England: Sutton Publishing (p. 173).
40. Wilson, S. (2004). *The Magical Universe: Everyday Ritual and Magic in Pre-Modern Europe*. New York, NY: Hambledon and London (pp. 135–136).
41. Ibid. p. 154.
42. Rawcliffe, C. (2003). "Women, Childbirth and Religion in Later Medieval England." In D. Wood (Ed.), *Women and Religion in Medieval England* (pp. 91–117). Oakville, CT: Oxbow Books (p. 91).
43. Ibid. p. 98.
44. Warner, M. (1976). *Alone of All Her Sex: The Myth and Cult of the Virgin Mary*. New York, NY: Vintage Books (p. 275).
45. Rawcliffe, C. (2003). "Women, Childbirth and Religion in Later Medieval England." In D. Wood (Ed.), *Women and Religion in Medieval England* (pp. 91–117). Oakville, CT: Oxbow Books (p. 107).
46. Leyser, H. (1995). *Medieval Women: A Social History of Women in England 450–1500*. New York, NY: St. Martin's Press (p. 129).
47. Elsakkers, M. (2004). "In Pain You Shall Bear Children (Gen. 3:16): Medieval Prayers for a Safe Delivery." In A.M. Korte (Ed.), *Women and Miracle Stories: A Multidisciplinary Exploration* (pp. 179–209). Boston, MA: Brill Press (p. 184).
48. Ibid. pp.194–195.
49. Rawcliffe, C. (2003). "Women, Childbirth and Religion in Later Medieval England." In D. Wood (Ed.), *Women and Religion in Medieval England* (pp. 91–117). Oakville, CT: Oxbow Books (pp. 98–104).
50. Wilson, S. (2004). *The Magical Universe: Everyday Ritual and Magic in Pre-Modern Europe*. New York, NY: Hambledon and London (p. 227).
51. Ibid. p. 253.
52. Leyser, H. (1995). *Medieval Women: A Social History of Women in England 450–1500*. New York, NY: St. Martin's Press (pp. 129–130).
53. Warner, M. (1976). *Alone of All Her Sex: The Myth and Cult of the Virgin Mary*. New York, NY: Vintage Books (p. 204).
54. Ibid. pp. 198–200.
55. Atkinson, C. (1991). *The Oldest Vocation: Christian Motherhood in the Middle Ages*. Ithaca, NY: Cornell University Press (p. 60).
56. Ibid. p. 189.
57. Harline, C. (2003). *Miracles at the Jesus Oak: Histories of the Supernatural in Reformation Europe*. New York, NY: Doubleday (p. 58).
58. Ibid. pp. 53–60.
59. Ibid. p. 70.
60. Ibid. pp. 62–78.
61. Warner, M. (1976). *Alone of All Her Sex: The Myth and Cult of the Virgin Mary*. New York, NY: Vintage Books (pp. 143–144).
62. Atkinson, C. (1991). *The Oldest Vocation: Christian Motherhood in the Middle Ages*. Ithaca, NY: Cornell University Press (p. 153).
63. Warner, M. (1976). *Alone of All Her Sex: The Myth and Cult of the Virgin Mary*. New York, NY: Vintage Books (p. 182).
64. Atkinson, C. (1991). *The Oldest Vocation: Christian Motherhood in the Middle Ages*. Ithaca, NY: Cornell University Press (p. 162).
65. Ibid. p. 123.

Chapter 6

1. Gibson, G.M. (1990). "Saint Anne and the Religion of Childbed: Some East Anglian Texts and Talismans." In K. Ashley and P. Sheingorn (Eds.), *Interpreting Cultural Symbols: Saint Anne in Late Medieval Society* (pp. 95–110). Athens, GA: University of Georgia Press (p. 98).
2. Wilson, S. (2004). *The Magical Universe: Everyday Ritual and Magic in Pre-Modern Europe*. New York, NY: Hambledon and London (p. 128).
3. Byzantines.net. "Glorious St. Anne: Mother of the Theotokos." 24 January 2007, <http://www.byzantines.net/saints/st%20anne.htm> (pp. 2–3).
4. Cunneen, S. (1996). *In Search of Mary: The Woman and the Symbol*. New York: Ballantine Books (p. 191).
5. Nixon, V. (2004). *Mary's Mother: St. Anne in Late Medieval Europe*. University Park, PA: Pennsylvania State University Press (p. 71).
6. Sheingorn, P. (1990). "Appropriating the Holy Kinship: Gender and Family History." In K. Ashley and P. Sheingorn (Eds.), *Interpreting Cultural Symbols: Saint Anne in Late Medieval Society* (pp. 169–198). Athens, GA: University of Georgia Press (p. 176).
7. Ibid. p. 180.
8. Ibid. p. 178.

9. Ashley, K. (1990). "Image and Ideology: Saint Anne in Late Medieval Drama and Narrative." In K. Ashley and P. Sheingorn (Eds.), *Interpreting Cultural Symbols: Saint Anne in Late Medieval Society* (pp.111–130). Athens, GA: University of Georgia Press (p. 119).
10. Sautman, F. (1990). "Saint Anne in Folk Tradition: Late Medieval France." In K. Ashley and P. Sheingorn (Eds.), *Interpreting Cultural Symbols: Saint Anne in Late Medieval Society* (pp. 69–94). Athens, GA: University of Georgia Press (pp. 70–71).
11. Orth, M.D. (1990). "'Madame Saint Anne': The Holy Kinship, the Royal Trinity, and Louise of Savoy." In K. Ashley and P. Sheingorn (Eds.), *Interpreting Cultural Symbols: Saint Anne in Late Medieval Society* (pp. 199–227). Athens, GA: University of Georgia Press (p. 212).
12. Ibid. pp. 204–205.
13. Sautman, F. (1990). "Saint Anne in Folk Tradition: Late Medieval France." In K. Ashley and P. Sheingorn (Eds.), *Interpreting Cultural Symbols: Saint Anne in Late Medieval Society* (pp. 69–94). Athens, GA: University of Georgia Press (p. 80).
14. Ibid. p. 81.
15. Ibid. p. 77.
16. Brandenbarg, T. (1995). "Saint Anne: A Holy Grandmother and Her Children." In A.B. Mulder-Bakker (Ed.), *Sanctity and Motherhood: Essays on Holy Mothers in the Middle Ages* (pp. 31–65). New York, NY: Garland (p. 33).
17. Ibid. pp. 33–34.
18. Nixon, V. (2004). *Mary's Mother: St. Anne in Late Medieval Europe*. University Park, PA: Pennsylvania State University Press (pp. 11–16).
19. Brandenbarg, T. (1995). "Saint Anne: A Holy Grandmother and Her Children." In A.B. Mulder-Bakker (Ed.), *Sanctity and Motherhood: Essays on Holy Mothers in the Middle Ages* (pp. 31–65). New York, NY: Garland (p. 43).
20. Tilmans, K. (1995). "Sancta Mater Versus Sanctus Doctus: Saint Anne and the Humanists." In A.B. Mulder-Bakker (Ed.), *Sanctity and Motherhood: Essays on Holy Mothers in the Middle Ages* (pp. 330–351). New York, NY: Garland (p. 334).
21. Brandenbarg, T. (1995). "Saint Anne: A Holy Grandmother and Her Children." In A.B. Mulder-Bakker (Ed.), *Sanctity and Motherhood: Essays on Holy Mothers in the Middle Ages* (pp. 31–65). New York, NY: Garland (p. 334).
22. Ibid. p. 58.
23. Sautman, F. (1990). "Saint Anne in Folk Tradition: Late Medieval France." In K. Ashley and P. Sheingorn (Eds.), *Interpreting Cultural Symbols: Saint Anne in Late Medieval Society* (pp. 69–94). Athens, GA: University of Georgia Press (p. 84).
24. Warner, M. (1976). *Alone of All Her Sex: The Myth and Cult of the Virgin Mary*. New York, NY: Vintage Books (p. 26).
25. Nixon, V. (2004). *Mary's Mother: St. Anne in Late Medieval Europe*. University Park, PA: Pennsylvania State University Press (p. 16).
26. Brandenbarg, T. (1995). "Saint Anne: A Holy Grandmother and Her Children." In A.B. Mulder-Bakker (Ed.), *Sanctity and Motherhood: Essays on Holy Mothers in the Middle Ages* (pp. 31–65). New York, NY: Garland (p. 55).
27. Wilson, S. (2004). *The Magical Universe: Everyday Ritual and Magic in Pre-Modern Europe*. New York, NY: Hambledon and London (p. 136).
28. Ibid. 178.
29. Sautman, F. (1990). "Saint Anne in Folk Tradition: Late Medieval France." In K. Ashley and P. Sheingorn (Eds.), *Interpreting Cultural Symbols: Saint Anne in Late Medieval Society* (pp. 69–94). Athens, GA: University of Georgia Press (p. 82).
30. Keyes, F.P. (1955). *St. Anne: Grandmother of Our Saviour*. New York, NY: Julian Messner. (p. 121).
31. Ronan, R.M.V. (1927). *S. Anne: Her Cult and Shrines*. London, England: Sands. (pp. 41–68).
32. Warner, M. (1976). *Alone of All Her Sex: The Myth and Cult of the Virgin Mary*. New York, NY: Vintage Books (pp. 30–31).
33. Ronan, R.M.V. (1927). *S. Anne: Her Cult and Shrines*. London, England: Sands. (p. 70).
34. Ibid. p. 71.
35. Nixon, V. (2004). *Mary's Mother: St. Anne in Late Medieval Europe*. University Park, PA: Pennsylvania State University Press (p. 46).
36. Ronan, R.M.V. (1927). *S. Anne: Her Cult and Shrines*. London, England: Sands. (p. 4).
37. Nixon, V. (2004). *Mary's Mother: St. Anne in Late Medieval Europe*. University Park, PA: Pennsylvania State University Press (p. 47).
38. Tilmans, K. (1995). "Sancta Mater Versus Sanctus Doctus: Saint Anne and the Humanists." In A.B. Mulder-Bakker (Ed.), *Sanctity and Motherhood: Essays on Holy Mothers in the Middle Ages* (pp. 330–351). New York, NY: Garland (p. 334).
39. Cunneen, S. (1996). *In Search of Mary: The Woman and the Symbol*. New York: Ballantine Books (p. 207).
40. Messadie, G. (1996). *A History of the Devil*. New York, NY: Kodansha International (p. 305).
41. Warner, M. (1976). *Alone of All Her Sex: The Myth and Cult of the Virgin Mary*. New York, NY: Vintage Books (p. 246).
42. Cristiani, L. (1962). *Evidence of Satan in the Modern World*. New York, NY: Macmillan. (Translated by Cynthia Rowland from 1959 ed.) (p. 57).
43. Ibid. pp. 80–81.
44. Ibid. p. 145.
45. Ibid. p. 83.
46. Gregg, J.Y. (1997). *Devils, Women and Jews: Reflections of the Other in Medieval Sermon Stories*. Albany, NY: State University of New York Press (pp. 156–157).
47. Ibid. pp. 162–164.
48. Russell, J.B. (1988). *The Prince of Darkness: Radical Evil and the Power of Good in History*. Ithaca, NY: Cornell University Press (p. 117).
49. Trachtenberg, J. (1943). *The Devil and the Jews: The Medieval Conception of the Jew and its Relation to Modern Anti-Semitism*. Philadelphia, PA: The Jewish Publication Society of America (p. 119).
50. Ibid. p. 186.
51. Gregg, J.Y. (1997). *Devils, Women and Jews: Reflections of the Other in Medieval Sermon Stories*.

Albany, NY: State University of New York Press (pp. 230–231).
52. Ibid. p. 228.
53. Tilmans, K. (1995). "Sancta Mater Versus Sanctus Doctus: Saint Anne and the Humanists." In A.B. Mulder-Bakker (Ed.), *Sanctity and Motherhood: Essays on Holy Mothers in the Middle Ages* (pp. 330–351). New York, NY: Garland (pp. 334–335).
54. Phillips, J.A. (1984). *Eve: The History of an Idea*. San Francisco, CA: Harper and Row (p. 139).
55. Dehau, P.T. (1958). *Eve and Mary* (Dominican Nuns of the Perpetual Rosary, Trans.). St. Lous, MO: B. Herder Book Co. (p. 71).
56. Cunneen, S. (1996). *In Search of Mary: The Woman and the Symbol*. New York: Ballantine Books (pp. 63–64).
57. Phillips, J.A. (1984). *Eve: The History of an Idea*. San Francisco, CA: Harper and Row (pp. 135–136).
58. Anderson, G.A. (2001). *The Genesis of Perfection: Adam and Eve in Jewish and Christian Imagination*. Louisville, KY: Westminster John Knox Press (p. 97).
59. Ibid. p. 92.
60. Warner, M. (1976). *Alone of All Her Sex: The Myth and Cult of the Virgin Mary*. New York, NY: Vintage Books (p. 60).
61. Ibid. p. 106.
62. Cunneen, S. (1996). *In Search of Mary: The Woman and the Symbol*. New York: Ballantine Books (p. 164).
63. Anderson, G.A. (2001). *The Genesis of Perfection: Adam and Eve in Jewish and Christian Imagination*. Louisville, KY: Westminster John Knox Press (p. 89).
64. Ibid. pp. 2–7.
65. Cunneen, S. (1996). *In Search of Mary: The Woman and the Symbol*. New York: Ballantine Books (p. 258).
66. Dehau, P.T. (1958). *Eve and Mary* (Dominican Nuns of the Perpetual Rosary, Trans.). St. Lous, MO: B. Herder Book Co. (p. 157).
67. Ibid. p. 41.
68. Ibid. p. 217.
69. Ibid. p. 155.
70. Ibid. p. 61.
71. Fitzgerald, K.K. (2002). "The Eve-Mary Typology and Women in the Orthodox Church: Reconsidering Rhodes." *Anglican Theological Review, LXXXIV*(3), pp. 627–644. (pp. 629–630).
72. Weyermann, M. (2002). "The Typologies of Adam-Christ and Eve-Mary, and Their Relationship to One Another." *Anglican Theological Review, LXXXIV*(3), pp. 609–626. (p. 625).
73. Ibid. p. 626.
74. Garside, C. (1973). "Good and Evil for Women." In J.P. Goldenberg and J.A. Romero (Eds.) *Women and Religion 1973: Pre-Printed papers for the Working Group on Women and Religion* (pp.104–124). Tallahassee, FL: American Academy of Religion. (p. 113).
75. Cunneen, S. (1996). *In Search of Mary: The Woman and the Symbol*. New York: Ballantine Books (p. 295).
76. Phillips, J.A. (1984). *Eve: The History of an Idea*. San Francisco, CA: Harper and Row (p. 142).
77. Ibid. pp. 142–145.
78. Filas, F.L. (1944). *The Man Nearest to Christ: Nature and Historic Development of the Devotion to St. Joseph*. Milwaukee, WI: Bruce Publishing (pp. 62–67).
79. O'Rafferty, N. (1951). *Discourses on St. Joseph: For the Month of March, St. Joseph's Feasts, and Similar Occasions*. Milwaukee, WI: Bruce Publishing (p. 58).
80. Ibid. pp. 57–58.
81. Wilson, C.C. (2001). *St Joseph in Italian Renaissance Society and Art: New Directions and Interpretations*. Philadelphia, PA: Saint Joseph's University Press (p. 3).
82. Ibid. p. 5.
83. Ibid. p. 14.
84. Filas, F.L. (1944). *The Man Nearest to Christ: Nature and Historic Development of the Devotion to St. Joseph*. Milwaukee, WI: Bruce Publishing (p. 138).
85. Ibid. p. 105.
86. Wilson, C.C. (2001). *St Joseph in Italian Renaissance Society and Art: New Directions and Interpretations*. Philadelphia, PA: Saint Joseph's University Press (pp. 17–19).
87. Mueller, R.J. (1952). *The Fatherhood of St. Joseph*. St. Lous, MO: B. Herder Book Co. (p. 6).
88. Wilson, C.C. (2001). *St Joseph in Italian Renaissance Society and Art: New Directions and Interpretations*. Philadelphia, PA: Saint Joseph's University Press (p. 3).
89. Warner, M. (1976). *Alone of All Her Sex: The Myth and Cult of the Virgin Mary*. New York, NY: Vintage Books (p. 26).
90. Filas, F.L. (1944). *The Man Nearest to Christ: Nature and Historic Development of the Devotion to St. Joseph*. Milwaukee, WI: Bruce Publishing (p. 33).
91. O'Rafferty, N. (1951). *Discourses on St. Joseph: For the Month of March, St. Joseph's Feasts, and Similar Occasions*. Milwaukee, WI: Bruce Publishing (p. 64).
92. Mueller, R.J. (1952). *The Fatherhood of St. Joseph*. St. Lous, MO: B. Herder Book Co. (p. 203).
93. Ibid. p. 221.
94. O'Rafferty, N. (1951). *Discourses on St. Joseph: For the Month of March, St. Joseph's Feasts, and Similar Occasions*. Milwaukee, WI: Bruce Publishing (p. 208).
95. Mueller, R.J. (1952). *The Fatherhood of St. Joseph*. St. Lous, MO: B. Herder Book Co. (pp. 17–19).
96. Filas, F.L. (1959). *St. Joseph and Daily Christian Living*. New York, NY: Macmillan (p. 34).
97. Ibid. pp. 38–39.
98. Ibid. p. 43.

Chapter 7

1. Wiseman, D.V., O.P. (2001). "Devotion to Mary Among the Dominicans in the Thirteenth Century." *Marian Studies, 52*, 246–263 (p. 251).

Notes—Chapter 7

2. Amt, E. (Ed.), (1993). *Women's Lives in Medieval Europe: A Sourcebook*. New York, NY: Routledge (p. 221).

3. Leyser, H. (1995). *Medieval Women: A Social History of Women in England 450–1500*. New York, NY: St. Martin's Press (p. 190).

4. Bynum, C.W. (1987). *Holy Feast and Holy Fast: The Religious Significance of Food to Medieval Women*. Berkeley, CA: University of California Press (p. 14).

5. Ibid. p. 6.

6. Shahar, S. (1983). *The Fourth Estate: A History of Women in the Middle Ages*. New York, NY: Methuen (p. 30).

7. Mooney, C.M. (1999). "Imitatio Christi or Imitatio Mariae? Clare of Assisi and Her Interpreters." In C.M. Mooney (Ed.), *Gendered Voices: Medieval Saints and Their Interpreters*. Philadelphia, PA: University of Pennsylvania Press (pp. 52–77). (p. 53).

8. Ibid. pp. 58–59.

9. Ibid. p. 60.

10. Ibid. pp. 75–76.

11. Ibid. pp. 70–73.

12. Gambero, L. (2000). *Mary in the Middle Ages: The Blessed Virgin Mary in the Thought of Medieval Latin Theologians* (T. Buffer, Trans.). San Francisco, CA: Ignatius Press (p. 69).

13. Abbott, E. (2000). *A History of Celibacy*. New York, NY: Scribner (p. 122).

14. Strasser, U. (2004). *State of Virginity: Gender, Religion and Politics in an Early Modern Catholic State*. Ann Arbor, MI: University of Michigan Press (p. 126).

15. Warner, M. (1976). *Alone of All Her Sex: The Myth and Cult of the Virgin Mary*. New York, NY: Vintage Books (p. 128).

16. McDannell, C. & Lang, B. (1988). *Heaven: A History*. New Haven, CT: Yale University Press (p. 101).

17. Ibid. pp. 102–106

18. Abbott, E. (2000). *A History of Celibacy*. New York, NY: Scribner (p. 94).

19. Shahar, S. (1983). *The Fourth Estate: A History of Women in the Middle Ages*. New York, NY: Methuen (p. 26).

20. Oliva, M. (1998). *The Convent and the Community in Late Medieval England: Female Monasteries in the Diocese of Norwich 1350–1540*. Rochester, NY: Boydell Press (p. 63).

21. Filax, E. (1995). "A Female I-deal: Chaucer's Second Nun." In M. Whitaker (Ed.), *Sovereign Lady: Essays on Women in Middle English Literature* (pp. 133–156). New York, NY: Garland (p. 140).

22. Ibid. pp. 144–145.

23. Underhill, E. (1905). *The Miracles of Our Lady Saint Mary*. London, England: William Heinemann (p. 195).

24. Warren, N.B. (2001). *Spiritual Economies: Female Monasticism in Later Medieval England*. Philadelphia, PA: University of Pennsylvania Press (p. 77).

25. Herolt, J. (1928). *Miracles of the Blessed Virgin Mary* (C.C. S. Bland, Trans.). New York, NY: Harcourt, Brace (Original Work published 1440.) (pp. 42–45).

26. Warner, M. (1976). *Alone of All Her Sex: The Myth and Cult of the Virgin Mary*. New York, NY: Vintage Books (p. 133).

27. Abbott, E. (2000). *A History of Celibacy*. New York, NY: Scribner (pp. 133–135).

28. Brown, J.C. (1999). "Everyday Life, Longevity and Nuns in Early Modern Florence." In P. Fumerton & S. Hunt (Eds.), *Renaissance Culture and the Everyday* (pp.115–138). Philadelphia, PA: University of Pennsylvania Press (pp. 124–132).

29. McNamara, J.A.K. (1996). *Sisters in Arms: Catholic Nuns Through Two Millennia*. Cambridge, MA: Harvard University Press (p. 199).

30. Ibid. p. 200.

31. Warner, M. (1976). *Alone of All Her Sex: The Myth and Cult of the Virgin Mary*. New York, NY: Vintage Books (pp. 30, 323).

32. Spretnak, C. (2004). *Missing Mary: The Queen of Heaven and Her Re-Emergence in the Modern Church*. New York, NY: Palgrave MacMillan (pp. 91–92).

33. Cunneen, S. (1996). *In Search of Mary: The Woman and the Symbol*. New York, NY: Ballantine Books (pp. 162–165).

34. Warren, N.B. (2001). *Spiritual Economies: Female Monasticism in Later Medieval England*. Philadelphia, PA: University of Pennsylvania Press (pp. 11–12).

35. Ibid. p. 123.

36. Ibid. pp. 45–48

37. Ibid. p. 116.

38. Ibid. pp. 117–119.

39. Ibid. p. 107.

40. Sperling, J. G. (1999). *Convents and the Body Politic in Late Renaissance Venice*. Chicago, Ill: University of Chicago Press (pp. 83, 96).

41. Laven, M. (2002). *Virgins of Venice: Broken Vows and Cloistered Lives in the Renaissance Convent*. New York, NY: Penguin Books (pp. 67–68).

42. Abbott, E. (2000). *A History of Celibacy*. New York, NY: Scribner (pp. 138–140).

43. Laven, M. (2002). *Virgins of Venice: Broken Vows and Cloistered Lives in the Renaissance Convent*. New York, NY: Penguin Books (pp. 3–4).

44. Ibid. p. 150.

45. Watson, R. N. (1998). "The State of Life and the Power of Death: Measure for Measure." In G.M. Kendall (Ed.), *Shakespearean Power and Punishment: A Volume of Essays* (pp. 130–156). Madison, NJ: Farleigh Dickinson University Press (pp. 144–145).

46. Andrew, S.M.M., RSM (1960). *Journal for Mary*. Boston, MA: Christopher Publishing House (pp. 16–17).

47. Lester, R. J. (2005). *Jesus in Our Wombs: Embodying Modernity in a Mexican Convent*. Berkeley, CA: University of California Press (pp. 101–102).

48. Ibid. p. 81.

49. Ibid. pp. 73–76.

50. Ibid. p. 160.

51. *Dictionary of Mary*. (1985). New York, NY: Catholic Book Publishing (p. 341).

Chapter 8

1. Frolich, M. (2001). "Christian Mysticism in Postmodernity: Therese of Lisieux as a Case Study." In D.B. Perrin (Ed.), *Women Christian Mystics Speak to Our Times* (pp. 157–171). Franklin, WI: Sheed and Ward (p. 158–159).
2. Haliczer, S. (2002). *Between Exaltation and Infamy: Female Mystics in the Golden Age of Spain.* New York, NY: Oxford University Press (p. 4).
3. Schutte, A.J. (2001). *Aspiring Saints: Pretense of Holiness, Inquisition and Gender in the Republic of Venice 1618–1750.* Baltimore, MD: Johns Hopkins University Press (p. 55).
4. Christian, W.A., Jr. (1981). *Apparitions in Late Medieval and Renaissance Spain.* Princeton, NJ: Princeton University Press (p. 190).
5. Haliczer, S. (2002). *Between Exaltation and Infamy: Female Mystics in the Golden Age of Spain.* New York, NY: Oxford University Press (pp. 54–55).
6. Christian, W.A., Jr. (1981). *Apparitions in Late Medieval and Renaissance Spain.* Princeton, NJ: Princeton University Press (p. 197).
7. Schutte, A.J. (2001). *Aspiring Saints: Pretense of Holiness, Inquisition and Gender in the Republic of Venice 1618–1750.* Baltimore, MD: Johns Hopkins University Press (p. 56).
8. Bremner, E. (1992). "Margery Kempe and the Critics: Disempowerment and Deconstruction." In S.J. McEntire (Ed.), *Margery Kempe: A Book of Essays* (pp. 117–135). New York, NY: Garland (pp. 120–129).
9. Christian, W.A., Jr. (1981). *Apparitions in Late Medieval and Renaissance Spain.* Princeton, NJ: Princeton University Press (p. 192).
10. Ibid. p. 198.
11. Abbott, E. (2000). *A History of Celibacy.* New York, NY: Scribner (pp. 232–233).
12. Cunneen, S. (1996). *In Search of Mary: The Woman and the Symbol.* New York, NY: Ballantine Books (p. 159).
13. Brown, R. (1994). *Saints Who Saw Mary.* Rockford, Ill.: Tan Books and Publishers (p. 59).
14. Haliczer, S. (2002). *Between Exaltation and Infamy: Female Mystics in the Golden Age of Spain.* New York, NY: Oxford University Press (pp. 89–90).
15. Clark, A.L. (2002). "The Priesthood of the Virgin Mary: Gender Trouble in the Twelfth Century." *Journal of Feminist Studies in Religion, 18* (1), 5–24 (pp. 18–21).
16. Elkins, S. (1997). "Gertrude the Great and the Virgin Mary. *Church History, 66* (4), 720–734 (p. 723).
17. Ibid. pp. 724–731.
18. Sahlin, C. L. (2001). *Birgitta of Sweden and the Voice of Prophecy.* (Studies in Medieval Mysticism, Vol. 3) Rochester, NY: Boydell Press (pp. 78–79).
19. Ibid. p. 83.
20. Birgitta, S. (1984). *Revelations of St. Bridget on the Life and Passion of Our Lord and the Life of His Blessed Mother.* Rockford, Ill: Tan Books and Publishers (Original Work Published 1611.) (p. 14).
21. Abbott, E. (2000). *A History of Celibacy.* New York, NY: Scribner (p. 59).
22. Bechtold, J. "St. Birgitta: The Disjunction between Women and Ecclesiastical Power." *Equally in God's Image: Women in the Middle Ages,* chapter two. 18 Feb. 2006, <www.umilta.net/equal2.html>. (pp. 37–43).
23. Birgitta, S. (1984). *Revelations of St. Bridget on the Life and Passion of Our Lord and the Life of His Blessed Mother.* Rockford, Ill: Tan Books and Publishers (Original Work Published 1611.) (p. 23).
24. Atkinson, C.W. (1983). *Mystic and Pilgrim: The Book and the World of Margery Kempe.* Ithaca, NY: Cornell University Press (pp. 176–178).
25. Newman, B. (1999). "Intimate Pieties: Holy Trinity and Holy Family in the Late Middle Ages." *Religion and Literature, 31* (1), 77–102 (pp. 89–90).
26. Hutchison, A.M. (2004). "Reflections on the Spiritual Impact of St. Birgitta, the Revelations and the Bridgettine Order in Late Medieval England." In E.A. Jones (Ed.), *The Medieval Mystical Tradition in England: Exeter Symposium VII* (pp. 69–82). Rochester, NY: D.S. Brewer (p. 78).
27. Kempe, M. (1998). *The Book of Margery Kempe* (J. Skinner, Trans.). New York, NY: Image Books (Original work published 1438.) (pp. 40–41).
28. Ibid. p. 111.
29. Ibid. p. 245.
30. Ibid. p. 229.
31. Christian, W.A., Jr. (1981). *Apparitions in Late Medieval and Renaissance Spain.* Princeton, NJ: Princeton University Press (p. 188).
32. Sahlin, C.L. (2001). *Birgitta of Sweden and the Voice of Prophecy.* (Studies in Medieval Mysticism, Vol. 3) Rochester, NY: Boydell Press (p. 83).
33. Christian, W.A., Jr. (1981). *Apparitions in Late Medieval and Renaissance Spain.* Princeton, NJ: Princeton University Press (p. 98).
34. Ibid. p. 47.
35. Honore, J. "The Tide of Vain Credulity: The Church's Role in Apparitions." *Catholic Culture,* 23 Feb. 2006, <www.catholicculture.org/docs/doc_view.cfm?recnum=1047>.
36. Schwebel, L.J. (2004). *Apparitions, Healings and Weeping Madonnas: Christianity and the Paranormal."* Mahwah, NJ: Paulist Press (pp. 122–131).
37. Durham, M.S. (1995). *Miracles of Mary: Apparitions, Legends and Miraculous Works of the Blessed Virgin Mary.* San Francisco, CA: HarperCollins (p. 145).
38. Abbott, E. (2000). *A History of Celibacy.* New York, NY: Scribner (p. 59).
39. Crapez, R.E., C.M. (1918). *Venerable Catherine Laboure: Daughter of Charity of Saint Vincent de Paul 1806–1876.* Emmitsburg, MD: St. Joseph's (pp. 12–14).
40. Ibid. p. 26.
41. Durham, M.S. (1995). *Miracles of Mary: Apparitions, Legends and Miraculous Works of the Blessed Virgin Mary.* San Francisco, CA: HarperCollins (pp. 143–144).
42. Ibid. pp. 86–88.
43. Warner, M. (1976). *Alone of All Her Sex: The*

Myth and Cult of the Virgin Mary. New York, NY: Vintage Books (p. 223).
44. Ibid. pp. 216–218.
45. Durham, M.S. (1995). *Miracles of Mary: Apparitions, Legends and Miraculous Works of the Blessed Virgin Mary*. San Francisco, CA: HarperCollins. Page number?
46. Ibid. pp. 174–175.
47. Rutkoff, A. & Oats, D. "Housewife's Vision Breaks Out Bayside Hills Turf War." *Queens Tribune*, 27 Feb. 2006 <http://www.queenstribune.com/anniversary2003/baysidehillsturfwar.htm>
48. Laurentin, R. (1990). *The Apparitions of the Blessed Virgin Mary Today*. Dublin, Ireland: Veritas Publications (p. 141).
49. Harline, C. (2003). *Miracles at the Jesus Oak: Histories of the Supernatural in Reformation Europe*. New York, NY: Doubleday (p. 12).
50. Ibid. p. 13.
51. Garnett, J. & Rosser, G. (2004). "The Virgin Mary and the People of Liguria: Image and Cult." In R.N. Swanson (Ed.), *The Church and Mary* (pp. 280–288). Rochester, NY: Boydell Press (pp. 280–281).
52. Harline, C. (2003). *Miracles at the Jesus Oak: Histories of the Supernatural in Reformation Europe*. New York, NY: Doubleday (p. 71).
53. Ibid. p. 84.
54. Carroll, M.P. (1992). *Madonnas That Maim: Popular Catholicism in Italy Since the Fifteenth Century*. Baltimore, MD: Johns Hopkins University Press (p. 19).
55. Carroll, M.P. (1996). *Veiled Threats: The Logic of Popular Catholicism in Italy*. Baltimore, MD: Johns Hopkins University Press (p. 59).
56. Ibid. p. 45.
57. Ibid. p. 21.
58. Ibid. p. 22.
59. Aston, M. (1988). *England's Iconoclasts: Laws Against Images*. New York, NY: Clarendon Press (pp. 107–109).
60. Ibid. p. 109.
61. Ibid. pp. 138–139.
62. Dolan, F.E. (1999). *Whores of Babylon: Catholicism, Gender and Seventeenth-Century Print Culture*. Notre Dame, Indiana: University of Notre Dame Press (p. 111).
63. Aston, M. (1988). *England's Iconoclasts: Laws Against Images*. New York, NY: Clarendon Press (p. 278).
64. Harline, C. (2003). *Miracles at the Jesus Oak: Histories of the Supernatural in Reformation Europe*. New York, NY: Doubleday (p. 189).
65. Zavjalova, M. "Folk Knowledge: Lithuanian Spells." 4 October, 2006, <http://ausis.gf.vu.lt/eka/spells.html> (pp. 3–4).
66. Carroll, M.P. (1992). *Madonnas That Maim: Popular Catholicism in Italy Since the Fifteenth Century*. Baltimore, MD: Johns Hopkins University Press (pp. 114–115).
67. Zavjalova, M. "Folk Knowledge: Lithuanian Spells." 4 October, 2006, <http://ausis.gf.vu.lt/eka/spells.html> (pp. 5–6).
68. Harline, C. (2003). *Miracles at the Jesus Oak: Histories of the Supernatural in Reformation Europe*. New York, NY: Doubleday (pp. 157–158).
69. Michael, P.K. (2004). *The Serpent and the Moon: Two Rivals for the Love of a Renaissance King*. New York, NY: Touchstone Books (p. 200).
70. Warner, M. (1976). *Alone of All Her Sex: The Myth and Cult of the Virgin Mary*. New York, NY: Vintage Books (p. 308).
71. Monter, E.W. (1987). *Enforcing Morality in Early Modern Europe*. London, England: Variorum Reprints (p. 128).
72. Warner, M. (1976). *Alone of All Her Sex: The Myth and Cult of the Virgin Mary*. New York, NY: Vintage Books (p. 323).
73. Underhill, E. (1905). *The Miracles of Our Lady Saint Mary*. London, England: William Heinemann (pp. 257–270).
74. McCleery, I. (2004). "The Virgin and the Devil: The Role of the Virgin Mary in the Theophilus Legend and its Spanish and Portuguese Variants." In R.N. Swanson (Ed.), *The Church and Mary* (pp. 147–156). Rochester, NY: Boydell Press (p. 151).
75. Ibid. p. 154.
76. Fanger, C. (1998). "Plundering the Egyptian Treasure: John the Monk's Book of Visions and Its Relation to the Ars Notoria of Solomon." In C. Fanger (Ed.), *Conjuring Spirits: Texts and Traditions of Medieval Ritual Magic* (pp. 216–235). University Park, PA: Pennsylvania State University Press (p. 217).
77. Evans-Wentz, W.Y. (2004). *The Fairy Faith in Celtic Countries*. Franklin Lakes, NJ: New Page Books (Original work published 1911.) (p. 122).
78. Ibid. p. 112.
79. Ibid. pp. 112–113.
80. Ibid. p. 72.
81. Harline, C. (2003). *Miracles at the Jesus Oak: Histories of the Supernatural in Reformation Europe*. New York, NY: Doubleday (p. 207).

Chapter 9

1. Johnson, E.A. (2003). *Truly Our Sister: A Theology of Mary in the Communion of Saints*. New York, NY: Continuum (p. 75).
2. Spretnak, C. (2004). *Missing Mary: The Queen of Heaven and Her Re-Emergence in the Modern Church*. New York, NY: Palgrave MacMillan (pp. 152–153).
3. Kramer-Rolls, D. (2004). ""The Emergence of the Goddess Mary."" *The Pomegranate*, 6 (1), pp. 34–50 (p. 42).
4. Cooper, K. (1998). "Contesting the Nativity: Wives, Virgins and Pulcheria's Imitatio Mariae." *The Scottish Journal of Religious Studies*, 19 (1), pp. 31–43 (p. 37).
5. Ibid. pp. 31–35.
6. Benko, S. (1993). *The Virgin Goddess: Studies in the Pagan and Christian Roots of Mariology*. New York, NY: E.J. Brill (p. 264).
7. Ibid. p. 176.

8. Spretnak, C. (2004). *Missing Mary: The Queen of Heaven and Her Re-Emergence in the Modern Church*. New York, NY: Palgrave Macmillan (p. 185).
9. Benko, S. (1993). *The Virgin Goddess: Studies in the Pagan and Christian Roots of Mariology*. New York, NY: E.J. Brill (p. 174).
10. Jordan, M. (2003). *The Historical Mary: Revealing the Pagan Identity of the Virgin Mother*. Berkeley, CA: Seastone Press (p. 182).
11. Benko, S. (1993). *The Virgin Goddess: Studies in the Pagan and Christian Roots of Mariology*. New York, NY: E.J. Brill (pp. 176–186).
12. Wilson, S. (2004). *The Magical Universe: Everyday Ritual and Magic in Pre-Modern Europe*. New York, NY: Hambledon and London (p. 18).
13. Ibid. p. 46.
14. Berger, P. (1985). *The Goddess Obscured: Transformation of the Grain Protectress from Goddess to Saint*. Boston, MA: Beacon Press (p. 138).
15. Ibid. p. 90.
16. Burdick, L.D. (1905). *Magic and Husbandry: The Folk-Lore of Agriculture*. Binghamton, NY: Otseningo Publishing (p. 50).
17. Berger, P. (1985). *The Goddess Obscured: Transformation of the Grain Protectress from Goddess to Saint*. Boston, MA: Beacon Press (p. 89).
18. Ibid. pp. 93–94.
19. Ibid. p. 16.
20. Ibid. p. 141.
21. Polinska, W. (2004). "In Woman's Image: An Iconography." *Feminist Theology, 13* (1), pp. 40–61 (p. 50).
22. Jordan, M. (2003). *The Historical Mary: Revealing the Pagan Identity of the Virgin Mother*. Berkeley, CA: Seastone Press (p. 199).
23. Burdick, L.D. (1905). *Magic and Husbandry: The Folk-Lore of Agriculture*. Binghamton, NY: Otseningo Publishing (p. 49).
24. Warner, H. (1976). *Alone of All Her Sex: The Myth and Cult of the Virgin Mary*. New York, NY: Vintage Books (pp. 282–283).
25. Burdick, L.D. (1905). *Magic and Husbandry: The Folk-Lore of Agriculture*. Binghamton, NY: Otseningo Publishing (pp. 104–105).
26. Wilson, S. (2004). *The Magical Universe: Everyday Ritual and Magic in Pre-Modern Europe*. New York, NY: Hambledon and London (p. 84).
27. Ibid. p. 80.
28. Berger, P. (1985). *The Goddess Obscured: Transformation of the Grain Protectress from Goddess to Saint*. Boston, MA: Beacon Press (p. 115).
29. MacGregor, A. (2002). "Candlemas: A Festival of Roman Origin." *Maria: A Journal of Marian Studies, 2* (1), pp. 26–45 (p. 34).
30. Ibid. pp. 36–39.
31. Benko, S. (1993). *The Virgin Goddess: Studies in the Pagan and Christian Roots of Mariology*. New York, NY: E.J. Brill (p. 221).
32. Ibid. p. 212–214.
33. Kramer-Rolls, D. (2004). "The Emergence of the Goddess Mary." *The Pomegranate, 6* (1), pp. 34–50 (pp. 40–41).
34. Benko, S. (1993). *The Virgin Goddess: Studies in the Pagan and Christian Roots of Mariology*. New York, NY: E.J. Brill (p. 225).
35. Ibid. p. 225.
36. Kramer-Rolls, D. (2004). "The Emergence of the Goddess Mary." *The Pomegranate, 6* (1), pp. 34–50 (pp. 37–38).
37. Benko, S. (1993). *The Virgin Goddess: Studies in the Pagan and Christian Roots of Mariology*. New York, NY: E.J. Brill (p. 214).
38. Carroll, M.P. (1999). *Irish Pilgrimage: Holy Wells and Popular Catholic Devotion*. Baltimore, MD: Johns Hopkins University Press (p. 57).
39. Spretnak, C. (2004). *Missing Mary: The Queen of Heaven and Her Re-Emergence in the Modern Church*. New York, NY: Palgrave Macmillan (pp. 106–107).
40. Carroll, M.P. (1999). *Irish Pilgrimage: Holy Wells and Popular Catholic Devotion*. Baltimore, MD: Johns Hopkins University Press (p. 55).
41. Vrudny, K. (1999). "Medieval Fascination with the Queen: Esther as the Queen of Heaven and Host of the Messianic Banquet." *Arts: The Arts in Religious and Theological Studies, 11* (2), pp. 36–43 (pp. 37–40).
42. Cunneen, S. (1996). *In Search of Mary: The Woman and the Symbol*. New York, NY: Ballantine Books (p. 199).
43. Ruether, R.R. (2005). *Goddesses and the Divine Feminine: A Western Religious History*. Berkeley, CA: University of California Press (p. 221).
44. Cunneen, S. (1996). *In Search of Mary: The Woman and the Symbol*. New York, NY: Ballantine Books (p. 201).
45. Ruether, R. R. (2005). *Goddesses and the Divine Feminine: A Western Religious History*. Berkeley, CA: University of California Press (p. 225).
46. Pelikan, J. (1996). *Mary Through the Centuries: Her Place in the History of Culture*. New Haven, CT: Yale University Press (p. 161).
47. Hackett, H. (1995). *Virgin Mother, Maiden Queen: Elizabeth I and the Cult of the Virgin Mary*. New York, NY: St. Martin's Press (pp. 29–32).
48. Ibid. p. 34.
49. Wizeman, W., SJ. (2004). "The Virgin Mary in the Reign of Mary Tudor." In R.N. Swanson (Ed.), *The Church and Mary* (pp. 239–248). Rochester, NY: Boydell Press (p. 245).
50. Hackett, H. (1993). "Rediscovering Shock: Elizabeth I and the Cult of the Virgin Mary." *The Critical Quarterly, 35* (3), pp. 30–42. (p. 36).
51. Dolan, F.E. (1999). *Whores of Babylon: Catholicism, Gender and Seventeenth-Century Print Culture*. Notre Dame, Indiana: University of Notre Dame Press (pp. 111–112).
52. Levin, C. (1994). *The Heart and Stomach of a King: Elizabeth I and the Politics of Sex and Power*. Philadelphia, PA: University of Pennsylvania Press (pp. 28–30).
53. Ibid. p. 104.
54. Cunneen, S. (1996). *In Search of Mary: The Woman and the Symbol*. New York, NY: Ballantine Books (p. 205).
55. Dolan, F.E. (1999). *Whores of Babylon: Catholicism, Gender and Seventeenth-Century Print*

Culture. Notre Dame, Indiana: University of Notre Dame Press (pp. 97–98).
56. Ibid. p. 99.
57. Ibid. pp. 125–126.
58. Ibid. pp. 131–132.
59. Ibid. pp. 148–149.
60. Ibid. p. 152.
61. Ruether, R.R. (2005). *Goddesses and the Divine Feminine: A Western Religious History*. Berkeley, CA: University of California Press (p. 274).
62. Wolfteich, C.E. (2002). *Navigating New Terrain: Work and Women's Spiritual Lives*. Mahwah, NJ: Paulist Press (p. 61).
63. Ibid. p. 108.
64. Ibid. p. 159.
65. Ibid. p. 152.

Chapter 10

1. Reidy, M.T. "Fiction Trumps Fact: 8 Reasons Why 'Da Vinci Code' Remains so Popular." May 27, 2006, *Catholic Online*. 29 June 2006 <http://www.catholic.org/php?id=19994&section=Cathcom> (p.2).
2. Alaimo, K. "'Da Vinci code' Lifts Lid on Goddess Scholarship." May 21, 2006. *Women's Enews*. 29 June 2006, <http://www.womensnews.org/article.cfm?aid=2748> (pp. 1–2).
3. Haskins, S. (1993). *Mary Magdalen: Myth and Metaphor*. New York, NY: Riverhead Books (p. 387).
4. Lightbourn, F.C. (1959). "Mary Magdalene in Scripture and Tradition." *Religion in Life*, XXVIII(2), pp. 273–280. (p. 273).
5. Ibid. p. 280.
6. Knutson, G.C. (1997). "The Feast of Saint Mary Magdalene." *Worship*, 71(3), (pp. 205–220) (p. 206).
7. Ibid. pp. 212–213.
8. Ibid. pp. 214–216.
9. Cantavella, R. (1990). "Medieval Catalan Mary Magdalen Narratives." In J.E. Connolly, A. Deyermond & B. Dutton (Eds.), *Saints and Their Authors: Studies in Medieval Hispanic Hagiography in Honor of John K. Walsh* (pp. 27–36). Madison, WI: The Hispanic Seminary of Medieval Studies (p. 32).
10. Ibid. p. 33.
11. Nolan, L. (1990). "Is She Dancing? A New Reading of Lucas van Leyden's Dance of the Magdalene of 1519." In J.B. Holloway, C.S. Wright & J. Bechtold (Eds.), *Equally in God's Image: Women in the Middle Ages* (pp. 233–250). New York, NY: Peter Lang (p. 236).
12. Schaberg, J. (1992). "How Mary Magdalene Became a Whore." *Bible Review*, VIII(5), (pp. 30–37, 51–52). (p. 51).
13. Garth, H.M. (1950). *Saint Mary Magdalene in Medieval Literature*. Baltimore, MD: Johns Hopkins Press (pp. 105–106).
14. Ibid. p. 80.
15. Haskins, S. (1993). *Mary Magdalen: Myth and Metaphor*. New York, NY: Riverhead Books (p. 171).
16. Grieco, S.F.M. (1999). "Models of Female Sanctity in Renaissance and Counter-Reformation Italy." In L. Scaraffia and G. Zarri (Eds.), *Women and Faith: Catholic Life in Italy from Late Antiquity to the Present* (pp. 159–175). Cambridge, MA: Harvard University Press (p. 167).
17. Jansen, K.L. (2000). *The Making of the Magdalen: Preaching and Popular Devotion in the Later Middle Ages*. Princeton, NJ: Princeton University Press (pp. 286–287).
18. Haskins, S. (1993). *Mary Magdalen: Myth and Metaphor*. New York, NY: Riverhead Books (p. 138).
19. Visser. D. (1992). "Faith and Love: The Iconography of Mary Magdalene, 1450–1650." In M. P. Fleischer (Ed.), *The Harvest of Humanism in Central Europe: Essays in Honor of Lewis W. Spitz* (pp. 281–302). St. Louis, MO: Concordia Publishing House (p. 293).
20. Haskins, S. (1993). *Mary Magdalen: Myth and Metaphor*. New York, NY: Riverhead Books (p. 156).
21. Ibid. p. 199.
22. Ibid. p. 201.
23. Karras, R.M. (1996). *Common Women: Prostitution and Sexuality in Medieval England*. New York, NY: Oxford University Press (pp. 115–117).
24. Haskins, S. (1993). *Mary Magdalen: Myth and Metaphor*. New York, NY: Riverhead Books (p. 132).
25. Jansen, K.L. (2000). *The Making of the Magdalen: Preaching and Popular Devotion in the Later Middle Ages*. Princeton, NJ: Princeton University Press (p. 300).
26. Ibid. p. 303.
27. Haskins, S. (1993). *Mary Magdalen: Myth and Metaphor*. New York, NY: Riverhead Books (pp. 212–213).
28. Jansen, K.L. (2000). *The Making of the Magdalen: Preaching and Popular Devotion in the Later Middle Ages*. Princeton, NJ: Princeton University Press (p. 294).
29. Ibid. p. 298.
30. Haskins, S. (1993). *Mary Magdalen: Myth and Metaphor*. New York, NY: Riverhead Books (pp. 324–325).
31. Jansen, K.L. (2000). *The Making of the Magdalen: Preaching and Popular Devotion in the Later Middle Ages*. Princeton, NJ: Princeton University Press (p. 260).
32. Ibid. p. 271.
33. Garth, H.M. (1950). *Saint Mary Magdalene in Medieval Literature*. Baltimore, MD: Johns Hopkins Press (p. 99).
34. Jansen, K.L. (2000). *The Making of the Magdalen: Preaching and Popular Devotion in the Later Middle Ages*. Princeton, NJ: Princeton University Press (p. 256).
35. Koenig, E.K.J. (1993). "Julian of Norwich, Mary Magdalene and the Drama of Prayer." *Horizons*, 20(1), pp. 23–43. (p. 27).
36. Ibid. pp. 37–40.

37. Jansen, K.L. (2000). *The Making of the Magdalen: Preaching and Popular Devotion in the Later Middle Ages.* Princeton, NJ: Princeton University Press (pp. 119–121).
38. Ibid. pp. 304–305.
39. Garth, H.M. (1950). *Saint Mary Magdalene in Medieval Literature.* Baltimore, MD: Johns Hopkins Press (p. 438).
40. Jansen, K.L. (2000). *The Making of the Magdalen: Preaching and Popular Devotion in the Later Middle Ages.* Princeton, NJ: Princeton University Press (pp. 322–323).
41. Haskins, S. (1993). *Mary Magdalen: Myth and Metaphor.* New York, NY: Riverhead Books (pp. 303–305).
42. Jansen, K.L. (2000). *The Making of the Magdalen: Preaching and Popular Devotion in the Later Middle Ages.* Princeton, NJ: Princeton University Press (p. 308).
43. Haskins, S. (1993). *Mary Magdalen: Myth and Metaphor.* New York, NY: Riverhead Books (p. 152).
44. Jansen, K.L. (2000). *The Making of the Magdalen: Preaching and Popular Devotion in the Later Middle Ages.* Princeton, NJ: Princeton University Press (pp. 276–277).
45. Ibid. p. 273.
46. Ibid. pp. 262–263.
47. Ibid. pp. 279–282.
48. Karras, R.M. (1996). *Common Women: Prostitution and Sexuality in Medieval England.* New York, NY: Oxford University Press (p. 121).
49. Jansen, K.L. (2000). *The Making of the Magdalen: Preaching and Popular Devotion in the Later Middle Ages.* Princeton, NJ: Princeton University Press (p. 250).
50. Ibid. p. 159.
51. Slim, H.C. (1992). "Music and Dancing with Mary Magdalen in a Laura Vestalis." In C. A. Monson (Ed.), *The Crannied wall: Women, Religion and the Arts in Early Modern Europe* (pp. 139–160). Ann Arbor, MI: University of Michigan Press (p. 143).
52. Ibid. p. 145.
53. Nolan, L. (1990). "Is She Dancing? A New Reading of Lucas van Leyden's Dance of the Magdalene of 1519." In J.B. Holloway, C.S. Wright & J. Bechtold (Eds.), *Equally in God's Image: Women in the Middle Ages* (pp. 233–250). New York, NY: Peter Lang (pp. 240–243).
54. Jansen, K.L. (2000). *The Making of the Magdalen: Preaching and Popular Devotion in the Later Middle Ages.* Princeton, NJ: Princeton University Press (pp. 250–251).
55. Kruppa, P.S. (1992). "'More Sweet and Liquid Than Any Other': Victorian Images of Mary Magdalene." In R.W. Davis & R.J. Helmstadter (Eds.), *Religion and Irreligion in Victorian Society: Essays in Honor of R.K. Webb* (pp. 117–132). New York, NY: Routledge (p. 118).
56. Ibid. pp. 125–126.
57. Haskins, S. (1993). *Mary Magdalen: Myth and Metaphor.* New York, NY: Riverhead Books (pp. 167–170).
58. Kruppa, P.S. (1992). "'More Sweet and Liquid Than Any Other': Victorian Images of Mary Magdalene." In R.W. Davis & R.J. Helmstadter (Eds.), *Religion and Irreligion in Victorian Society: Essays in Honor of R.K. Webb* (pp. 117–132). New York, NY: Routledge (p. 122).
59. Haskins, S. (1993). *Mary Magdalen: Myth and Metaphor.* New York, NY: Riverhead Books (p. 242).
60. Kruppa, P.S. (1992). "'More Sweet and Liquid Than Any Other': Victorian Images of Mary Magdalene." In R.W. Davis & R.J. Helmstadter (Eds.), *Religion and Irreligion in Victorian Society: Essays in Honor of R.K. Webb* (pp. 117–132). New York, NY: Routledge (p. 124).
61. Haskins, S. (1993). *Mary Magdalen: Myth and Metaphor.* New York, NY: Riverhead Books (p. 360).
62. Benko, S. (1993). *The Virgin Goddess: Studies in the Pagan and Christian Roots of Mariology.* New York, NY: E.J. Brill (p. 81).
63. Ibid. p. 227.
64. Ibid. p. 264.
65. Baring, A. & Cashford, J. (1991). *The Myth of the Goddess: Evolution of an Image.* New York, NY: Viking Arkana (p. 547).
66. Ibid. p. 556.
67. Ibid. pp. 556–593.
68. Ruether, R. R. (2005). *Goddesses and the Divine Feminine: A Western Religious History.* Berkeley, CA: University of California Press (pp. 302–303).
69. Matter, E.A. (1983). "The Virgin Mary: A Goddess?" In C. Olson (Ed.), *The Book of the Goddess Past and Present: An Introduction to Her Religion.* New York, NY: Crossroad (p. 94).
70. Ibid. p. 93.
71. Reis-Habito, M. (1993). "The Bodhisattva Guanyin and the Virgin Mary." *Buddhist-Christian Studies, 13* pp. 61–69 (pp. 61–62).
72. Ibid. p. 66.
73. Lin, X. (2001). "Seeing the Place: The Virgin Mary in a Chinese Lady's Inner Chamber." In K.M. Comerford and H.M. Pabel (Eds.), *Early Modern Catholicism: Essays in Honour of John W. O'Malley, S.J.* (pp. 183–210). Buffalo, NY: University of Toronto Press (pp. 201–202).
74. Cleary, T. & Aziz, S. (2000). *Twilight Goddess: Spiritual Feminism and Feminine Spirituality.* Boston, MA: Shambhala Publications (p. 236).
75. Ibid. pp. 238–241.
76. Ibid. p. 241.

Bibliography

Abbott, E. (1999). *A History of Celibacy*. New York: Scribner.

Alaimo, K. "'Da Vinci Code' Lifts Lid on Goddess Scholarship." May 21, 2006, *Women's Enews*. 29 June 2006, <http://www.Women senews.org/article.cfm?aid=2748>.

Alban, K. (2005). "The Character and Influence of Carmelite Devotion to Mary in Medieval England." *Maria, 2*, pp. 73–104.

Amt, E., (Ed.), (1993). *Women's Lives in Medieval Europe: A Sourcebook*. New York, NY: Routledge.

Anderson, G.A. (2001). *The Genesis of Perfection: Adam and Eve in Jewish and Christian Imagination*. Louisville, KY: Westminster John Knox Press.

Andrew, S.M.M., RSM (1960). *Journal for Mary*. Boston, MA: Christopher Publishing House.

Apolito, P. (2005). *The Internet and the Madonna: Religious Visionary Experience on the Web* (A. Shugar, Trans.). Chicago, Ill: University of Chicago Press.

Aradi, Z. (1954). *Shrines to Our Lady Around the World*. New York, NY: Farrar, Straus and Giroux.

Ashley, K. (1990). "Image and Ideology: Saint Anne in Late Medieval Drama and Narrative. In K. Ashley and P. Sheingorn (Eds.), *Interpreting Cultural Symbols: Saint Anne in Late Medieval Society* (pp. 111–130). Athens, GA: University of Georgia Press.

Astell, A.W. (1990). *The Song of Songs in the Middle Ages*. Ithaca, NY: Cornell University Press.

Aston, M. (1988). *England's Iconoclasts: Laws Against Images*. New York, NY: Clarendon Press.

Atkinson, C.W. (1983). *Mystic and Pilgrim: The Book and the World of Margery Kempe*. Ithaca, NY: Cornell University Press.

Atkinson, C. (1991). *The Oldest Vocation: Christian Motherhood in the Middle Ages*. Ithaca, NY: Cornell University Press.

Averintsev, S.S. (1994). The Image of the Virgin Mary in Russian Piety. *Gregorianum, 75* (4), pp. 611–622.

Baring, A. & Cashford, J. (1991). *The Myth of the Goddess: Evolution of an Image*. New York, NY: Viking Arkana.

Bechtold, J. St. Birgitta: "The Disjunction Between Women and Ecclesiastical Power." *Equally in God's Image: Women in the Middle Ages*, chapter two. 18 Feb. 2006, <www.umilta.net/equal2.html>.

Bell, S.G. (1988). "Medieval Woman Book Owners: Arbiters of Lay Piety and Ambassadors of Culture." In M. Erler & M. Kowaleski (Eds.), *Women and Power in the Middle Ages* (pp. 149–187). Athens, GA: University of Georgia Press.

Benko, S. (1993). *The Virgin Goddess: Studies in the Pagan and Christian Roots of Mariology*. New York, NY: E.J. Brill.

Berger, P. (1985). *The Goddess Obscured: Transformation of the Grain Protectress from Goddess to Saint*. Boston, MA: Beacon Press.

Berryman, E. (2001). "Medjugorje's Living Icons: Making Spirit Matter (for Sociology)." *Social Compass, 2*, pp. 593–610.

Birgitta, S. (1984). *Revelations of St. Bridget on the Life and Passion of our Lord and the Life of His Blessed Mother*. Rockford, Ill: Tan Books and Publishers. (Original Work Published 1611.)

Boissarie, D. (1933). *Healing at Lourdes*. Baltimore, MD: John Murphy Company.

Boyer, M.G. (1993). *Mary's Day — Saturday: Meditations for Marian Celebrations*. Collegeville, MN: Liturgical Press.

Brandenbarg, T. (1995). "Saint Anne: A Holy Grandmother and Her Children." In A.B.

Mulder-Bakker (Ed.), *Sanctity and Motherhood: Essays on Holy Mothers in the Middle Ages* (pp. 31–65). New York, NY: Garland.

Bremner, E. (1992). "Margery Kempe and the Critics: Disempowerment and Deconstruction." In S.J. McEntire (Ed.), *Margery Kempe: A Book of Essays* (pp. 117–135). New York, NY: Garland.

Bridges, L.M. (1999). "Brigid, Mary, and Lotte: An Irish American Baptist Woman of the South Looks at the Blessed Virgin Mary." *Review and Expositor*, 96, pp. 565–580.

Bridgett, T.E. (1875). *Our Lady's Dowry: Or How England Gained and Lost That Title*. London: Burns and Oates.

Brown, J.C. (1999). "Everyday Life, Longevity and Nuns in Early Modern Florence." In P. Fumerton & S. Hunt (Eds.), *Renaissance Culture and the Everyday* (pp. 115–138). Philadelphia, PA: University of Pennsylvania Press.

Brown, R. (1994). *Saints Who Saw Mary*. Rockford, Ill.: Tan Books and Publishers.

Brown, R.E., Donfried, K.P., Fitzmyer, J.A., Reumann, J. (Eds.) (1978). *Mary in the New Testament*. Philadelphia, PA: Fortress Press.

Buck, P.F., S.J. (1980). "The Marian Interpretation of the 'Song of Songs' in the Middle Ages (A.D. 1100–1500). *Acta Congressus Mariologici-Mariani Internationalis Romae Anno 1975 Celebrati: Vol. IV. De culto mariano apud scriptores ecclesiasticos saec. XII-XIII*, 69–96.

Burdick, L.D. (1905). *Magic and husbandry: The Folk-Lore of Agriculture*. Binghamton, NY: Otseningo Publishing.

Butler, M.A. (1967). *Twice Queen of France: Anne of Brittany*. New York: Funk & Wagnalls.

Bynum, C.W. (1987). *Holy Feast and Holy fast: The Religious Significance of Food to Medieval Women*. Berkeley, CA: University of California Press.

Byzantines.net. "Glorious St. Anne: Mother of the Theotokos." 24 January 2007, <http://www.byzantines.net/Saints/st%20anne.htm>

Cadegan, U. (1995). "Images of Mary in Popular Periodicals." *Marian Studies*, XLVI, 87–107.

Cantavella, R. (1990). "Medieval Catalan Mary Magdalen Narratives." In J.E. Connolly, A. Deyermond & B. Dutton (Eds.), *Saints and Their Authors: Studies in Medieval Hispanic Hagiography in Honor of John K. Walsh* (pp. 27–36). Madison, WI: Hispanic Seminary of Medieval Studies.

Carroll, E.R. (2001). "Medieval Devotion to Mary Among the Carmelites. *Marian Studies*, LII, pp. 219–228.

Carroll, M.P. (1999). *Irish Pilgrimage: Holy Wells and Popular Catholic Devotion*. Baltimore, MD: Johns Hopkins University Press.

Carroll, M.P. (1992). *Madonnas That Maim: Popular Catholicism in Italy since the Fifteenth Century*. Baltimore, MD: Johns Hopkins University Press.

Carroll, M.P. (1996). *Veiled Threats: The Logic of Popular Catholicism in Italy*. Baltimore, MD: Johns Hopkins University Press.

Christian, W.A., Jr. (1981). *Apparitions in Late Medieval and Renaissance Spain*. Princeton, NJ: Princeton University Press.

Clark, A L. (2002). "The Priesthood of the Virgin Mary: Gender Trouble in the Twelfth Century. *Journal of Feminist Studies in Religion*, 18 (1), 5–24.

Cleary, T. & Aziz, S. (2000). *Twilight Goddess: Spiritual Feminism and Feminine Spirituality*. Boston, MA: Shambhala Publications.

Colahan, C. (1988). "Mary of Agreda, the Virgin Mary and Mystical Knowing." *Studia Mystica*, 9 (3), pp. 53–65.

Condren, M. (1999). *The Serpent and the Goddess: Women, Religion, and Power in Celtic Ireland*. San Francisco, CA: HarperCollins.

Cooper, K. (1998). "Contesting the Nativity: Wives, Virgins and Pulcheria's Imitatio Mariae." *The Scottish Journal of Religious Studies*, 19(1), pp. 31–43.

Crapez, R.E., C.M. (1918). *Venerable Catherine Laboure: Daughter of Charity of Saint Vincent de Paul 1806–1876*. Emmitsburg, MD: St. Joseph's.

Creasman, A.F. (2002). "The Virgin Mary Against the Jews: Anti-Jewish Polemic in the Pilgrimage to the Schone Maria of Regensburg, 1519–25." *The Sixteenth Century Journal* 33, (4), 963–980.

Cristiani, L. (1962). *Evidence of Satan in the Modern World*. New York, NY: Macmillan. (Translated by Cynthia Rowland from 1959 ed.)

Cunneen, S. (1999). "Breaking Mary's Silence: A Feminist Reflection on Marian Piety. *Theology Today*, 56 (3), pp. 319–335.

Cunneen, S. (1996). *In Search of Mary: The Woman and the Symbol*. New York: Ballantine Books.

Cunningham, L. (1982). *Mother of God*. San Francisco, CA: Harper and Row.

Dehau, P.T. (1958). *Eve and Mary* (Dominican Nuns of the Perpetual Rosary, Trans.). St. Louis, MO: B. Herder Book Co.

Dickinson, J.C. (1956). *The Shrine of Our Lady of Walsingham*. Cambridge, England: Cambridge University Press.

Dictionary of Mary. (1985). New York, NY: Catholic Book Publishing.

Dolan, F.E. (1999). *Whores of Babylon: Catholicism, Gender and Seventeenth-Century Print Culture*. Notre Dame, Indiana: University of Notre Dame Press.

Donofrio, B. (2000). *Looking for Mary: Or the Blessed Mother and Me*. New York: Viking Compass.

Durham, M.S. (1995). *Miracles of Mary: Apparitions, Legends and Miraculous Works of the Blessed Virgin Mary*. San Francisco, CA: HarperCollins.

Elkins, S. (1997). "Gertrude the Great and the Virgin Mary." *Church History*, 66 (4), 720–734.

Elkins, S. (2001). "The Virgin Mary in the Visions of Hildegard of Bingen (1098–1179)." In D.B. Perrin (Ed.), *Women Christian Mystics Speak to Our Times* (pp. 143–155). Franklin, WI: Sheed and Ward.

Elliott, D. (1993). *Spiritual Marriage: Sexual Abstinence in Medieval Wedlock*. Princeton, NJ: Princeton University Press.

Elsakkers, M. (2004). "'In Pain You Shall Bear Children' (Gen 3:16): Medieval Prayers for a Safe Delivery." In A.M. Korte (Ed.), *Women and Miracle stories: A Multidisciplinary Exploration* (pp. 179–209). Boston, MA: Brill Press.

Evans-Wentz, W.Y. (2004). *The Fairy Faith in Celtic Countries*. Franklin Lakes, NJ: New Page Books (Original work published 1911).

Fanger, C. (1998). "Plundering the Egyptian Treasure: John the Monk's Book of Visions and Its Relation to the Ars Notoria of Solomon." In C. Fanger (Ed.), *Conjuring Spirits: Texts and Traditions of Medieval Ritual Magic* (pp. 216–235). University Park, PA: Pennsylvania State University Press.

Filas, F.L. (1959). *St. Joseph and Daily Christian Living*. New York, NY: Macmillan.

Filas, F.L. (1944). *The Man Nearest to Christ: Nature and Historic Development of the Devotion to St. Joseph*. Milwaukee, WI: Bruce Publishing.

Filax, E. (1995). "A Female I-deal: Chaucer's Second Nun." In M. Whitaker (Ed.), *Sovereign Lady: Essays on Women in Middle English Literature* (pp. 133–156). New York, NY: Garland.

Fitzgerald, K.K. (2002). "The Eve-Mary Typology and Women in the Orthodox Church: Reconsidering Rhodes." *Anglican Theological Review*, LXXXIV(3), pp. 627–644.

Florendo, A.O. (2004). *The Liturgy of Flowers in a Mary Garden: A Contemplation*. New York, NY: Rosetti della Virgine Books.

Foley, D.J. "Mary Gardens." 29 March 2006, <http://www.mgardens.org/DF-MG-HE.html>.

Frolich, M. (2001). "Christian Mysticism in Postmodernity: Therese of Lisieux as a Case Study." In D.B. Perrin (Ed.), *Women Christian Mystics Speak to Our Times* (pp. 157–171). Franklin, WI: Sheed and Ward.

Galot, J., S.J. (1965). *Mary in the Gospel* (S.M. Constance, Trans.). Westminster, MD: Newman Press.

Gambero, L. (2000). *Mary in the Middle Ages: The Blessed Virgin Mary in the Thought of Medieval Latin Theologians* (T. Buffer, Trans.). San Francisco, CA: Ignatius Press.

Garnett, J. & Rosser, G. (2004). "The Virgin Mary and the People of Liguria: Image and Cult." In R.N. Swanson (Ed.), *The Church and Mary* (pp. 280–288). Rochester, NY: Boydell Press.

Garside, C. (1973). "Good and Evil for Women." In J.P. Goldenberg and J.A. Romero (Eds.), *Women and Religion 1973: Pre-Printed Papers for the Working Group on Women and Religion* (pp. 104–124). Tallahassee, FL: American Academy of Religion.

Garth, H.M. (1950). *Saint Mary Magdalene in Medieval Literature*. Baltimore, MD: Johns Hopkins Press.

Gaventa, B.R. (1995). *Mary: Glimpses of the Mother of Jesus*. Columbia, SC: University of South Carolina Press.

Gibson, G.M. (1990). "Saint Anne and the Religion of Childbed: Some East Anglian Texts and Talismans." In K. Ashley and P. Sheingorn (Eds.), *Interpreting Cultural Symbols: Saint Anne in Late Medieval Society* (pp. 95–110). Athens, GA: University of Georgia Press.

Gill, S. (2004). "Marian Revivalism in Modern English Christianity: The Example of Walsingham." In R.N. Swanson (Ed.), *The Church and Mary*. Rochester, NY: Boydell Press.

Graef, H. (1963). *Mary: A History of Doctrine and Devotion* (Vol. 1). New York: Sheed and Ward.

Gregg, J.Y. (1997). *Devils, Women and Jews: Reflections of the Other in Medieval Sermon Stories*. Albany, NY: State University of New York Press.

Grieco, S.F.M. (1999). "Models of Female Sanctity in Renaissance and Counter-Reformation Italy." In L. Scaraffia and G. Zarri (Eds.), *Women and Faith: Catholic Life in Italy from*

Late Antiquity to the Present." Cambridge, MA: Harvard University Press (pp. 159–175).

Hackett, H. (1993). "Rediscovering Shock: Elizabeth I and the Cult of the Virgin Mary." *The Critical Quarterly, 35* (3), pp. 30–42.

Hackett, H. (1995). *Virgin Mother, Maiden Queen: Elizabeth I and the Cult of the Virgin Mary.* New York, NY: St. Martin's Press.

Haliczer, S. (2002). *Between Exaltation and infamy: Female Mystics in the Golden Age of Spain.* New York, NY: Oxford University Press.

Hallissy, M. (1993). *Clean Maids, True Wives, Steadfast Widows: Chaucer's Women and Medieval Codes of Conduct.* Westport, CN: Greenwood Press.

Harline, C. (2003). *Miracles at the Jesus Oak: Histories of the Supernatural in Reformation Europe.* New York, NY: Doubleday.

Harrington, P.A. (1984). "Mary and Femininity: A Psychological Critique." *Journal of Religion and Health, 23* (3), pp. 204–217.

Harrington, P. (1988). "Mother of Death, Mother of Rebirth: The Mexican Virgin of Guadalupe." *Journal of the American Academy of Religion, LVI* (1), pp. 25–50.

Harris, R. (1999). *Lourdes: Body and Spirit in the Secular Age.* New York, NY: Penguin Compass.

Harthan, J. (1977). *Books of Hours and Their Owners* London: Thames and Hudon.

Haskins, S. (1993). *Mary Magdalen: Myth and Metaphor.* New York, NY: Riverhead Books.

Haughton, R. (1976). *Feminine Spirituality: Reflections on the Mysteries of the Rosary.* New York: The Missionary Society of St. Paul the Apostle.

Heimann, M. (1995). *Catholic Devotion in Victorian England.* New York, NY: Oxford University Press.

Herolt, J. (1928). *Miracles of the Blessed Virgin Mary* (C.C. S. Bland, Trans.). New York, NY: Harcourt Brace (Original Work published 1440).

Hicks, M.A. (1987). "The Piety of Margaret, Lady Hungerford (d. 1478)." *Journal of Ecclesiastical History, 38* (1), pp. 19–38.

Honore, J. "The Tide of Vain Credulity: The Church's Role in Apparitions. *Catholic Culture,* 23 Feb. 2006, <www.catholicCulture.org/docs/doc_view.cfm?recnum=1047>.

Hopper, S. (2002). *To Be a Pilgrim: The Medieval Pilgrimage Experience.* Gloucestershire, England: Sutton Publishing.

Hutchison, A.M. (2004). "Reflections on the Spiritual Impact of St. Birgitta, the Revelations and the Bridgettine Order in Late Medieval England." In E.A. Jones (Ed.), *The Medieval mystical tradition in England: Exeter symposium VII* (pp. 69–82). Rochester, NY: D.S. Brewer.

Jansen, K.L. (2000). *The Making of the Magdalen: Preaching and Popular Devotion in the Later Middle Ages.* Princeton, NJ: Princeton University Press.

Johnson, E. A. (1985) "The Marian Tradition and the Reality of Women." *Horizons 12* (1), 116–135.

Johnson, E.A. (2003). *Truly Our Sister: A Theology of Mary in the Communion of Saints.* New York: Continuum.

Jordan, M. (2003). *The Historical Mary: Revealing the Pagan Identity of the Virgin Mother.* Berkeley, CA: Seastone Press.

Karras, R.M. (1996). *Common Women: Prostitution and Sexuality in Medieval England.* New York, NY: Oxford University Press.

Karras, R.M. (1990). "Holy Harlots: Prostitute Saints in Medieval Legend." *Journal of the History of Sexuality, 1,* pp. 3–32.

Kaufman, S.K. (2005). *Consuming Visions: Mass Culture and the Lourdes Shrine.* Ithaca, NY: Cornell University Press.

Kempe, M. (1998). *The Book of Margery Kempe* (J. Skinner, Trans.). New York, NY: Image Books (Original work published 1438).

Keyes, F.P. (1955). *St. Anne: Grandmother of Our Saviour.* New York, NY: Julian Messner.

Knutson, G.C. (1997). "The Feast of Saint Mary Magdalene." *Worship, 71* (3), pp. 205–220.

Koenig, E.K.J. (1993). "Julian of Norwich, Mary Magdalene and the Drama of Prayer." *Horizons, 20*(1), pp. 23–43.

Kramer-Rolls, D. (2004). "The Emergence of the Goddess Mary." *The Pomegranate, 6* (1), pp. 34–50.

Kruppa, P.S. (1992). "'More Sweet and Liquid Than Any Other': Victorian Images of Mary Magdalene." In R.W. Davis & R.J. Helmstadter (Eds.), *Religion and Irreligion in Victorian society: Essays in honor of R.K. Webb* (pp. 117–132). New York, NY: Routledge.

Kraus, H. (1982). "Eve and Mary: Conflicting Images of Medieval Woman." In N. Broude & M.D. Garrard (Eds.), *Feminism and Art History: Questioning the Litany* (pp. 79–99). New York: Harper & Row.

Krymow, V. (2002). *Mary's Flowers: Gardens, Legends and Meditations.* Cincinnati, OH: St. Anthony Messenger Press.

Laurentin, R. (1990). *The Apparitions of the Blessed Virgin Mary Today.* Dublin, Ireland: Veritas Publications.

Laven, M. (2002). *Virgins of Venice: Broken Vows*

and *Cloistered Lives in the Renaissance Convent*. New York, NY: Penguin Books.
Lester, R.J. (2005). *Jesus in Our Wombs: Embodying Modernity in a Mexican Convent*. Berkeley, CA: University of California Press.
Levin, C. (1994). *The Heart and Stomach of a King: Elizabeth I and the Politics of Sex and Power*. Philadelphia, PA: University of Pennsylvania Press.
Leyser, H. (1995). *Medieval Women: A Social History of Women in England 450–1500*. New York, NY: St. Martin's Press.
Lightbourn, F.C. (1959). "Mary Magdalene in Scripture and Tradition." *Religion in Life*, XXVIII(2), pp. 273–280.
Lin, X. (2001). "Seeing the Place: The Virgin Mary in a Chinese Lady's Inner Chamber." In K.M. Comerford and H.M. Pabel (Eds.), *Early Modern Catholicism: Essays in Honour of John W. O'Malley, S.J.* (pp. 183–210). Buffalo, NY: University of Toronto Press.
MacGibbon, D. (1933). *Jean Bourdichon: A Court Painter in the Fifteenth Century*. Glasgow: Robert Maclehose.
MacGregor, A. (2002). "Candlemas: A Festival of Roman Origin." *Maria: A Journal of Marian Studies*, 2(1), pp. 26–45.
Matter, E.A. (1983). "The Virgin Mary: A Goddess?" In C. Olson (Ed.), *The Book of the Goddess Past and Present: An Introduction to Her Religion*. New York, NY: Crossroad.
Matter, E.A. (1990). *The Voice of my Beloved: The Song of Songs in Western Medieval Christianity*. Philadelphia, PA: University of Pennsylvania Press.
McClain, L. (2004). *Lest We Be Damned: Practical Innovation and Lived Experience Among Catholics in Protestant England, 1559–1642*. New York, NY: Routledge.
McCleery, I. (2004). "The Virgin and the Devil: The Role of the Virgin Mary in the Theophilus Legend and Its Spanish and Portuguese Variants." In R.N. Swanson (Ed.), *The Church and Mary* (pp. 147–156). Rochester, NY: Boydell Press.
McDannell, C. & Lang, B. (1988). *Heaven: A History*. New Haven, CT: Yale University Press.
McHugh, J. (1975). *The Mother of Jesus in the New Testament*. Garden City, NY: Doubleday.
McNamara, J.A.K. (1996). *Sisters in Arms: Catholic Nuns Through Two Millennia*. Cambridge, MA: Harvard University Press.
Messadie, G. (1996). *A History of the Devil*. New York, NY: Kodansha International.
Michael, P. K. (2004). *The Serpent and the Moon: Two Rivals for the Love of a Renaissance King*. New York, NY: Touchstone Books.
Miller, J.D. (2002). *Beads and Prayers: The Rosary in History and Devotion*. London: Burns and Oates.
Moldenke, H.N. "Flowers of the Madonna." Dec., 1953, *HortiCulture*. 29 March 2006, <http://www.mgardens.org/HM-FOTM-HO.html>.
Monter, E.W. (1987). *Enforcing Morality in Early Modern Europe*. London, England: Variorum Reprints.
Mooney, C.M. (1999). "Imitatio Christi or Imitatio Mariae? Clare of Assisi and her Interpreters." In C.M. Mooney (Ed.), *Gendered Voices: Medieval Saints and Their Interpreters* (pp. 52–77). Philadelphia, PA: University of Pennsylvania Press.
Mueller, R.J. (1952). *The Fatherhood of St. Joseph*. St. Louis, MO: B. Herder Book Co.
Newman, B. (1999). "Intimate Pieties: Holy Trinity and Holy Family in the Late Middle Ages." *Religion and Literature*, 31(1), pp. 77–102.
Nixon, V. (2004). *Mary's Mother: St. Anne in Late Medieval Europe*. University Park, PA: Pennsylvania State University Press.
Nolan, L. (1990). "Is She Dancing? A New Reading of Lucas van Leyden's Dance of the Magdalene of 1519." In J.B. Holloway, C.S. Wright & J. Bechtold (Eds.), *Equally in God's Image: Women in the Middle Ages* (pp. 233–250). New York, NY: Peter Lang.
Oliva, M. (1998). *The Convent and the Community in Late Medieval England: Female Monasteries in the Diocese of Norwich 1350–1540*. Rochester, NY: Boydell Press.
O'Rafferty, N. (1951). *Discourses on St. Joseph: For the Month of March, St. Joseph's Feasts, and Similar Occasions*. Milwaukee, WI: Bruce Publishing.
Orth, M.D. (1990). "'Madame Saint Anne': The Holy Kinship, the Royal Trinity, and Louise of Savoy." In K. Ashley and P. Sheingorn (Eds.), *Interpreting Cultural Symbols: Saint Anne in Late Medieval Society* (pp. 199–227). Athens, GA: University of Georgia Press.
Os, H. van (1994). *The Art of Devotion in the Late Middle Ages in Europe 1300–1500*. Princeton, NJ: Princeton University Press.
Pelikan, J. (1996). *Mary Through the Centuries: Her Place in the History of Culture*. New Haven, CT: Yale University Press.
Penkneth, S. (1997). "Women and Books of Hours." In L. Smith & J.H.M. Taylor (Eds.), *Women and the Book: Assessing the Visual*

Evidence (pp. 266–281). London: The British Library.
Pereyra, A. (1997). "The Virgin of Guadalupe: History, Myth and Spirituality." *Currents in Theology and Mission, 24* (4), pp. 348–354.
Peters, C. (2003). *Patterns of Piety: Women, Gender and Religion in Late Medieval and Reformation England.* New York, NY: Cambridge University.
Petitot, F.H., OP. (1950). *The True Story of Saint Bernadette.* Westminster, MD: Newman Press.
Phillips, J.A. (1984). *Eve: The History of an Idea.* San Francisco, CA: Harper and Row.
Pizan, C. de (1989) *A Medieval Woman's Mirror of Honor: The Treasury of the City of Ladies* (C.C. Willard, Trans.). Tenafly, NJ: Bard Hall Press (Original work published 1405).
Polinska, W. (2004). "In Woman's Image: An Iconography." *Feminist Theology, 13* (1), pp. 40–61.
Poos, L.R. (1988). "Social History and the Book of Hours." In R.S. Wieck (Ed.), *The Book of Hours in Medieval Art and Life* (pp. 33–38). London: George Braziller.
Porcher, J. (1959). *The Rohan Book of Hours.* New York: Thomas Yoseloff.
Rawcliffe, C. (2002). "Curing Bodies and Healing Souls: Pilgrimage and the Sick in Medieval East Anglia." In C. Morris and P. Roberts (Eds.), *Pilgrimage: The English Experience from Becket to Bunyan* (pp. 108–140). Cambridge, UK: Cambridge University Press.
Rawcliffe, C. (2003). "Women, Childbirth and Religion in Later Medieval England." In D. Wood (Ed.), *Women and Religion in Medieval England* (pp. 91–117). Oakville, CT: Oxbow Books.
Reed, T. (2003). *Shadows of Mary: Reading the Virgin Mary in Medieval Texts.* Cardiff, Wales: University of Wales Press.
Reidy, M.T. "Fiction Trumps Fact: 8 Reasons Why 'Da Vinci Code' Remains so Popular." May 27, 2006, *Catholic Online.* 29 June 2006, <http://www.catholic.org/php?id=19994&section=Cathcom>.
Reimer, S. "Women in the Mary Garden Feed a Flowering of Spirit." *The Baltimore Sun,* Sunday, May 14, 1995. 29 March 2006, <http://www.mgardens.org/SR-SOD-BS.html>.
Reis-Habito, M. (1993). "The Bodhisattva Guanyin and the Virgin Mary." *Buddhist-Christian Studies, 13,* pp. 61–69.
Riani, P.R. (1955). *Mary in the Twelfth Chapter of the Apocalypse.* Baltimore, MD: St. Mary's Seminary and University.

Ronan, R.M.V. (1927). *S. Anne: Her Cult and Shrines.* London, England: Sands.
Roten, J.G. (1998). "Mary and the Way of Beauty." *Marian Studies, XLIX,* pp. 109–127.
Ruether, R.R. (2005). *Goddesses and the Divine Feminine: A Western Religious History.* Berkeley, CA: University of California Press.
Russell, J.B. (1988). *The Prince of Darkness: Radical Evil and the Power of Good in History.* Ithaca, NY: Cornell University Press.
Rutkoff, A. & Oats, D. "Housewife's Vision Breaks Out Bayside Hills Turf War." *Queens Tribune,* 27 Feb. 2006. <http://www.Queenstribune.com/anniversary2003/baysidehillsturfwar.htm>
Saenger, P. (1985). "Books of Hours and the Reading Habits of the Later Middle Ages." *Scrittura e Civilta, 9,* 239–269.
Sahlin, C.L. (2001). *Birgitta of Sweden and the Voice of Prophecy* (Studies in Medieval Mysticism, Vol. 3). Rochester, NY: Boydell Press.
Saint-Jacques, D.P. "Women on Pilgrimage." Mar. 2004, *Terre Entiere.* (C. Buuck, Trans.) 29 Mar. 2006, <http://www.Saint-jacques.info/Women>.
Sautman, F. (1990). "Saint Anne in Folk Tradition: Late Medieval France." In K. Ashley and P. Sheingorn (Eds.), *Interpreting Cultural Symbols: Saint Anne in Late Medieval Society* (pp. 69–94). Athens, GA: University of Georgia Press.
Schaberg, J. (1992). "How Mary Magdalene Became a Whore." *Bible Review, VIII*(5), (pp. 30–37, 51–52).
Schoemperlen, Diane (2001). *Our Lady of the Lost and Found: A Novel.* New York: Viking.
Schutte, A.J. (2001). *Aspiring Saints: Pretense of holiness, Inquisition and Gender in the Republic of Venice 1618–1750.* Baltimore, MD: Johns Hopkins University Press.
Schwebel, L.J. (2004). *Apparitions, Healings and Weeping Madonnas: Christianity and the Paranormal.* Mahwah, NJ: Paulist Press.
Sered, S.S. (1986). "Rachel's Tomb and the Milk Grotto of the Virgin Mary: Two Women's Shrines in Bethlehem." *Journal of Feminist Studies in Religion, 2*(2), pp. 7–22.
Shahar, S. (1983). *The Fourth Estate: A History of Women in the Middle Ages.* New York, NY: Methuen.
Sheingorn, P. (1990). "Appropriating the Holy Kinship: Gender and Family History. In K. Ashley and P. Sheingorn (Eds.), *Interpreting Cultural Symbols: Saint Anne in Late Medieval Society* (pp. 169–198). Athens, GA: University of Georgia Press.
Sison, A.D. (2004). "Himala: The Temptress, the

Virgin and the Elusive Miracle." *Crosscurrents, 54* (1), pp. 48–64.
Slim, H.C. (1992). "Music and Dancing with Mary Magdalen in a Laura Vestalis." In C. Monson (Ed.), *The Crannied Wall: Women, Religion and the Arts in Early Modern Europe* (pp. 139–160). Ann Arbor, MI: University of Michigan Press.
Sperling, J.G. (1999). *Convents and the Body Politic in Late Renaissance Venice.* Chicago, Ill: University of Chicago Press.
Spretnak, C. (2004). *Missing Mary: The Queen of Heaven and Her Re-Emergence in the Modern Church.* New York, NY: Palgrave MacMillan.
Stokes, J.S. "Mary Gardener of Love." 1997. 29 March 2006, <http://www.mgardens.org/JS-MGOL-MG.html>.
Stokes, J.S. "Mary Gardens' Historical Perspective." 1995. 29 March 2006, <http://www.mgardens.org/JS-HP-MG.html>.
Tavard, G.A. (1997). "The Virgin Mary and the Baroque Image." *Marian Studies, XLVIII,* pp. 60–86.
Tilmans, K. (1995). "Sancta Mater Versus Sanctus Doctus: Saint Anne and the Humanists. In A.B. Mulder-Bakker (Ed.), *Sanctity and Motherhood: Essays on Holy Mothers in the Middle Ages* (pp. 330–351). New York, NY: Garland.
Trachtenberg, J. (1943). *The Devil and the Jews: The Medieval Conception of the Jew and Its Relation to Modern Anti-Semitism.* Philadelphia, PA: The Jewish Publication Society of America.
Underhill, E. (1905). *The Miracles of Our Lady Saint Mary: Brought Out of Divers Tongues and Newly Set Forth in English.* London: William Heinemann.
Van Biema, D. (2005). "Hail, Mary." *Time, 165* (12), pp. 60–69.
Van Scott, M. (1998) *Encyclopedia of Hell.* New York, NY: Thomas Dunne Books.
Visser. D. (1992). "Faith and Love: The Iconography of Mary Magdalene, 1450–1650." In M.P. Fleischer (Ed.), *The Harvest of Humanism in Central Europe: Essays in Honor of Lewis W. Spitz* (pp. 281–302). St. Louis, MO: Concordia Publishing House.
Voragine, J. de (1941). *The Golden Legend of Jacobus de Voragine* (G. Ryan and H, Ripperger, Trans.). New York: Longmans, Green. (Original work published 1298).
Vrudny, K. (1999). "Medieval Fascination with the Queen: Esther as the Queen of Heaven and Host of the Messianic Banquet." *Arts: The Arts in Religious and Theological Studies, 11* (2), pp. 36–43.

Warner, M. (1983). *Alone of All Her Sex: The Myth and Cult of the Virgin Mary.* New York: Vintage Books.
Warren, N.B. (2001). *Spiritual Economies: Female Monasticism in Later Medieval England.* Philadelphia, PA: University of Pennsylvania Press.
Watson, R.N. (1998). "The State of Life and the Power of Death: Measure for Measure." In G.M. Kendall (Ed.), *Shakespearean Power and Punishment: A Volume of Essays* (pp. 130–156). Madison, NJ: Farleigh Dickinson University Press.
Webb, D. (2002). *Medieval European Pilgrimage.* New York, NY: Palgrave.
Webb, D. (2001). *Pilgrimage in Medieval England.* New York, NY: Hambledon and London.
Westerfield, N.G. (1999). "Mary of the Mirrors." *Theology Today, 56* (3), 399.
Weyermann, M. (2002). "The Typologies of Adam-Christ and Eve-Mary, and Their Relationship to One Another. *Anglican Theological Review, LXXXIV*(3), pp. 609–626.
Wickham, V. "Chaucer's Prioress: Simple and Conscientious, or Shallow and Counterfeit?" 14 April, 2006, <http://www.luminarium.org/medit/wickham.htm>.
Wieck, R.S. (1988). *The Book of Hours in Medieval Art and Life.* London: George Braziller.
Wilson, C.C. (2001). *St. Joseph in Italian Renaissance Society and Art: New Directions and Interpretations.* Philadelphia, PA: Saint Joseph's University Press.
Winston-Allen, A. (1997). *Stories of the Rose: The Making of the Rosary in the Middle Ages.* University Park, PA: Pennsylvania State University Press.
Wiseman, D.V., O.P. (2001). "Devotion to Mary Among the Dominicans in the Thirteenth Century." *Marian Studies, 52,* 246–263.
Wizeman, W., SJ. (2004). "The Virgin Mary in the Reign of Mary Tudor." In R.N. Swanson (Ed.), *The Church and Mary* (pp. 239–248). Rochester, NY: Boydell Press.
Wolfteich, C.E. (2002). *Navigating New Terrain: Work and Women's Spiritual Lives.* Mahwah, NJ: Paulist Press.
Yalom, M. (1997). *A History of the Breast.* New York: Alfred A. Knopf.
Zavjalova, M. "Folk Knowledge: Lithuanian Spells." 4 October, 2006, <http://ausis.gf.vu.lt/eka/spells.html>.
Zimdars-Swartz, S.L. (1989). "Popular Devotion to the Virgin: The Marian Phenomenon at Melleray, Republic of Ireland." *Archives de Sciences Sociales Des Religions, 67* (1), pp. 125–144.

Index

Abelard, Peter 120
Abstention from sex 86, 88
Acts of the Apostles 32
Albert the Great 18
Alcuin 81
Ambrose (Saint) 173
Amulets 93, 94, 150
Angels 17
Anne (Saint) 15, 97–105
Anne of Brittany 44–47
Annunciation 24, 83, 84
Anselm of Canterbury 10
Antoninus of Florence 71
Augustine (Saint) 18, 109

Bede (Saint) 61
Bernadette Soubirous (Saint) 59, 74, 76, 58, 105
Bernard of Clairvaux (Saint) 34, 69, 112
Birgitta of Sweden (Saint) 98, 124, 137, 139–141
Black Madonnas 34, 161
Black Plague 16, 145
Boleyn, Anne 163, 165
Boniface (Saint) 72
Boniface IX (Pope) 73
Books of Hours 36, 37, 39–47, 57, 60
Brandon (Saint) 12
Breastfeeding 15, 22, 80, 94, 95
Breasts 12
Brigittines 124, 125, 139
Brown, Dan 168, 169, 179, 180
Buddhism 181

Candlemas 82, 83, 94
Candles 83, 160
Canterbury Tales 52, 68, 71, 121
Cathars 49, 95, 96
Catherine Laboure (Saint) 142, 144
Catherine of Siena (Saint) 176, 177
Charles Stuart I 166, 167
Charles Stuart II 167
Chaucer, Geoffrey 52, 68, 71, 121
Childbirth 40, 70, 72, 93, 102, 137, 160, 167, 181
Clare (Saint) 117, 118
Collyridians 155
Conrad of Saxony 10
Crucifixion 31, 172, 173

The Da Vinci Code 168–170, 176, 180
Dancing 97, 177, 178
De Agreda, Maria 17
De Pizan, Christine 41, 117
D'Etaples, Jacques Lefeure 99
De Rupe, Alanus 49, 53
Devil 12, 15, 103–108, 111, 132, 137, 151, 152, 173
De Vitry, Jacques 96
De Voragaine, Jacobus 16, 17, 20, 172
Divination 97
Divine Feminine 169, 180, 182
Dominic (Saint) 49, 59, 115

Eadmer 10, 18
Education: of children 40, 41, 104; lack of 182; of nuns 124–126
Eleanor of Acquitaine (Queen) 172
Elizabeth (Saint) 15
Elizabeth of Schonau (Saint) 134, 135
Elizabeth Tudor I 57, 151, 163, 165, 166
Enclosure 117, 118, 120, 122
Ephesus 154
Epiphanius 20
Esther (Queen) 162
Eve 20, 21, 46, 93, 108–111, 151, 172

Fairies 133, 152
Feminism 25, 28
Flagellants 16
Flowers 9, 61, 64, 68, 103, 135, 160; lilies 61, 64; roses 53, 61, 64
Food 84–86, 140, 156
Francis of Assisi (Saint) 117

Gabriel (Angel) 24
Garden Enclosed 20, 34, 46
Gardens 64, 68
Gerson, Jean 112, 133
Gertrude the Great (Saint) 120, 134, 135
Goddesses 153–156, 160–162, 167, 180–182
Godfrey of Admont 18
Golden Legend 16, 17, 20, 35, 100, 172
Gratian 87
Gregory the Great 171

209

Index

Henrietta Maria (wife of Charles I) Stuart 166, 167
Hildegard of Bingen 21, 109, 124, 134
Holy Family 96
Holy Kinship 20, 97, 101
Holy Spirit 17
Hours of Anne of Brittany 44–47
Hroswitha of Gandersheim 21, 124

Iannuso, Antonina 144
Iconoclasts 107, 149, 150, 166
Iconography 61, 165
Immaculate Conception 74, 85, 101, 105, 139, 142, 144
Infertility 9, 47, 80, 89, 93, 101, 102, 150, 151, 174
Innocent I (Pope) 86
Innocent III (Pope) 160, 178
Innocent VIII (Pope) 112
Ireland 58, 152

Jerome (Saint) 20, 86, 108
Jesus 18; discovery at the temple 28; miracles of 10, 29, 30; Resurrection of 17
Jews 70, 71, 107, 108
Joan of Arc (Saint) 132, 134
John (Saint) 28
John Paul II (Pope) 161, 180
John the Baptist (Saint) 15
John XXIII (Pope) 5
Joseph (Saint) 20, 88, 111–114, 139
Judas 12
Judgment Day 12, 104, 114
Julian of Norwich (Saint) 96, 174
Justin Martyr 108

Kempe, Margery 22, 133, 139, 140

Lady Godiva 51
Leo XIII (Pope) 49, 113
Leuken, Veronica 145, 146
Lilies 61, 64
Lombard, Peter 87
Lourdes, France 74, 76, 78–80, 105
Luke (Saint) 24
Luther, Martin 25, 148, 163

Magi 27
Magic 147, 150–152
Magnificat 25, 93
Mark (Saint) 23
Marriage 86–88, 95–99, 109, 118, 163
Martyrs 86, 87
Mary Magdalene (Saint) 17, 168–180, 182, 184
Mary Tudor I 150, 165
Matthew (Saint) 27
May (Month of Mary) 81, 82
Measure for Measure 126, 127
Menstruation 89
Mexico 127
Miraculous Medal 142
Motherhood 89, 98, 174

Nativity 26
Nature 110
Nuns 21, 96, 114, 115, 117, 118, 12–123, 125–127, 130, 134, 135, 142, 144, 163, 175

Ordination of Women 110, 111, 176
Origen 111
Our Lady of Walsingham 53, 69, 70, 73, 74, 89, 151, 163

Paul (Saint) 20, 23, 154
Paul VI (Pope) 31
Pentecost 17, 32
Pilgrimage 68–73, 79
Pius V (Pope) 56
Pius IX (Pope) 113, 142
Pius X (Pope) 74
Pius XII (Pope) 33, 103
Polo, Marco 51
Prayer 36, 37, 40, 42, 43, 51, 53, 56, 131
Prophecy 27, 144
Prosperity 99, 100
Prostitution 170, 171, 175, 177–179
Protestantism 25, 56–58, 95, 148, 163
Protoevangelium of James 100
Psalters 37
Pubs 9
Pulcheria 154, 155

Radbertus, Paschasius 34
Rain 160
Reading 43
Relics 69
Repentance 170, 172, 176, 178, 179
Revelations of John 33
Rohan Hours 44–46
Rosary 5, 6, 9, 12, 47–49, 51–53, 56–60, 151
Rosary Confraternities 56
Roses 53, 61, 64
Rupert of Deutz 18, 34

Saints (Female) 94
Saturday (Mary's Day) 81, 85, 86, 105
Seven Sorrows 16
Sexuality 88, 98, 99, 108, 122, 172, 177, 179
Shakespeare, William 126, 127
Shrines 9, 69–75, 76, 78–80, 89, 95, 102, 103 112, 147–149, 162, 171, 174
Sickness 40, 76, 78–80, 88, 102, 123, 174
Simeon 27
Song of Songs 10, 18, 20, 33, 34, 64
Sprenger, Jakob 53
Sufis 181, 182

Tertullian 109
Theophilus 124, 151, 152
Theresa of Avila (Saint) 114
Thomas (Saint) 18
Thomas Aquinas (Saint) 87, 111
Thomas More (Saint) 72, 148
Thomas of Perseigne 10
Treasury of the City of Ladies 41

Urban VI (Pope) 97

Vatican II 5
Virgin Mary: Assumption of 17, 18, 61, 84; as behavioral ideal 19, 21, 98, 109–111, 114, 117, 121, 130, 168, 171, 175; birth of 85, 166; as Bride of Christ 18, 35, 118; coronation of 18; day of (Saturday) 81, 85, 86, 105; as devil's adversary 106, 108, 151; as disciple 33; as distant figure 8; as Ecclesia 17, 32, 112; and feminism 6, 7; as handmaid of the Lord 7, 25, 87; humanity of 15, 22, 45, 46, 96; as Intercessor 9, 10, 12, 135, 162, 167; Liturgical Feasts of 82–85; as Madonna 8; marriage to Saint Joseph 88, 111–114; as Mater Dolorosa 16, 31, 145; miracles of 76, 78, 79, 94, 95, 106, 107, 122, 123, 144, 147–149, 156, 160, 173; month of (May) 81, 82; as mother 8, 31, 89, 135, 137, 140, 152; as obedient 20; poverty of 26; and Protestantism apparitions of 59, 146; Purification of 27; as Queen of Heaven 17, 45, 46, 135, 161; relationship with Jesus 29, 30; silence of 23, 26; suffering of 16; as Theotokos 154; as virgin 7, 8, 20, 24, 82, 108, 130, 155; women's identification with 44
Virginity 8, 21, 87, 118, 122, 123, 134, 173
Visionaries 22, 131–135, 141, 142, 146, 147, 174

Wedding at Cana 10, 29, 30
Weeping Madonnas 144, 145
Wells 70, 102, 103, 162
William of Newburgh 18
Wills 39
Wine 10, 29, 85, 99
Woman Clothed with the Sun 33

Yolanda of Aragon 44–46

www.ingramcontent.com/pod-product-compliance
Ingram Content Group UK Ltd.
Pitfield, Milton Keynes, MK11 3LW, UK
UKHW042000140426
5217IPUK00015B/899